Decade of Fear

Decade

Michelle Shephard

of Fear

REPORTING
FROM TERRORISM'S
GREY ZONE

Douglas & McIntyre
D&M PUBLISHERS INC.
Vancouver/Toronto/Berkeley

Douglas & McIntyre
An imprint of D&M Publishers Inc.
2323 Quebec Street, Suite 201
Vancouver BC Canada V5T 4S7
www.douglas-mcintyre.com

Cataloguing data available from Library and Archives Canada
ISBN 978-1-55365-658-6 (cloth)
ISBN 978-1-55365-659-3 (ebook)

Editing by Trena White
Jacket and text design by Jessica Sullivan
Jacket photographs (top to bottom): 1. Warrick Page/Getty Images
News/Getty Images; 2. AFP/ Getty Images; 3. Michelle Shephard/
Toronto Star; 4. Michelle Shephard; 5. Michelle Shephard/Toronto Star;
6. Rizwan Tabassum/AFP/Getty Images; 7. AFP/ Getty Images;
8. AFP/Getty Images; 9. same as #2; 10. same as #6
Printed and bound in Canada by Friesens
Text printed on acid-free, 100% post-consumer paper
Distributed in the U.S. by Publishers Group West

We gratefully acknowledge the financial support of the Canada Council
for the Arts, the British Columbia Arts Council, the Province of British
Columbia through the Book Publishing Tax Credit and the Government
of Canada through the Canada Book Fund for our publishing activities.

To Ismail, my hero
and
To Jimmie, my love

Contents

Somewhere at Sea: An Introduction

ELEVEN FLOORS ABOVE the churning Atlantic Ocean, with Fort Lauderdale long faded and the island of Grand Turk looming, former Central Intelligence Agency boss Porter Goss is justifying the waterboarding of self-professed 9/11 mastermind Khalid Sheikh Mohammed. He is using salted bar nuts as a prop.

We are on a mammoth Holland America cruise ship, sitting in a swanky bar called the Silk Den, which is serviced by solicitous Filipino wait staff who stand at ease with legs spread and hands clasped. Sitting to the right of the former spy chief is U.S. General Michael Hayden, the retired head of the American electronic eavesdropping agency, the National Security Agency, and Goss's predecessor at the CIA. The New York Times once called Hayden the "thinking man's spy." Former U.S. president George W. Bush notes in his memoir: "Mike has a calming personality."

To Goss's left is Hayden's wife Jeanine, who nods emphatically at each point made by the former spy bosses, sometimes adding comments, suggesting that perhaps she had been a domestic advisor of sorts. To her left stands Porter Goss's forty-something-year-old son Chauncey, a mild-mannered fiscal policy consultant who acts

1

as an awkward sentry for our group, appearing as though he will quickly extricate his father if the waiters, or my questions, become threatening.

Over the decade that I have covered terrorism and national security for the *Toronto Star*, dozens of moments have seemed so bizarre that I later wondered if I had somehow imagined them. This November 2010 evening aboard the "Spy Cruise" is one of those times.

Themed cruises are common enough. Mickey Mouse and Donald Duck have their sea legs. Fitness wannabes Cruise to Lose and gyrate to Richard Simmons before the buffet. Even Elvis impersonators can indulge their passion on the ocean (can you imagine the "Thank Yous" at the buffet line?). So why not mix terrorism and tourism?

Why not, asked Bart Bechtel as he created his SpyCruise® series after 9/11. SpySkipper Bart, as he likes to be called, is a true red-white-and-blue-bleeding patriot who worries that Americans may forget the horror of 9/11 and become complacent in their security fears. Bart was once a CIA operations officer, recruited when he was working in a California liquor store in the 1970s. "I thought, if I can sell a bottle of Jack Daniel's, I can sure as hell sell America," he told me on more than one occasion.

I had just returned home from my twenty-third trip to Guantanamo Bay when a friend sent me an email about cruising the western Caribbean. The idea of two former intelligence heavyweights trapped aboard a ship, not to mention the vaudevillian idea of cruising with spies, was too much to pass up.

On the ship of about a thousand passengers, there were only about a hundred of us "spy cruisers"—an eclectic mix of intelligence types, students, "consultants" (including one odd, raspy fellow who warned that if I wrote about him there would be "consequences," even though I was just making small talk because I felt bad he was sitting alone), and some very sharp and genial retirees. We were given little pins with the U.S. Secret Service symbol embedded into an American flag.

During the days at sea, we sat in a stuffy third-floor conference room listening to terrorism talk, as coffee sloshed back and forth in our china cups from the unusually high swells. On breaks, we discussed the Patriot Act, the trouble with Iran and whether those discreet seasick-remedy patches behind our ears actually calmed the queasiness. In the evening "off-hours," or at port stops, we were free to be tourists. It always seemed awkward running into the speakers. Stumbling upon Hayden on the Lido deck in his sandals and khaki shorts as he dined with his wife, while bikini-clad cruisers got drunk in a nearby hot tub, somehow felt voyeuristic.

Hayden and Goss were not thrilled that three reporters were on board, but they were generous with their time and had agreed to meet us in the Silk Den that evening. For most of the meeting my friend Colin Freeze, who covers national security for the *Globe and Mail*, was on the edge of his seat, leaning forward, with a big mischievous grin and his fingers constantly running through his curly blond hair as he talked. Colin was extremely knowledgeable about terrorism issues and had a thirst for security information that bordered on obsession. I liked to tease him that he was the Columbo of journalists, always getting the story, but only by asking questions that jockeyed in and out like a frustrated driver determined to parallel park.

Colin had just called Hayden and Goss "doubting Thomases." I wasn't sure where he was going with that angle, but the fidgety Colin certainly had the former spy bosses' rapt attention. Thomas, the most circumspect apostle, he explained, demanded to see Christ's wounds before acknowledging that he had been crucified. Could Hayden and Goss still be denying that terrorism suspects were tortured in the Middle Eastern prisons where the CIA had sent them for interrogation (a controversial process known as "rendition") when it was well documented that prisoners were whipped with cables, beaten, threatened with rape, or held in grave-like cells in those detention centres? Hayden seemed amused but told Colin he was Catholic and the comment was out of line. The CIA, he said emphatically, as Goss and Jeanine Hayden nodded, never encouraged, never acquiesced and never engaged in torture either directly, or with a nod or a wink.

That was when I raised the question of waterboarding KSM.

Khalid Sheikh Mohammed, KSM as he was widely known, was arguably the biggest al Qaeda fish captured by 2010. Junior in al

Qaeda's hierarchy only to Osama bin Laden and Egyptian doctor Ayman al-Zawahiri, KSM was fingered as the architect of the
September 11, 2001, attacks. The Pentagon claimed he was also
responsible for a variety of other plots, including the kidnapping
and beheading of Wall Street Journal correspondent Daniel Pearl. KSM
had been held at one of the CIA secret prisons overseas known as
"black sites" before his transfer to Guantanamo Bay in 2006. He was
an arrogant self-professed murderer and one of three "high-value
detainees" who had been interrogated using the CIA's post-9/11
"enhanced" technique of waterboarding, which means he was
strapped on a gurney, his body inclined, his face covered with a cloth
while his interrogators poured cold water up his nose for up to forty
seconds. The purpose is to induce the sensation of drowning. KSM
had undergone 183 waterboarding sessions.

In January 2009, newly elected U.S. president Barack Obama
called waterboarding "torture." Goss, a former CIA officer and
Republican congressman from Florida who had been appointed
head of the spy agency in 2004, called it "effective."

"But 183 times?" I asked him. The number was not the point, but
it made the scenario seem even more ludicrous.

This is how the bar nuts came into play.

"Do you know what 183 means?" Goss asked.

Out plopped an almond. "One." A cashew. "Two." Peanut. "Three."

It looked so benign while cruising the Atlantic.

Waterboarding predated Goss's two-year term at the CIA, but
he was there in 2005 when the agency destroyed tapes recording
its practice. A criminal investigation followed but the U.S. Justice
Department did not lay any charges. The CIA said the tapes needed
to be destroyed to protect the interrogators. Critics accused the
agency of covering up illegal acts.

"Enhanced interrogation techniques" were not used during
Hayden's tenure either, and he closed the black sites and transferred
the remaining detainees to Guantanamo in 2006. But Hayden said
he was also weary of "self-righteous" criticism and second-guessing.

"I understand there are moral judgments to be made and honest
men differ," Hayden told me on another day, as passengers in tacky

Hawaiian shirts strolled past. "What I'm saying, however, is that process resulted in valuable intelligence that made America and citizens of the West safe. So you don't get to say, 'I don't want you doing it and it didn't work anyway.' The front half of that sentence is yours, as a human being, the back half of that sentence is based on fact, and the facts are it did work. So the sentence you get to say is, 'Even though it may have worked, I don't want you doing it.' I understand that sentence. It's a very noble sentence."

When I later pressed Porter Goss on Hayden's point, asking how journalists, who were paid to be doubting Thomases, could simply accept their assertions that "harsh interrogations" saved lives, that waterboarding provided actionable intelligence, or that renditions had worked in "Ninety-eight per cent of cases," Goss looked exasperated.

"We are a clandestine intelligence service," he said one afternoon as we sat on chaise longues. Then he leaned forward. "Clandestine intelligence. Clandestine intelligence. Clandestine intelligence. Clandestine intelligence. What about that is it that the media doesn't get?"

The thing is, I do understand the intelligence idiom of "need-to-know" and accept that not everything can be made public. Sources need protection and some interrogation methods do also. And I understand that we rarely hear about successful intelligence operations. We almost always hear about the failures. I also respect the value of good intelligence and have met spies, cops and members of armed forces worldwide whom I greatly admire.

And I am not naive to the horrors of ruthless, radical organizations that do not respect any rule of law. A teenager had his limbs amputated because he wouldn't join the cause; a thirteen-year-old girl was stoned to death on charges of adultery; and a beautiful pregnant woman from Toronto was widowed because al Qaeda decided to target the World Trade Center. Their names are Ismail, Asho and Cindy.

But I have also seen the power of al Qaeda propagandists and know where faulty intelligence can lead. I have interviewed many men whose reputations were destroyed by false claims of terrorism. Nothing, except perhaps being erroneously labelled a pedophile, is harder to shake. Bush wrote in his memoir that his "blood was boiling" on 9/11. "We were going to find out who did this, and kick their ass," he wrote. But ass-kicking had consequences. Why did it seem that all too often efforts to make the world safer only made it more dangerous?

Since the evening of September 11, 2001, standing amid the remains of the World Trade Center, I have been envious of those who see issues of national security as black and white. As a journalist, lucky enough to have extensively travelled seeking answers, I have the curse, and blessing, of seeing the world in shades of grey.

As it was for many, 9/11 was the first time I had tried to understand how world events could puncture our own bubble of security. As a twenty-nine-year-old crime reporter for the *Toronto Star* I knew more at the time about the Bloods and Crips than Osama bin Laden. On September 10 I had written about a sixteen-year-old gun-toting purse-snatcher and questioned why his elderly victim had not come forward.

Everyone has his or her own 9/11 story. Some missed one of the four hijacked flights and would spend their lives wondering why a traffic jam or last-minute emergency allowed them to be spared. Some watched the towers fall and would never be the same again. People remember exactly where they were and how they found out, the event seared in memory like that of the first moon landing, or the assassinations of Martin Luther King Jr. or John F. Kennedy. A friend of mine in Toronto said she ran to her children's school and brought them home to keep them close.

After the first plane hit, I grabbed my passport and called our assignment editor, offering to go to Manhattan. Running from my downtown Toronto apartment, I hailed a cab to Pearson International Airport, slapped five full-fare Air Canada tickets to LaGuardia on my Visa for the colleagues I thought would follow, dashed from counter to counter as airline after airline shut down, and begged bar owners to turn on the TV so I could see what was happening (they said they couldn't, citing airport policy). Eventually I ran outside to take a taxi back to the *Star*; joined two reporters waiting impatiently for me; drove to a border crossing, just getting through before it shut; and arrived in Manhattan, where I was stopped by a frazzled cop who believed in the lovely constitutionally enshrined right to freedom of the press and nodded at our cheaply laminated *Star* credentials. We raced into the city on an emergency road marked by flares, dumped the car, jogged the more than fifty blocks from our hotel down to Ground Zero, and some twelve hours after that first plane hit, finally stopped at the feet of a firefighter slumped on the sidewalk, who, after hours of searching the gruesome, twisted metal wreckage known as "the pile," could not move or speak.

Pulverized pieces of the World Trade Center still fell from the sky. A dusty film coated my arms and filled my lungs. For a few minutes, I stood with *Star* reporters Bill Schiller and Dale Brazao, just looking at the backlit facade of the towers, trying to remember exactly how they had once stood.

The paper blizzard was haunting. At St. Paul's Chapel on Broadway at Fulton Street, where George Washington had worshipped following his inauguration, the snow-like drift was almost knee-deep. Somehow, the church's 235-year-old bricks had absorbed the impact of the crumbling towers, but the gravestones in the adjacent cemetery were cracked and covered white with bills, business cards, charred unfinished reports and letters: the contents of thousands of filing cabinets and desktops now blanketing New York. All of it work people had laboured over, or had kept them awake at night, or had caused panic in the morning, and now it was just the debris of the dead.

For a couple of weeks after the attacks, I was one of hundreds of journalists who tried to make sense of the tragedy by telling stories of the dead, the living, the heroes and the villains. Relatives of the missing would press pictures into my hands, their eyes red and puffy, hoping that this young Canadian reporter could help them find their husband, child, lover, sister, mother, uncle, friend, still alive, perhaps with amnesia, somewhere recovering in hospital, or trapped in a pocket of air under the rubble. The struggle each day was not to find *a* story but to decide *which* to tell. I carried tissues or napkins with me because people cried openly.

At night, I would walk in a daze back to 6th Avenue and West 44th Street, to the Algonquin Hotel, where seven decades earlier a club of great writers and actors, including the acerbic Dorothy Parker (who famously said, "I don't care what's written about me so long as it isn't true"), met for boozy lunches. I would say goodnight to Matilda, a snotty Persian cat who lolled on the front counter and would accept my pats with cool detachment. After filing my stories, I'd call my husband, Jim Rankin, a photojournalist at the *Star*, who had been dispatched to Boston, where two of the flights originated. We had left so suddenly it wasn't until hours after we'd both got on the road that we remembered our poor new kitten—and I called my sister to see if she could look after him. Eventually, I'd crawl into bed sometime after midnight or one or two or three, and turn on NY1, sometimes crying as I watched the footage before falling asleep with the TV on.

There were a few voices preaching about the horrors of American foreign policy and a smattering of joyful rallies around the world celebrating that the great U. S. of A. was finally feeling their pain. But generally there was unprecedented international support. If not empathy, at least there was sympathy, or perhaps just fear about what would happen now that the United States had been brought to her knees.

The good thing about covering 9/11 was that you could do something when others felt helpless. It also provided the comfortable detachment so many journalists relish—writing about reality to avoid it. But in those first frenzied weeks I was just a scribe, recording what people told me, trying to put in words the heartache, or how a sickening metallic stench hung over Battery Park, or what it sounded like when Manhattan didn't sound like Manhattan. The roar of patrolling F-16s echoed off the skyscrapers, which now looked like looming towers of death. I covered funerals and wrote obituaries before relatives acknowledged their loved ones were gone. All the while the dead watched us, hundreds of eyes looking out from walls and lampposts and restaurant windows and anywhere there was space to plaster the "Have You Seen" posters. It really was no different from the crime stories I had written for most of my career, only on a massive scale.

For the next decade, I went in search of the hows and whys, try-ing to define terrorism and understand its roots. In Yemen, Osama bin Laden's former bodyguard explained why he admired one of the world's most reviled men. In Syria, guards standing outside the notorious Far Falestine prison denied that it was a jail, let alone a place where people were tortured. Interviewing elusive Islamists on the UN terrorist list in Mogadishu and Karachi helped me under-stand just how differently each region viewed the world. It took more than twenty visits to Guantanamo Bay to discover that the world's most famous detention centre was almost indescribable.

Sometimes I didn't need to go far. In Toronto, eighteen young men and teenagers were arrested for plotting to blow up financial and government buildings a ten-minute walk from my newsroom. I drank many cups of coffee with the police mole in the case, trying to understand why someone who hadn't reached puberty before 9/11 would a few years later vow to blow himself up. Comedian Jon Stew-art said what many were thinking the night of the dramatic June 2006 Toronto arrests: "You hate Canada? That's like saying, 'I hate toast.'"

During my ten years of putting pieces of the national security puzzle together I was never posted to a particular region and always returned to my home in Toronto. Nor was I a war reporter embedded in Iraq or Afghanistan. The benefit I got from the exotic and varied travel—and my return to the Western cities, politicians and public who would often determine the fate of those countries in turmoil—was a global view of terrorism and security. It helped me experience the great divide. It became easy during my travels to see all the disas-trous missteps. It was harder to look ahead and see the way forward.

In the media we jump from story to story, from one crisis to the next—*If it bleeds, it leads*—with brief commercial breaks for philan-dering politicians, crack-addicted celebrities and a sporting event or two. Trying to understand the aftermath of 9/11 was different. It was a big, ugly, complicated, misunderstood, politically and financially motivated, sometimes humorous, sometimes sexy, sometimes dull, often devastating story.

On this night aboard the Spy Cruise, somewhere in the middle of the Atlantic, I left the Silk Den with that sinking feeling I often had after talking with people in positions of authority, where the underlying, unspoken message was, *We know more than you, so just trust us.* There is little doubt Porter Goss and General Michael Hayden knew much more about terrorism than I did, but I learned quickly in this beat that the greater the position of authority, the higher the level of skepticism I should have.

I retreated to my eighth-floor windowless "state cabin," which was neither stately nor the size of a cabin. I couldn't tell if it was the swelling ocean that caused the hangers in my closet to clang from side to side as I tried to sleep, or if my head was spinning from the evening's conversation. Either way, I just felt woozy.

Six months after the cruise, Osama bin Laden was killed in Pakistan. So many hard lessons had been learned in the ten years since 9/11 and yet the immediate debate in the wake of his death felt like a step back in time. "Well, that didn't take long," journalist Jane Mayer wrote in the *New Yorker* on May 2, 2011. "It may have taken nearly a decade to find and kill Osama bin Laden, bit it took less than twenty-four hours for torture apologists to claim credit for his downfall." Enhanced interrogation techniques were once again at the forefront of the news. Former Bush administration officials claimed waterboarding was the reason al Qaeda's leader had finally been exterminated. I replayed the cruise conversations and still couldn't help but wonder. KSM was waterboarded in 2003 and bin Laden was killed eight years later. I thought of what had happened in those eight years. Even if KSM had provided a nugget of intelligence (which was later largely discounted) is that what Goss and others called "effective"?

The problem with the national security beat is that the more you know, the more you wonder. All I have been certain about is that "the war on terror" was a ridiculous name for a war in the first place.

This is not a memoir or an exhaustive analysis, but a ten-year trip through the national security grey zone, which ends where it began— at Ground Zero. It is a glimpse at a decade of terror inflicted by both individuals and the state. It is an introduction to the people I met who instilled that terror, and to the victims they left in their wake.

1 New York

IT WAS MIDNIGHT on September 14, 2001, and
Times Square was eerily quiet. The few people milling about had
their chins dipped, eyes downcast, and if the knock-off Gucci hand-
bag vendors had been out earlier, there was no sign of them now.
Broadway was dark. No inebriated late-night diners. No tourists.
Times Square was like a wrinkly and weary prostitute, resigned to
her fate, and longing for a client just to escape the tedium. Only the
Lipton Cup-a-Soup high above, spewing its curly stream of smoke
into the warm night, seemed oblivious to what had happened three
days earlier.

Standing alone at Broadway and 46th, I was trying to decide if a
doughy pretzel passed for dinner and wishing there was somewhere
I could buy a new T-shirt that didn't say *I Love New York*—even if I did.
I had worn the same pants and shirt since the morning of September 11, washing the Ground Zero dust off them at night, using the
hair dryer on them in the morning. High above me was a gargan-
tuan billboard for Arnold Schwarzenegger's next action Hollywood
blockbuster, *Collateral Damage*.

The news of the day had been U.S. President George W. Bush's trip to Ground Zero. Finally. Bush had been in Sarasota, Florida, at Emma E. Booker Elementary School the morning of 9/11. Five minutes before he walked into a classroom, National Security Advisor Condoleezza Rice called him from the White House to say a commercial aircraft had struck the World Trade Center, adding, "That's all we know right now, Mr. President." Ten minutes later Bush was reading "The Pet Goat" to the class of eager youngsters when White House Chief of Staff Andrew Card whispered in Bush's ear, "A second plane hit the second tower. America is under attack."

Bush later wrote in his memoir that his instinct was to stay calm, so he remained in the classroom reading for another seven minutes. "The nation would be in shock; the president could not be," he wrote. "If I stormed out hastily, it would scare the children and send ripples of panic throughout the country." But in a video clip that aired endlessly, Bush looked less like the sanguine commander-in-chief he imagined himself to be and more like a deer in headlights. Osama bin Laden recalled this moment before Bush's 2004 re-election. "Because it seemed to him that occupying himself by talking to the little girl about the goat and its butting was more important than occupying himself with the planes and their butting of the skyscrapers, we were given three times the period required to execute the operations. All praise is due to Allah," al Qaeda's leader said in a video.

While Bush was criticized for maintaining that stunned demeanour in the days that followed, he was reborn amid the debris of the towers on that Friday as exhausted firefighters and cops started cheering "U-S-A, U-S-A!" The image of Bush with raised bullhorn, standing among New York's finest, was beamed around the world. The swaggering Texan told the crowd that the world was listening. "And the people who knocked these buildings down will hear all of us soon," he thundered.

I didn't see Bush that day, but instead was writing a profile on the man emerging as New York's real hero, Mayor Rudy Giuliani. Giuliani was at the World Trade Center ten minutes before the first building collapsed and remained at the epicentre of the tragedy during the week that followed. He became New York's trauma counsellor, public information minister and cheerleader. "He seems both concerned and calm, and appears to be in control of an uncontrollable situation. Usually I cringe when I hear politicians speaking. But this hasn't been the case with the mayor," New Yorker Molly Hammerberg told me as we walked along Canal Street in the pounding rain.

Just a week earlier, New Yorkers had not particularly liked Giuliani, lamenting the scandals in the city's police department and the mayor's well-publicized affair, but 9/11 had transformed the thin-skinned Giuliani into the fifty-seven-year-old big-hearted Teflon Rudy. He had even spontaneously hugged the largely unhuggable New York Senator Hillary Rodham Clinton at a press conference. Friday, September 14, may have been Bush's day to shine, but New Yorkers were praising Giuliani. He would later become *Time* magazine's Person of the Year and Queen Elizabeth II herself would knight him.

As I searched for dinner after writing about Saint Rudy, my cellphone rang. "Hi, doll." It was Lorrie Logan.

AT THE TORONTO STAR there was once a secret we called "switchboard." All *Star* journalists who worked in the pre-Internet, pre-cellphone, pre-BlackBerry, -Twitter, -Facebook and -24-hour-news-coverage days, have a switchboard story or favourite operator who saved their career. I loved Lorrie because aside from being a workaholic she had this way of talking that made you feel like a cherished niece. Whenever I was somewhere feeling homesick, my eyes would well up when I heard her say, "Oh, dolly, what can I do for you?"

The CIA really should have employed *Star* operators. Switchboard could track anyone. For years, they worked manically, hidden in a third-floor room that looked as if it belonged to an autistic mathematician. Every inch of wall space was carefully covered in numbers. Shelves were lined with phone books from around the world or obscure tomes on cooking, or wildlife, or Tajikistan. These incredible women—because except for the rare male interloper the staff were predominantly women—had found hostages and gunmen, presidents and criminals and more than one *Star* reporter who didn't want to be found. They weren't just operators even though they also connected calls. They were relentless and charming investigators, bloodhounds, who could go toe-to-toe with the most dogged investigative journalist.

One famous story goes back to November 23, 1963, when the *Star*'s managing editor desperately needed our Washington correspondent, Martin Goodman. It was less than twenty-four hours after U.S. President John F. Kennedy had been assassinated and Lyndon Johnson inaugurated. Goodman had covered Johnson's swearing in, but still hadn't filed his story and editors were panicking. Switchboard was dispatched to track the wayward scribe. Within minutes, they had a map of Johnson's post-inauguration parade route and the names of all the shops along the motorcade's path. They called a drugstore and persuaded a pharmacist to go outside and shout Goodman's name from the sidewalk as the press cars passed. Goodman heard, was told by the helpful druggist to call his *Star* boss, and he did.

Linda Diebel, our former Latin America correspondent, recalls one time when in a panic she dialled switchboard on a Thursday night, trying to track a Canadian government official for a weekend story. The man was on vacation. Somehow, within the next twelve hours, switchboard not only discovered that the official was in London, England, but had uncovered what he was going to do, where he was travelling, how he would get there and what he looked like. When the bureaucrat got off the Tube at a south end station that Friday morning, some guy held out a pay phone asking if he was from Ottawa, Canada, because he had a call. True story. There were hundreds.

Journalists were fiercely protective of our switchboard and mourned their "downsizing" in 2010. But in the weeks after 9/11 they were working overtime, and on this night switchboard had found Cindy Barkway.

THERE WERE 2,982 9/11 victims. Twenty-four were Canadian. David Michael Barkway was one. As the managing director for Toronto's office of BMO Nesbitt Burns, he had been on a three-day business trip to Manhattan. He was meeting with the bond-trading firm Cantor Fitzgerald on the 105th floor of the north tower when American Airlines Flight 11 hit. David was a family man who loved his cottage, golfing, practical jokes, fine cigars, action films, his university sweetheart Cindy, and Jamie, their two-year-old son. Friends called him "Barky." He would sit with his giggling toddler on his lap as they listened over and over, and then over again to the Baha Men singing "Who Let the Dogs Out?" Somehow the song's *woof woof woof woof* just got funnier every time. David was one of those guys who possessed a kinetic energy that allowed him to suck out of life all he could, and his energy was contagious.

His wife, Cindy, was five months pregnant with their second son when she accompanied him to New York that week. They had flown together the day after David's 34th birthday, on September 9. At 7:40 the morning of the 11th, they said goodbye as David left for meetings and Cindy prepared for a day of shopping. She was in SoHo when the first plane hit.

But none of this story had been told yet and all I knew was that one of David's friends had called our newsroom to say David was among the missing and his wife Cindy was somewhere in New York. Before I had started trailing Giuliani that afternoon I called switchboard. "Can you find Cindy?" Of course they did, and this time it was quite simple, albeit time-consuming. Lorrie just called every New York hotel until she found a Barkway reservation.

"She's at the Times Square Hilton," Lorrie told me. Cindy was three blocks from where I stood, so I passed on the pretzel and went directly to the hotel, only remembering when I got there that it was after midnight.

Like Times Square, the Hilton's second-floor lobby was nearly empty and depressing. Sitting in one of the overstuffed chairs, I started scribbling a letter, explaining to Cindy who I was, that I was staying at a nearby hotel and that I wanted to tell her husband's story, but understood if she didn't want to talk and hoped the letter didn't compound her grief.

I always dreaded trying to talk to relatives of someone who had just died—something I had done far too often in my years as a crime reporter. It never got easier. My first journalism assignment after just three days of "orientation" at the paper—which back then consisted roughly of "and here's the women's washroom, and the cafeteria. Human resources need you to fill out this form and pee in a cup"—had been to interview a woman whose baby had died after the doctor had dropped him on the delivery room floor. She lived in Hamilton, about a ninety-minute drive from our downtown news-room, and by the time I got to her door I was so filled with dread that I was delighted no one was home. An editor told me to stay put, so I sat in one of the company cars staring at her front door. When she arrived home an hour later, I reluctantly went again, and knocked gently, perhaps hoping she wouldn't hear. When she did, the sight of her reduced me to tears. After I choked out an introduction and apologies for being there, the poor woman took such pity on my snotty face that she brought me inside for tea and told me about her baby Michael. In the end, the Star was the only paper to get an inter-view but despite the editors' praise, I still felt sick. The only saving grace was that eventually the publicity surrounding the case helped push for an investigation into hospital policies regarding newborns and recommendations were implemented, including the mandatory swaddling of babies in a towel before moving them.

Sometimes telling crime stories did make a difference, and I really did believe that as journalists we shared the motto posted in the hall of Toronto's coroner's office: "We Speak for the Dead to Protect the Living." Of my dozens of "pick ups," as they're known because essentially we go and "pick up" a picture of the deceased, only a handful of relatives ever closed the door without talking. But the times that they did, that noble mission of making the world a better place by violating someone's private grief just sounded hol-low and I felt ghoulish. Besides, these days, as news gets delivered faster, most stories, no matter how tragic, have a shelf life of only a few days before the next tragedy makes them expire.

Of course, 9/11 was different because the grief was so widespread and public. But for Cindy, like the other relatives, it was a personal loss. I promised in my letter not to bother her if she didn't call back and included my hotel and cell numbers at the bottom, before convincing a kind hotel clerk to take the note to her room and slide it quietly under the door.

I HAD JUST fallen asleep at the Algonquin Hotel as the sun came up, when the phone rang. In a steady and clear voice, Cindy Barkway told me she had my note and she would be happy to talk. But she was leaving New York. Could I come now? After a quick phone call to *Star* photographer Vinnie Talotta, who had been in New York shooting Fashion Week on the 11th, we ran to the hotel in time to greet Cindy as she came off the elevator. Cindy's blond hair was smooth and styled. She wore a twin sweater set that looked cashmere and was accentuated by a string of small pearls. I felt embarrassed at what a mess the two of us were beside this beautiful widow. Cindy's whole world had collapsed in those towers, but what I would better understand later is that grief affects everyone uniquely, at different times, and Cindy had somehow grasped something so many other relatives couldn't yet believe. She realized her husband was gone. She knew David wasn't in a hospital, or trapped alive under the rubble. She said she could *feel* it and needed to get home to her son Jamie to tell him. But first, she would tell us. We had only about twenty minutes before she had to join her parents in the idling Lincoln Town Car that had been sent by David's company to drive her to Toronto.

She was remarkably composed. She said she was thankful for the two days she had had with David in New York, roaming the city, dining at the Gramercy Tavern and a steak house on Avenue of the Americas, thinking it would have been so much harder had she been forced to watch it all from Toronto. "He loved his son more than anything in the world," she said, touching her stomach, which held the baby her husband would not meet. "My children are going to grow up without a father. But I'm going to make sure they know what a wonderful dad they had."

Cindy had been playing the cruel "what if" game in her head since the towers were hit. What if the planes had struck twenty minutes later, when David was due in another meeting and would have left the building, or what if they had crashed into another skyscraper, far away from the World Trade Center? At first, Cindy believed David had escaped since he was in the north tower, which collapsed second, and perhaps he had time to climb down the 105 flights. He had sent an email to a colleague in Toronto that said, "We need help. This is not a joke," so it was clear he had not been killed upon impact.

But by the morning of September 12, when David had not returned to the hotel, Cindy went to the missing persons bureau. She was given number 180. She wanted instead to go south and claw through the pile herself, but no one would let her near Ground Zero, and they cautioned her about being outside at all with the questionable air quality. The day before I met her, she had taken David's toothbrush to the centre for DNA testing.

"I haven't wanted to leave because that's admitting David is gone," Cindy said as she clutched a picture of her husband and walked toward the car. "But it is time to go home."

None of David's remains would ever be recovered.

THE FIRST CALL from the newsroom came shortly after we filed the story and photos. I vividly recall Vinnie's face as he talked. The conversation went something like this:

"Are there any *other* pictures?"

"I sent what I have," replied Vinnie, defensive.

"It's just, well, she doesn't look, *sad*."

"She was. That's how she looked."

"But aren't there any, where she's, you know, *crying*?"

Vinnie grew up in Toronto, the eldest son of a first generation Italian household where his mother did not speak English and his father loved to sit in the backyard under a canopy of grape vines, wearing a white undershirt and straw hat as he drank coffee or grappa and embarrassing the hell out of the teenaged Vinnie. Perhaps it is more accurate to say Vinnie grew up on the street. And even though Toronto is heralded for its low crime rate, Vinnie always drove around, and likely still does today, with a small pocket knife tucked somewhere under his seat.

Vinnie joined the *Star* in 1988 as a "copy boy." It was a position that has retained its name today even though the duties now entail general office administration. Since computers replaced typewriters, copy boys were no longer needed to run stories from the reporters' hands to editors, then cram the stories into oblong containers that would be suctioned along tubes to the engravers and eventually to the printing presses.

Over the years, Vinnie got to know everyone at the *Star*, and everyone knew Vinnie. But it was the photographers he studied and wanted most to befriend. Vinnie learned about journalism in the newsroom, not the classroom, and in 1997 the paper rewarded him with a job as staff photographer. I loved working with Vinnie as a crime reporter because he had a gift for putting anyone at ease. I watched him charm politicians, dignitaries, housewives, CEOs, drag queens (and I bet the Queen herself should he meet her), drug dealers and chiefs of police. In Compton, California, where we once did a series on gangs, I interviewed a six-foot-five Crip serving two life sentences for murder, and it was Vinnie whom the gang leader felt more comfortable talking with. Ditto the cops. Yes, Vinnie had charisma and treated everyone as equals, but if pushed too far, he also had a short Italian fuse, and on the phone that day I watched it ignite.

The editors wanted to know if he could go back to photograph Cindy again. I had to wonder what that would involve. Would we keep probing and prodding, and if that didn't bring her to tears perhaps I would pinch her?

"No," Vinnie said. "She's on her way back to Toronto."

"Could we get her here?"

The call was over.

In the end, David Barkway's story ran on the Sunday front, the pictures inside.

A DAY AFTER interviewing Cindy, I wandered into an empty Afghan Kebab House at 9th Avenue and 51st Street and met Mohammad Nasir. Taped to the window outside the restaurant were yellow ribbons and an American flag, just like those that hung at almost every other Manhattan restaurant. But there was also a handwritten note on yellow lined paper. "To our neighbors, fellow New Yorkers and everyone affected by the terrible tragedy at the World Trade Center. Please accept our sincere and heartfelt condolences. We also feel such shock and horror." The *also* was not underlined but that was the point.

Mohammad was a twenty-three-year-old waiter serving tables to help pay for tuition at New York's City College. He told me in a soft voice that employees at the restaurant had been receiving death threats and that people would come in to stare at the flag of Afghanistan teary-eyed and shake their heads. Two of Mohammad's friends sold coffee from carts on the top floors of the twin towers and were missing, presumed dead. But unlike other New Yorkers who shared that intense kinship in grief, Mohammad felt alone and like an outsider for the first time since he left Pakistan.

Which was ironic, because Mohammad had always felt more at home in New York than he had growing up in Islamabad.

Mohammad's father was an officer with Pakistan's navy who told his two boys from a very young age that he didn't want his sons to live with the corruption of Pakistan's ruling elite. When they were old enough, he would find a way to send them abroad to study and work. Mohammad's chance came in 1995 when he travelled to Switzerland, where he studied hotel management, while his older brother left for Ireland. Even though he was only a teenager, Mohammad had been planning all his life ("I'm addicted to work," he liked to exclaim, throwing up his hands as if he had an undiagnosed medical condition that he had learned to live with). He hit his stride as soon as he arrived in Switzerland, quickly securing a hotel internship, freelancing with bartending and DJ gigs at night, and learning English and German to add to his list of languages that already included Punjabi, Farsi and passable Arabic. But while his living costs were taken care of through the internship, his jobs earned little, which meant he was unable to save for the career he sought. He wanted to be a doctor. He believed there was only one place where he could do that. "To me, it was always the land of opportunities," he said of New York. In 1998, he applied for a U.S. student visa and was delighted when he was accepted. He arrived in Manhattan soon after and found himself at the doorstep of the Afghan Kebab House, where he met Shafi Rouzy.

Shafi, the founder of the Afghan Kebab House chain, had also come to the United States in search of a new life, after fleeing his home in Mazar-e-Sharif, Afghanistan, in 1979 during the Soviet invasion. He received political asylum in the United States and became an American citizen. Shafi's first job was selling kebabs from a pushcart on the streets of Midtown during the 1980s. One night as he wearily parked his cart in the rundown garage on 9th Avenue, he imagined what could be. By the time he was able to sponsor his wife and children to get them out of Pakistan, to which they had fled, the wily businessman had established the Afghan Kebab House and already had a faithful clientele.

When the planes crashed into the World Trade Center, Shafi was in the Middle East trying to start a chain of restaurants and had left his 9th Avenue restaurant in the care of his son Yusuf. Yusuf had slept in the restaurant for a week following the 9/11 attacks, because travelling in and out of the city was too difficult with all the road restrictions, but Mohammad thought it was also to keep his family business safe. Mosques, stores, and Arab and South Asian homes were being vandalized. Within a week of the attacks, a Sikh owner of a gas station was shot dead in Arizona (reportedly because he "looked Middle Eastern"); a Pakistani store clerk was killed in Dallas; and Hassan Awdah of Gary, Indiana, a U.S. citizen born in Yemen, survived an attack at his gas station by a masked man wielding a high-powered rifle. Mourning was giving way to vengeance.

Shafi told employees in a conference call from Kuwait that he was considering dropping "Afghan" from the restaurant's name. He even mused that he wanted to close his restaurants and open a fried chicken chain instead.

Business was certainly bad for a long time after that, but in the end, Shafi wasn't forced to close his chain, and the Afghan Kebab House survived.

On an unusually warm spring night in 2010, I went back in search of Mohammad. Ready to use my best investigative skills to track him down, I went first to the restaurant hoping he had a friend still working there. Instead, I found Mohammad right where I had left him almost a decade earlier, waiting tables at 9th and 51st. Yusuf was there too, in the kitchen, slicing massive white pieces of cod into cubes.

The restaurant diners that night were the usual mix of the pre-theatre crowd, tourists with aching feet and bulging shopping bags, and women in pencil skirts, looking all business above the table, but underneath they had traded their spiky office heels for flip flops or running shoes. The restaurant didn't serve alcohol, but diners were allowed to bring their own. "Some people don't think it's right to have hard liquor every night. What's with that?" a twenty-something suit at the table beside me loudly exclaimed to his workmates as they clinked their corner store beer.

I had secured the only free table and spent a few minutes watching Mohammad before saying hello. He had lost a little hair and his black vest and dress pants seemed looser, I thought. He was busy, banging back and forth through the swinging kitchen doors, returning with fragrant trays of lamb, rice and fish, filling water glasses from wine decanters and returning with empty plates. There was no fried chicken on the menu.

"You're still here?" I said to Mohammad as I explained that we had met days after 9/11, handing him my business card.

"You came back!" he exclaimed. "I remember."

For Mohammad, a university degree was still the Holy Grail but his quest had ended a number of years ago when he could no longer afford rent for his 46th Avenue apartment near the restaurant and was forced to move to New Jersey. Trying to balance the commute, school and classes, with cost of tuition... "I'll go back," he said brightly.

A white-haired man came into the restaurant with a pack of smokes and handed them to Mohammad. "See? I didn't forget you," the man said before walking out with a smile. Mohammad later explained that he didn't know the man's name but knew his story. The eighty-six-year-old was a World War II veteran whose wife had died about five years earlier and who was down on his luck. He wandered in often, usually without money, and Mohammad took it upon himself to bring him a steaming bowl of lamb stew. Sometimes the man would come back with a pack of cigarettes to thank him, and Mohammad didn't have the heart to tell him he wasn't really a smoker.

Mohammad had other fans and a bunch of them were at a table at the front of the restaurant, wearing crisp suits and sitting with their backs to the wall in a defensive, erect posture that screamed police officers. "You write good things about him," one told me, winking at Mohammad as he paid the bill.

"You working with NYPD on 9/11?" I asked the baby-faced officer.

"Negative," he replied.

"They're good guys," Mohammad said once they were out of earshot. "Work for intelligence."

Then he added seemingly more to himself than to me, "You know, New York is a good place for good people and it's a bad place for bad people.

"I don't have anybody here but I don't feel lonely. This is my home. This is my place. This is my country."

A FEW BLOCKS from the Afghan Kebab House was the Pride of Midtown, the nickname for New York's busiest fire hall. Built more than one hundred years ago, it sits on the corner of 8th Avenue and 48th Street, close to Broadway and the theatres. The firefighters working in the red-brick building answer more than fourteen thousand emergency calls a year.

Engine 54, Ladder 4, Battalion 9 lost fifteen men on duty on 9/11: the three Mikes—Haub (the Hobbinator), Lynch and Brennan; the house "probie" and youngest at 24, Chris Santora; the "artist" Paul Gill; the athlete Sam Oitice. Chief Ed Geraghty, Joe Angelini, Len Ragaglia, Carl Asaro, Captain Dave Wooley, Jose Guadalupe, Lieutenant Danny O'Callaghan, John Tipping, Alan Feinberg. They answered the call at 9:04 AM, fourteen minutes after the first plane hit.

Just before the first anniversary of 9/11, I went back to the fire hall and spent a week doing a "ride along" with the men. This involved a lot of grocery store visits. The Pride of Midtown may be the busiest station in the city, but there always seemed time to get ingredients and create elaborate meals. It was almost inevitable, however, that the bell would ring just as the plates were served and the men would run cursing toward the trucks as mouthwatering scents wafting like fingers from the kitchen tried to pull them back to their seats.

The anniversary was hard on the New York City firefighters. They lost 343 members. Stories of some of their dead had reached near-mythical status. The commander, the rookie, the father and son under the rubble; sixty-eight-year-old Fire Chaplain Reverend Mychal F. Judge, who was killed by falling debris in the lobby of the north tower after giving the last rites to firefighter Daniel Suhr. The Reuters photo of Father Judge as he was carried out by firefighters on a tipped chair, his head slumped sideways, became one of the most enduring images of 9/11.

But at the Pride of Midtown in particular, the anniversary was excruciating. Firefighter Richard Kane came off a twenty-four-hour shift one day in early September 2002 and walked out bleary-eyed smack into a busload of earnest children, all gripping hand-drawn pictures and lined up shyly behind their teacher. They wanted to deliver the drawings and could they maybe hug the firefighters, the teacher asked? A few nights earlier, a group of inebriated women had come to buy commemorative 9/11 T-shirts that most of the stations sold for charity, and then just stared at the firefighters with drunken tears and slurred their admiration. On this morning, Kane looked down at the children and wanted to tell them to go away. He needed a shower and a bed.

In the first months after 9/11, the focus on the firefighters made it okay for the normally macho men to break down. It was expected that you would cry and more of an issue if you didn't. The Pride of Midtown became a shrine of candle wax and flowers that stretched from the driveway into the road, blocking two lanes of traffic. Whenever you passed that corner, all noise ceased. Even the cabbies wouldn't honk.

But then fall turned to winter, the missing became the dead, and the steady stream of well-meaning visitors and mourners turned into a daily sucker punch in the gut. *You're the ones who survived,* those well-meaning hugs and tears said. *Your buddies are all dead.* And if the firefighters didn't already think about that almost every minute at that fire hall, then all they had to do was look up at the Ladder 4 sign that had been brought back after it was discovered in the rubble of Ground Zero in the spring of 2002, twenty metres below ground. Or they would see O'Callaghan's spare coat, which remained where it was on the morning of 9/11. "All gave some, some gave all," screamed a sign read by only those who gave some. The firefighters were working, cursing, sweating, guilt-ridden, pissed-off actors in a living memorial.

"It's really the toughest place in the city to work. No one wants to say that because we're just so grateful for the public support we've received, but it has to end soon. Everybody just wants it to stop," Richard Kane said after smiling and accepting the drawings from the children. Seeing a penny on the ground, he kicked it absent-mindedly. I wrote in my notebook that Kane did not put that penny in his pocket. Probably just an act of frustration but it felt significant. *See a penny pick it up all day long you'll have good luck.* None of the firefighters wanted to talk about luck as the reason they survived.

So call it timing. Five trucks responded to the 9:04 call. Only one made it back—Kane's. His lieutenant turned around after realizing he had left his helmet behind. "Leave it, we've got to go, leave it," Kane remembered yelling. But they went back to get it and then their truck was stopped en route. They were two blocks away when the second tower fell.

FEW WOULD PREDICT how a terrorist attack on U.S. soil could usher in a such a dark, divisive period in history, one that not only failed to quash the threat of global terrorism, but instead created a whole new generation raised on war and rhetoric and bent on revenge.

In the early days, those few voices who called for a measured response and urged the United States to look inward and take a deep, collective breath were branded traitors and told they did not appreciate just how profoundly the world had changed. The world was indeed a different place. "Patriotic" and "anti-American" became buzzwords. A rabid new breed of so-called security experts hit the airwaves, talking in concise 15-second clips about the near and the far enemy that now, looking back, does not seem that different from the rhetoric Osama bin Laden spewed. I was part of the media machine that churned out these stories, which were heavy on drama and outrage, and light on analysis.

Hindsight makes it easy to judge how things went so disastrously wrong, how the goodwill for the United States turned to international condemnation. What is harder to recall and for many of us to admit now was how we felt then. People were scared. We wanted strong leaders. Many wanted revenge. The sepia-toned Western posters demanding Osama bin Laden be captured Dead or Alive were flying off the racks. I bought a roll of toilet paper with the al Qaeda's leader's face on every square above the words *Wipe Out Terrorism*.

Subways and tunnels turned ominous, as did tall buildings. No one wanted to fly and the airline industry, already hit by a recession, spiralled downward. On October 5, less than a month after the attacks, Robert Stevens, a sixty-three-year-old photo editor of the Boca Raton, Florida, tabloid, the *Sun*, inhaled anthrax spores after opening his mail. Targeting a newspaper, of course, also had the chilling effect of putting all journalists on alert and making them personally invested in the story. By mid-November, five people were dead or dying of anthrax, dozens injured. Senators and Supreme Court justices were also targeted. Everyone was on edge. The FBI began tracking leads from Washington to Florida and the fear grew that if al Qaeda had anthrax maybe they had smallpox too, or plans to poison the water supply. Maybe nuclear weapons? It would take a multi-million-dollar investigation and nearly seven years for the FBI to dismiss an al Qaeda connection to the anthrax and conclude that the likely perpetrator was an army scientist named Bruce Edwards Ivins, a troubled doctor who had helped develop an anthrax vaccine and had even been advising the FBI in its investigation. Dr. Ivins had been tormented by alcohol and mental illness and took his own life in 2008 when the FBI turned its focus on him.

Fear is a powerful motivator that our brains process in strange ways. We *know* that obesity and smoking are killers, but it's the idea that a murderer is lurking in the basement or under our bed that scares us. How often are nervous flyers told that they are more likely to die in an accident driving to the airport than flying? But knowing the statistics doesn't stop their palms from sweating during take-off. Even after 9/11, the risk of being struck by lightning was greater than dying in a terrorist attack in North America. But we had heard F-16s soar across Manhattan, and that was the thunder that made us shudder.

If you didn't feel afraid instinctively, then you were told you should. In fact we were bombarded with fear, warned to be in a constant state of readiness and to heed the colour-coded threat level. It was usually red (severe risk), sometimes on good days maybe orange (high risk). If you see a red flag on Hawaii's North Shore you probably don't go swimming. A black weather flag at a military base means it's not the smartest idea to run a marathon at noon. But how do you live with severe risk when you don't know what the risk is?

Fear explained the billions spent on airport security even though there is no way to plug all the holes. The box cutters used on 9/11 caused airlines to give us plastic cutlery on flights. Shoe bomber Richard Reid caused us to take off our footwear. In 2006, after British police thwarted a liquid bomb plot, water bottles were deemed dangerous. After the so-called underwear bomber failed to bring down a Detroit-bound flight on Christmas Day 2009, Canadian passengers flying to the United States had to put their hands in their pockets, rub them around and extend their palms for an explosives test. Minutes before undergoing this routine at Toronto's Pearson Airport in February 2010, I had stood in a customs line that snaked out the door to the check-in counters. No one had passed through security yet or checked their luggage. A bomb detonated there could have killed hundreds.

Fear helps explain why there was little debate over Canada's Anti-Terrorism Act or the sweeping October 2001 U.S. Patriot Act that undermined decades of civil rights protections. It had passed 96 to 1. Wisconsin Democratic Senator Russ Feingold was the one. "This was not, in my view, the finest hour for the United States Senate," he told Congress. "The debate on a bill that may have the most far-reaching consequences on civil liberties of the American people in a generation was a non-debate. The merits took a back seat to the deal." He was branded a traitor, which didn't deter him from later trying to censure Bush for wiretapping American citizens without court approval, from voting against the Iraq war or from becoming the first senator to call for the withdrawal of U.S. troops.

"The tragic events of September 11, 2001, changed more than Manhattan's skyline; it profoundly altered our political and legal landscape as well," Hunter S. Thompson wrote in his bestseller *Kingdom of Fear.* "Anyone who witnessed the desecration of those buildings and the heart-wrenching loss of life, who didn't want to run out and rip someone a new asshole, doesn't deserve the freedoms we still enjoy. However, anybody who thinks for one moment that giving up our freedoms is any way to preserve or protect those freedoms, is even more foolhardy."

And that's the thing. Everyone knows that fear can be irrational but many just resorted to the mantra "better safe than sorry."

But are we safer?

In April 2006, a National Intelligence Estimate said the United States wasn't. According to declassified portions of the report, the terrorist threat was in fact greater than it had been on September 10, 2001. This wasn't the bleeding-heart-socialist-civil-rights-activists-American-Civil-Liberties-Union-leftist-media talking. This was an NIE, a federal government document written by the National Intelligence Council, approved by the Director of National Intelligence and based on raw, uncensored information collected by the sixteen American intelligence agencies. Of course, as the name states, the reports are "estimates." But they are considered authoritative assessments and while typically bureaucratic or measured in tone, this one was blunt. Radical Islamic movements that aligned themselves with al Qaeda had not been quashed, but had metastasized and spread around the world. The report laid out the factors that were fuelling the movement: fear of Western domination leading to anger, humiliation and a sense of powerlessness when coupled with entrenched grievances such as corruption and injustice; the faulty intelligence that led to the Iraq war; the slow pace of economic, social and political reform in Muslim nations; and the pervasive anti-U.S. sentiment among Muslims and exploited by jihadists.

Two of the authors of a report issued by the 9/11 Commission (an independent, bipartisan committee created by congressional legislation to investigate the attacks) asked in a *Washington Post* editorial in 2007 how it was possible that the threat could remain so dire when billions had been spent, new laws enacted, wars fought.

"We face a rising tide of radicalization and rage in the Muslim world—a trend to which our own actions have contributed. The enduring threat is not Osama bin Laden but young Muslims with no jobs and no hope, who are angry with their own governments and increasingly see the United States as an enemy of Islam," wrote the former commission chair Thomas H. Kean, and vice chair Lee H. Hamilton.

Kean and Hamilton wrote that the West had lost the struggle of ideas.

"We have not been persuasive in enlisting the energy and sympathy of the world's 1.3 billion Muslims against the extremist threat. That is not because of who we are: Polling data consistently show strong support in the Muslim world for American values, including our political system and respect for human rights, liberty and equality. Rather, U.S. policy choices have undermined support." Military is essential, they wrote. "But if the only tool is a hammer, pretty soon every problem looks like a nail."

Fear drove so much of what happened after 9/11, and many political leaders were the masters of stoking it. The world was suddenly viewed only through the terrorism prism. There was no middle ground. As Bush famously said on September 20, 2001, "Either you are with us, or you are with the terrorists."

"If you lose where you're going,
you look back to where you've been."

TRADITIONAL SOMALI SAYING

2 Mogadishu

THERE MAY BE no country more cursed than Somalia, the archetypal failed state. Which is strange when you think that unlike so many other war-torn nations, Somalis share one language, religion, ethnicity and culture.

Somalia went into free fall in 1991 when warring clans deposed the military dictatorship of Mohamed Siad Barre and the incendiary fighting nurtured an entire generation on violence and poverty. Say Somalia and most think *Black Hawk Down*, three words that sum up the 1993 failed U.S. intervention that ingrained an image of a savage Somalia into the Western consciousness.

The U.S. Special Forces mission was an attempt to back a UN humanitarian mission trying to quell the chaos that followed Barre's ousting. What the U.S. administration did not appreciate in its attempt to capture Mohammed Farah Aideed, the ruthless warlord of the day, was Somalia's fierce clan structure and nationalistic pride. Nothing unites Somalis more than fending off a foreign force, which is why a militia in flip flops and armed with rocket-propelled grenades managed to shoot America's sturdy steel birds out of the sky and send its elite forces running for cover.

Black Hawk Down had always been my image of Somalia. Every time I walked down the newsroom corridor to my desk I saw the dusty, battered torso of U.S. Staff Sergeant William Cleveland. The *Toronto Star*'s Paul Watson risked his life to take that Pulitzer Prize–winning photo of Cleveland's corpse as it was dragged through the streets of Mogadishu by a cheering, dancing, frenzied mob on October 3, 1993. Paul would later write in his memoir, *Where War Lives*, that before he took the photo he "winced with each blow."

Paul's image of Cleveland, one of the eighteen American soldiers killed the day two U.S. Black Hawk helicopters were shot out of the sky (and hundreds of Somalis were killed in the fighting), changed the course of history, prompting U.S. President Bill Clinton to pull American forces out of the region. When it was announced the following year that Paul had become the first Canadian journalist to win a Pulitzer Prize, colleagues paraded him around the newsroom on their shoulders. The *Star* later created commemorative pewter coins about the diameter of hockey pucks depicting Paul with a disproportionately enormous forehead. "A pall of stunned silence fell over the room," Paul later told me, describing the moment when managers handed out the coins. "Then suddenly there was a single *thunk* of a coin hitting a plastic garbage bin, followed by another and then more, in a rippling wave of *thunks* as my oversized, memorialized forehead hit bottom across the *Star*." When I joined the newspaper as a summer student a year later, reporters who still had the coins had stashed them in their desk drawers and the consensus seemed to be that money spent on a big party would have been a better idea.

After 1993, Somalia largely fell off the world's radar as the fighting continued and thousands died of starvation and disease. The West became reluctant to get involved again, which brought disastrous consequences not just for Somalia but for the region. The Western world ignored the 1994 genocide in Rwanda until it was too late partly because of *Black Hawk Down* aftershocks and fears of becoming involved in African affairs. The little foreign help Somalia did receive throughout the 1990s came from Arab states, Saudi Arabia in particular, which helped fund schools and mosques and deliver humanitarian aid.

With 9/11 came fears that the Horn of Africa would harbour fleeing al Qaeda fighters from Afghanistan as it had in the past. U.S. forces set up a military base in nearby Djibouti, and Somalia's instability took on global significance. Conferences, summits, dialogues and reconciliation meetings were held in five-star hotels in neighbouring Kenya as UN officials and diplomats met with Somali warlords, politicians, businessmen and clan power brokers to discuss a way out of the mess. The meetings would end with much hand-shaking and ten- or fifteen- or twenty-point plans of action, and there would be brief periods of optimism before greed, corruption, ineptitude or bureaucratic bungling would scuttle any chances of peace.

Somalia had fascinated me as an important terrorism footnote, and with the majority of foreign reporting after 9/11 focused on the wars in Iraq and Afghanistan, Somalia was interesting for the simple reason that almost no one else was covering it. Somalia also held special significance for Canada, home to the world's largest Somali diaspora outside of Africa. It was one of the few countries in the world where the *Toronto Star* carried as much clout as the *New York Times*—and in some cases more. Many Somalia-born Canadians held positions of great influence in their birth country and had homes about a thirty-minute drive northwest of my newsroom.

For the first few years after 9/11, I concentrated on making contacts within Canada's diasporas, prominent Muslim organizations, the Canadian Security Intelligence Service and the Royal Canadian Mounted Police, trying to build the *Star*'s first national security beat. The timing for this new direction was good. In 2002, I was part of a team of *Star* reporters headed by my husband that wrote a series about racial profiling and Toronto's police force. Jimmie had spent two years fighting for access to a police database that would reveal patterns suggesting police in certain circumstances treated blacks more harshly than whites. The stories caused a major uproar. The police union sued our paper for $2.7 billion in a class action defamation suit. (We won the legal battle, with costs.) The series eventually resulted in important changes and was awarded the Governor General's Michener Award for public service journalism. But needless to say, covering city cops got a little more challenging after that, and I welcomed the change in beat.

One of the biggest Canadian national security stories when I started concerned Maher Arar, a Syrian-born Canadian citizen and Ottawa engineer who was detained in New York's JFK Airport during a stopover in 2002 and was covertly flown to Damascus for interrogation as part of the CIA's rendition program. In early 2004, after his release, I went to Syria to retrace his steps and learned more about another Canadian who had been held and tortured as a terrorism suspect. Later that summer, I spent almost every week in Ottawa covering a federal inquiry into Arar's case, which concluded that the RCMP had passed erroneous information to the United States, which influenced the decision to render him. Arar was vindicated and awarded a $10.5 million settlement.

By 2006, I was eager to do more foreign reporting and in particular to learn more about Somalia. I pitched a trip to Mogadishu. Somalis living all over the world were returning to the country's capital. For some, it was the first time in fifteen years they had felt safe enough to visit, weeping as they saw the African coastline where they grew up, or felt the heat, or introduced their Western-raised children to their homeland.

What had transformed the country's previously anarchic capital was a group called the Islamic Courts Union, a union of small Sharia courts throughout the south. The ICU was doing what no one else had managed: they took weapons off the streets, shut down the gun markets and chased away the warlords and dismantled their checkpoints, which had once dotted every block. Soon couples ventured out after dark. The airport opened. Kids played soccer on the streets. The ICU brought civility to a city that had seen none in fifteen years. The Transitional Federal Government had the backing of the UN but was led by unpopular warlord Abdullahi Yusuf Ahmed, and by 2006 most Somalis had given up hope that they could stabilize the country. When the ICU took over control of Mogadishu and much of the south, the TFG was pushed 250 kilometres west, to the town of Baidoa.

The secret to the ICU's success was that they had overcome sub-clan rivalry in Mogadishu. The majority of the ICU's senior members belonged to the powerful Hawiye clan, and the unifying forces were religion and a hatred of warlord Abdullahi Yusuf Ahmed (of rival Darod clan). Somalia had always been beholden to a complicated and fierce clan structure that was part of the reason past attempts at reconciliation had failed. But the ICU purported to have only Islam as the backbone of their organization, and in bringing all the sub-clans of Hawiye together, the ICU had done something no UN-backed, CIA-funded agreements (of which by this point there had been fourteen) could.

Then there was the other side of the story: the worrying fact that the ICU adhered to a strict interpretation of Islamic law. There were reports that thieves had their hands amputated and adulterers were stoned to death, music and theatre were banned, the media faced "regulations," and women were forced to cover their faces with the niqab or be penalized. There were also foreign ICU members with pedigrees earned in Afghanistan who appeared on the U.S. and UN terrorism watch lists. Some Western analysts compared the ICU to Afghanistan's Taliban. The conditions certainly looked similar. The Taliban had come to power in 1996 amid chaos as the world paid little attention.

Many Somalis, the majority of whom were Sunni Muslims following the Sufi traditions infused with dancing, art and the honouring of saints, were just as concerned about the ICU's Saudi-influenced doctrine that banned music and imposed harsh rules on women. The shooting death of two fans watching a World Cup soccer match made headlines around the world. A ban of the ubiquitous and much-loved leafy narcotic qat had many grumbling and in some cases mounting small protests. But even with these reservations, after years of bloodshed, most Somalis acquiesced since they were thankful for the stability.

When my editor gave the trip to Somalia a green light, I tried to recall the lessons I had learned a few months earlier in my "Hostile Environment Training" course. British ex-marines offered these sessions for journalists heading into conflict zones. (A course certificate also lowered the insurance rate our papers paid to cover us when we travelled.) Basically, it was a week in a Virginian field where the tough Brits beat the snot and scared the shit out of us. The first morning began with a surprise hostage-taking as "kidnappers" in balaclavas ran from the woods, stopped our car and hauled us out of the vehicle (I went by my pony tail since I was awkwardly stuck in the back), threw burlap sacks over our heads and then had us march, kneel, lie motionless face down in the dirt in a drill that felt all too real. The entire exercise was videotaped and later analyzed so we could learn what made a "good hostage" and a few other tricks. Other lessons that week included how to negotiate checkpoints, cover riots (wear natural, not manmade fabrics that could melt and stick to your skin if burned), identify different types of explosions and negotiate a minefield, as well as general orienteering, which was by far my worst session—not surprising, as I cannot read a map in Toronto, either, and lasted only two days in Girl Guides as a kid.

My favourite session was first aid, thanks partly to a background in lifeguarding, but also because I found our instructor endlessly amusing. Tall, lanky and right out of a Monty Python skit, his every sentence included the phrase "Happy with that?" As in "Your leg has been severed by a machete. Happy with that? What do you do now?" Or, "You've run out of water. Happy with that? Happy with that? Do you drink your piss?" The scenarios they set up for us were resplendent with fake blood and Oscar-worthy performances, and my hands shook every time I tended to the "victims" or used a Sharpie to write on someone's forehead the exact time I had tied the tourniquet so the doctors would know if the limb could be saved or if it had to be amputated. The only time I saw one of our instructors break role was when I tried to stop a femoral artery bleed. "Lovie, that's not working," said the smirking instructor as he pushed my quaking hands south of his crotch to his inner thigh.

I arrived at Washington's National Airport after that week with fake blood still on my cargo pants and my dirty hair tamed in two braids, so exhausted that I fell asleep at the gate. I woke only as my name was called over the speaker and ran breathless onto the flight. Startled passengers looked up and I am sure more than one thought, *Great, we're about to be hijacked by a deranged Pippi Longstocking.*

How any of this would help me in Somalia if things got bad I had no idea, but I packed a big first aid kit anyway. There were two such different versions of what was taking place on the ground, it was hard to know what to expect. Was this the long-awaited chance for peace, or the startup of al Qaeda's next franchise?

I could never have imagined that over the years my tour guides into this part of the world would be a Toronto grocer, a wanted terrorist, a stubborn tortoise, a primary school teacher who would become president, a Somali-Canadian journalist and a teenage boy named Ismail who broke my heart.

FLYING HIGH OVER Mogadishu's chiselled coastline, looking at the soft haze beyond the airplane window, I could imagine what once was: the beachfront cafés, lively soccer games and vibrant markets that only Somali elders nostalgically recall. At the safety of ten thousand feet, all that was visible were the outlines of the bone-white Italian architecture, built by the capital's former colonial rulers, and the turquoise Indian Ocean. Descend farther and see Mogadishu today: the broken, pockmarked, crumbling city of bombed-out buildings, the sun relentlessly beating down on arid red dirt, a city that has been ravaged by two decades of war.

I flew to Mogadishu from Nairobi with *Star* photographer Peter Power in October 2006 as the only foreigners on a commercial flight into the newly opened airport. Pete is an affable, tough Newfoundlander and an excellent partner. Aside from his mighty photography skills, he had spent a brief stint in the army before entering journalism, which came in handy in tense situations or when the military mindset confounded me to the point that I was ready to scream. Besides, Pete had a superhero-like last name that people loved wherever we travelled. Somalis especially delighted in greeting him and always seemed to do so with gusto: "Mr. Power! Time to go." "Welcome, Mr. Power!" "Mr. Power! Over here." It was hard not to like

Pete. He laughed often, talked openly (and incessantly), told bad jokes and after a few beers you might even hear traces of his New-foundland accent. Like most photographers he also possessed an endearing blend of bravado and insecurity.

Before leaving for Somalia, we had hired one of the country's best "fixers." That's a term used by journalists for local contacts who will fix everything from setting up interviews and security, arranging hotels, telling you what to wear, what to eat, providing translation, driving and, although it's not part of the job description, almost always becoming cherished friends. Foreign journalists are often only as good as their fixers. They're especially important when the journalist arrives in a country for the first time.

There have been cases since 9/11 when fixers have sold journal-ists to kidnappers offering a higher price. Others talk a bigger game than they deliver. But most fixers are respected local journalists, and hire themselves out as a lucrative side business.' The journalism com-munity worldwide is small (and more collegial than most would expect), so reputations—both bad and good—spread quickly. Fix-ers are paid well, but they put themselves at risk to help us. Aside from facing danger alongside us, fixers working with foreigners can be targeted as traitors. We have passports and go home. Most fixers have nowhere else to go.

Abdulahi Farah Duguf came highly recommended as a skilled and trusted fixer in Mogadishu. Even though the city was the safest it had been in years, there were always risks for foreigners. Swed-ish freelance photographer Martin Adler had been shot in the heart by hooded assailants as he covered a street protest just a couple of months before we arrived. Months before that, BBC producer Kate Peyton had been killed within hours of arriving in Mogadishu. Even the most prepared or experienced journalists can be killed or kid-napped, but having a good fixer was the first step in reducing risk.

Duguf was a close friend of Ali Sharmarke, a Somalia-born Cana-dian and a giant of journalism, and also a friend of mine. Ali came to Canada as a refugee in 1990 and built a life with his family in Ottawa, becoming a citizen and completing a master's degree in public administration at Carleton University. In 1999, Ali left a good job with the Canadian government's finance department, and with two other Somalia-born Canadians, started HornAfrik, Mogadishu's most popular radio station. Somehow HornAfrik had managed to survive amid the chaos. Ali was one of those people who always seemed untouchable, even physically, since he was taller and more robust than most Somali men. When he strode through my newsroom during a visit in the summer of 2006, people turned to watch because he had a presence—you just wanted to know who he was.

It wasn't hard to find Duguf as we disembarked from African Express Flight 525 and dozens of excited passengers ran onto the tarmac. He was the only person coming toward the plane. Duguf walked with arms outstretched, the morning sun bouncing off his bald head and a grin consuming the lower half of his face.

After brief introductions and hugs, he ushered us into a small office where, as the only two non-Somali visitors, we were told by bored-looking officials of the Islamic Courts Union that we would have to pay a "visa" fee of $250 U.S. They were not a governing force, but our passports were stamped anyway with a very professional-looking ICU symbol, an entry that would cause many raised eyebrows among airport immigration officials in the years that followed. Mogadishu's airport security consisted of having our bags thrown in a pile and being "inspected" by men armed with hand-held metal detectors, who, descending seemingly out of nowhere, pounced upon the luggage, eliciting a cacophony of beeps. I kept my knapsack on and one of the inspectors tentatively came over and waved his wand around my back as if he were conducting an opera, before nodding me on.

We climbed into our Jeep, with Duguf at the wheel. We were the middle car in a convoy of three we had hired, armed guards representing a variety of clans hanging out of Jeeps in front and behind us in case we had any troubles. We set out to meet "Somalia's Taliban."

THE BLUE DOORS of Al-Furqaan University opened to reveal a driveway with intricately laid chipped tiles, upon which a rusted red

Vespa was parked. It was an idyllic snapshot, with chirping birds and students, clutching books, who stopped to stare and smile at the foreigners. The cool breeze in this oasis of education brought relief from Mogadishu's sun-baked, sandy streets.

We were here to meet Canadian Abdullahi Afrah, known to friends by his nickname, "Asparo." His involvement in the ICU is what convinced my editors that the transformation of Somalia under the ICU was a story worth telling.

The *Star* may be Canada's largest circulation newspaper, but our readership is largely based in Toronto and the surrounding region, known as the Greater Toronto Area, or GTA. As with many papers, the *Star* gives precedence to stories with a local connection—which is why, after 9/11, I sought out Cindy Barkway. Many reporters like to poke fun at old-school *Star* editors who believe every foreign story needs a Toronto connection. How far would we go to seek our "GTA man"? Earthquake in Pakistan? Find that injured guy who once lived in Toronto or has a cousin in Mississauga and suddenly your story is moving from A17 to the front page. Crime wave in Mexico? Only important if Oakville tourists were hurt. Asparo was our GTA man in Mog.

Surya Bhattacharya, a *Star* intern and a friend of mine, had come across an ICU press release in August 2006, announcing the group's executive members. One of the leaders was Asparo, which surprised many in Toronto. Asparo had come to Canada in the early 1990s, and by all accounts he led a life in Toronto like that of many struggling newcomers. He was quiet—almost shy—and religious, but no more so than most Somalis. Asparo moved between jobs, working for a brief time as security supervisor at Toronto's Catholic school board, and he once ran a *hawala* bureau—a money transfer service popular for wiring funds home to Somalia—that would come under intense focus after 9/11. Ahmed Yusuf, a well-known community leader in Toronto, knew Asparo when he lived in Canada. "No one could believe it," he said about the ICU press release. "We thought it couldn't be the same man."

Asparo stood at the university's front doors, shaking Pete's hand and acknowledging me with a nod. He appeared neither annoyed nor pleased with our visit and was certainly in no hurry to talk. In fact, he was reluctant to speak at all. The fifty-four-year-old insisted that we visit one of the university's professors before our interview. Leading the way up the stairs, he laughed and said to no one in particular, "There are so many lost Canadians here." After introducing us to Professor Ibrahim Hassan Addou, he dipped his head and departed, leaving us to wonder if our GTA man would return.

Many were also surprised to see Professor Addou listed as one of the ICU's executive members, because, like Asparo, he was not considered an aspiring religious leader or politician. He was a Western-trained academic, a scholar, and that's exactly what he looked like standing behind a desk in his sunny classroom, with students' papers piled high on it and a chalkboard behind him. He gave us a wan smile as he peered over the rim of his owl-like glasses. We had a feeling we were about to get a lesson in Islam rather than an interview.

Addou had returned to Somalia in 2002, having lived for twenty-four years in Georgetown, where he worked as an administrator at Washington's American University. He was proud of his American citizenship and enjoyed life in D.C., but like many other expats he felt a responsibility to his country of birth. His philosophy? "Educate the lost generation," he said. Enlightenment was the only way out of poverty. He was also an environmentalist, which may have seemed like an insignificant vocation when war and poverty consumed Somalia. But Addou believed fixing problems such as deforestation, illegal commercial fishing or the polluting of Somalia's coast by foreign companies was key to securing a stable future.

Addou, like Asparo, was considered a "moderate Islamist," an ambiguous term that in Somalia generally meant the person supported a more tolerant interpretation of Sharia law. Before leaving Toronto, I had been in contact with Addou, since the only safe way to travel in Mogadishu was with the ICU's consent. Addou had emailed me a form titled "Visa Regulations by the Islamic Courts." The application stated that foreign nationals could not enter Mogadishu without written permission. Within ten working days, they would respond as to whether we could come—all very formal, professional. "Finally, please be informed," the form concluded, "foreign nationals who attempt to enter the country illegally as well as their sponsors (if any) will face swift penalty."

As Addou finished talking about the merits of education about an hour later, Asparo slipped silently back into the room. He seemed surprised that we still wanted to talk with him. Haltingly, he answered our questions, his eyes turned down to his hands or stroking his red, henna-dyed beard. His lined face looked older than fifty-four. He kept insisting he couldn't understand why we were curious about his involvement with the ICU. "This is something that just happened. When things happen, someone's lucky to be moved up. It's not something I was looking for. It's not something I even enjoy doing, but it's something I have to do."

He echoed what others were saying about how the ICU had transformed Mogadishu and brought order, and urged other Somalis around the world to return and help. "There's a bright future if things go on like this. We can say people will be saved, resources may come back, international relations may improve, construction may happen, people's trust in each other may be renewed. Many, many things that were happening before. People were running around doing whatever they wanted to do. Law and order may now be restored. Somali people are talented people if they get some sort of environment where they can work on their own. Somalis have something in their hearts that they're attached to their country even though they're better off over there. He has a nice car, a good life, but he needs to get back to see his broken home."

Like Addou, Asparo wasn't interested in answering questions about perceptions in the West about their group, or to debate the ICU's restrictions on women's rights and harsh punishment under Sharia law. Just exaggerations, he said.

Before we left, Asparo had one more message for me, something to put in the newspaper he used to read every day: "You have the power. Use your pen in the right way."

IF ASPARO AND ADDOU were considered the moderates, then Hassan Dahir Aweys was one of the ICU's radicals. The night before we left Nairobi, I sat with Pete in our hotel, discussing the trip on a conference call with our editors. One senior editor wanted to know how likely it was that we would get an interview with Aweys. When I said I had no idea, the reply was something to the effect of, "Well, can't you get his address and knock on his door?" I lied, unsure if he was joking or not. "Good idea."

The thing is, you don't drop in on Aweys. He lets you know if you are welcome, and when. Luckily, we were. While sitting on rugs in the shady cool comfort of HornAfrik's media compound, we got a call to see him. The call meant we had to leave now, before he changed his mind. "Go, go," yelled Ali Sharmarke, who was delighted and surprised that Aweys would meet a female reporter.

Duguf knew exactly where Aweys lived, but when everything started to look the same as we sped along the sandy streets, I was sure we were lost. Mogadishu's main street, named 21 October for the day General Mohamed Siad Barre seized power in a 1969 military coup, was lined with vendors' shacks hawking everything from goat carcasses to cellphones. Merchants stared as we passed. Ribbons of purple from the bougainvilleas, and the reds and blues of the women's abayas, created a colourful blur beyond the car window. Down a small alley off the unmarked Ballad Road, we neared Aweys's home. Children scattered as we roared in, except for one boy, who curiously cradled a dusty blender as he waved furiously with his free hand.

Two months after the 9/11 attacks, Aweys was put on the U.S. terrorist list because of his alleged connections to Osama bin Laden. He became one of the men U.S. President George W. Bush liked to call the "evildoers." The reclusive seventy-one-year-old former army commander was a well-known figure in Somalia. He was nicknamed "the Red Fox" because of his shrewd military career—but his red, scraggly beard and long face certainly didn't hurt.

Aweys had been a powerful leader with Al Itihaad al Islaam, a group that was formed in the final years of Barre's dictatorship, and fought against Somalia's most powerful warlords in the early 1990s—General Mohamed Farah Aideed and Colonel Abdullahi Yusuf Ahmed. (Aideed, of *Black Hawk Down* fame, was the warlord

U.S. Special Forces targeted during their disastrous 1993 mission. Ahmed became the unpopular president of the Transitional Federal Government. A month before we arrived, he survived an assassination attempt that killed his brother and several others; he publicly accused Aweys of orchestrating the attack.) Aweys and other former Al Itihaad leaders were some of the founders of the ICU and held sway in the various Islamic courts across the south.

On MSNBC's *Meet the Press*, three months before our trip, U.S. Senator Russ Feingold criticized the war in Iraq and inaction in Somalia during an interview with host Tim Russert: "You know, Tim, today it was announced that a guy named Hassan Dahir Aweys is now the head of the government that has taken over in Mogadishu, in Somalia. He is on the State Department's terrorist list. He is known as an al Qaeda operative or somebody that is connected with al Qaeda. While we are asleep at the switch; while we are bagged—bogged down in Iraq; while we are all focused on Iraq as if it is the be-all and end-all of our American foreign policy, we are losing the battle to al Qaeda because we're not paying attention. I asked Ambassador (Henry) Crumpton at a hearing the other day how many people in our federal government are working full-time on the problem in Somalia. He said one full-time person. We spent two million dollars on Somalia in the last year, while we're spending two billion dollars a week on Iraq. This is insanity, if you think about what the priorities are in terms of those who have attacked us and who are likely to attack us in the future."

The day we met, Aweys had the flu and sat listlessly in a stuffed velvet chair with a blue-and-white crocheted doily on one of the armrests. He didn't stand when we entered, but motioned to some chairs. His lethargy likely wasn't helped by the fact that we were visiting during Ramadan, so he had not eaten or had water since dawn. Flies buzzed around the house, which was humid and dark, except for a narrow ray of sunlight slicing through heavy gold and green curtains.

"Ask me anything," he began, peering through filmy round glasses.

But after more than an hour, it was clear that Aweys was happy to talk in circles. Many of our questions were met with questions.

"Ties with Osama bin Laden? If I met Osama bin Laden, did I make a mistake?"

"We don't care what they say," he said eventually, about reports of the ICU's formal allegiance to bin Laden. "We don't have any links to al Qaeda." Finally, exasperated, he almost pleaded: "Why don't they give us a chance?"

I snapped shut my notebook, and we emerged squinting in the punishing sun, saying our final goodbyes. We wanted to be careful not to overstay our welcome. Aweys had undoubtedly agreed to an interview because he wanted us to tell the story of Mogadishu's pacification. More than once, he mentioned the fact that he was meeting a Western woman as proof of his modernity. But despite this desire for good PR, Mogadishu was Mogadishu and not all of his followers appreciated our presence. The scowling faces of some of the youths lounging on soiled mattresses in Aweys's courtyard were starting to unnerve us. We were keen to get back to the guarded walls of Horn-Afrik, or to the Peace Hotel, where we were staying—its name made us feel safe.

As we turned to leave, however, shouting began. Or it sounded like shouting. Aweys was speaking loudly. Quickly. Passionately. I tensed, wondering what we had done wrong, self-consciously touching the rim of my hijab. Thinking we had been set up, I turned slowly around, locking eyes with Duguf before looking at Aweys. The Red Fox had come out onto the porch and was staring at my feet, which I had just slipped into my boots. He was grinning. In the bright sunlight his age was more apparent and he looked frail, and, well, goofy, with his toothy white smile slicing through his red beard. My eyes went to my scuffed Blundstones, durable if not fashionable Australian footwear popular among journalists. (The company motto is "Because Life's Tough.")

Soon Duguf was grinning too. "He likes your boots," he said. Aweys was nodding violently. The boys in the courtyard were snickering. For a second I contemplated slipping them off and giving them to the man the United States wanted dead—if for no other reason than I was so relieved. I started to laugh. Aweys laughed. Pete snapped a picture. I bowed my head and put my hand to my chest in an awkward goodbye, then quickly marched those Blundstones out of there.

WITH SHEIKH SHARIF SHEIKH AHMED, the soft-spoken teacher turned political leader of the ICU, agreeing to see us next, we managed to interview the leadership of the organization in less than twenty-four hours. Duguf would later call us the luckiest journalists he had ever worked with.

We met Sharif at Villa Somalia, the guarded presidential compound the ICU had commandeered. He sat in a room that looked as if a Saudi prince and California surfer had collaborated on the decor. The wood was polished, and burgundy drapes with gold stitching covered the windows. From the ceiling hung streamers, deflated balloons and beach balls bearing Fanta, Pepsi, 7Up and Coke logos. More than a dozen men lounged on cushions along the walls murmuring into their constantly ringing cellphones. Sharif nodded to me but did not offer his hand to shake.

Like Aweys, Sharif was happy to talk, but revealed little. He described the chaos that had reigned before the ICU took over and spoke of his newfound optimism for peace. "People were not anticipating there would be light at the end of the tunnel," he said, with a grandiose sweep of his arms.

Sharif may have comported himself like a politician, but he was born into a family of Sufi scholars, not powerbrokers. Sharif left Somalia in his twenties to study civil and Sharia law in Libya and Sudan. But when he returned to southern Somalia in 2002 and tried to set up an Islamic court, he faced bitter disagreements with a warlord from his own clan. He accepted the setback and returned to Mogadishu, where he gave up law and became a primary school teacher. One of his twelve-year-old students was kidnapped for ransom in the crime-prone city, and Sharif, along with the school principal, managed to negotiate the boy's rescue. That kidnapping became a defining moment in Sharif's life. He had brought about change in this one case; he could do it for his country. Believing that Islamic law was the only way to overcome clan differences, this time he focused on Mogadishu, with a goal of eventually uniting all the existing courts in the country. He had no following of his own, but aligned himself with Aweys. Though diplomatic in nature, Sharif was no pacifist, and his first step was to get rid of what stood in his way—the embattled UN-endorsed government. He found support among Somalis fed up with the cruelty of the warlords, some of whom were reportedly backed by the CIA. This foreign support for marauding militias only made the Somali-run courts more attractive.

Sharif became frustrated when I mentioned comparisons between the ICU and the Taliban during our interview. He also denied claims that foreign fighters were training recruits at ICU camps and said he had nothing to do with the recent audio statements by al Qaeda leaders about their "brothers" in Somalia. It was what we expected him to say and it was clear he would offer little else.

As we left Sharif's compound, Duguf suggested we see a remnant of one of the downed Black Hawk helicopters. Pete thought it could be a good photo and I was curious to see the site that Mark Bowden had described so vividly in his book *Black Hawk Down*, the scene that forever haunted my friend Paul Watson. As our convoy stopped on an empty street, a woman emerged from her home and a young girl with tassels hanging from her red hijab like a fringe of bangs stared at us. Duguf showed us an overgrown thorny bush decorated like a Christmas tree with bits of garbage. A piece of the wreck was supposed to be under there. But before we could look further, suddenly, people were shouting, the woman's hands were flailing and Duguf looked annoyed. Within seconds, the once empty street was packed. I got back in the Jeep as Pete went to get Duguf, who was arguing with the woman.

Dozens of men pressed up against the window and started yelling "American," laughing and banging the glass, trying to rock the Jeep. I smiled weakly, mouthing "Nooo... Cann-ehhh-di-ann," which made their jeers louder. Hmm. What had those British SAS guys taught me to do in a situation like this?

The crowd didn't believe me, or understand, or care if I was Canadian or American or Bhutanese, but I wasn't sure what else to do. So I just sat there smiling and pressing my blue passport against the window like a shield while Pete yelled at Duguf outside the Jeep. His lips looked like they were saying: "Time to go!" Once they made their way through the crowd back to our car, the convoy finally inched forward and then took off at high speed when in the clear. Duguf seemed calm but was shaking his head in disbelief.

"She wanted us to pay!" he finally said. The woman, who lived nearby and we later learned was called the "Black Hawk Lady," had wanted us to pay a fee to see the piece of helicopter. She wanted about $5, something we would have gladly paid for a "museum" fee, considering we had already paid $250 for a "visa." But Duguf was indignant. He considered us guests and was furious we were being taken advantage of. But it appeared few were on Duguf's side.

AS THE SUN SANK below the roof of the Peace Hotel that night, the clanking of plates and mewing of scrawny cats heralded the end of that day's Ramadan fast. Ali Sharmarke swirled his decaffeinated coffee slowly, cradling one cellphone to his ear while another jumped closer to the table's edge with each vibration. Hotel owner Bashir Yusuf Osman was famous for treating his foreign guests to lobster dinner on the roof, but on this night we sat under a tree in front of the hotel with a simple but delicious dinner of fish and rice. Business was booming at the Peace Hotel, where the generator rarely failed, with humanitarian workers, foreign journalists and businessmen tentatively coming back into the country. There were no vacancies when we arrived, but Bashir's younger brother kindly gave me his room and Pete found space with a couple of generous Japanese photographers.

"They just closed our station in Kismayo," Ali said, hanging up the phone. Earlier in the day, his HornAfrik reporters had covered an all-female protest against the ICU in the southern town. The ICU retaliated by shutting down the station. When I had asked Professor Addou about a free press earlier in the day, he had agreed wholeheartedly about its importance. But he added that journalists must work "with restrictions." In fact, there were thirteen. Rule 13: "The media must not employ the terms which infidels use to refer to Muslims, such as 'terrorist,' 'extremists,' etc." Journalists were not allowed to create "conflict" with their stories. "It's so arbitrary," Ali said, shaking his head.

As we discussed these problems, the heavy tin door to the hotel compound was in constant motion, opening to let in visitors like a curtain sliding back between acts of a play. We were afforded glimpses of the darkened street, where men strolled arm in arm or children ran alongside the odd goat. The evening's soundtrack that night was a murmur of voices and laughs, not the gunshots that Somalis had grown accustomed to.

Farah Muke could barely contain his excitement as he ran through the doors and up to our table, pumping my hand furiously. Farah was Canadian and like many of Toronto's Somali diaspora lived in the Rexdale neighbourhood north of the city. Also like many Somalia-born Canadians, Farah was a diehard patriot. "If I see any Canadians here, I have to meet them," he said, explaining that word had reached him that journalists from the *Star* were in town. "I love the *Toronto Star*!" Farah had returned to Mogadishu four months ago but missed his Canadian home and planned to return soon. "I fly a Canadian flag from my home and people are always asking why I do that, and I say, 'Because I like Canada so much!'" He asked if we could come see his flag, maybe take a picture the following day?

Throughout the night, visitors came to the hotel to see us: a Somali poet, other Canadians, curious neighbours of the hotel. And while this easy flow of people may not have seemed remarkable to us, Ali assured us that it was. Most people stayed home after dark in Mogadishu.

But Ali was still worried about the ICU's radical element. Young, bloodthirsty fighters like Sheikh Indha'adde and Sheikh Mukhtar Robbow, also known as Abu Mansour, were jockeying for power. There were frightening stories about how ICU members dispensed their own perverted sense of justice. Would these factions overwhelm Sheikh Sharif? What about Aweys, whom no one trusted?

But even Ali, indignant with the restrictions on his reporters, could not denounce the entire organization. It was simple. The ICU had delivered a break in the war, and for that, at least for now, Somalis were thankful.

SOMETIMES IT IS hard not to picture terrorists holed up in caves, with AK-47s resting against the muddy walls and generators powering broadcasts of Fox News, around which they all huddle. Giggling. Rubbing their hands. "This is making our job too easy," one would exclaim. Gifts for al Qaeda recruiters: the Iraq war, the abuse of prisoners at Abu Ghraib, the burning of Qur'ans, the tortured death of an Afghan taxi driver in Bagram, waterboarding, misguided predator drones, faulty intelligence. In this theme of disastrous reactions to disastrous events comes the next chapter in Somalia's history.

U.K.-born, Canadian-raised analyst Matt Bryden, who has lived much of his adult life in Somalia and neighbouring countries and speaks Somali fluently without a trace of an English accent, was among those who tried to warn what would happen if fears about the ICU led to their removal by force. "After more than a decade of political disengagement from Somalia, the United States has plunged back in with an approach that threatens to produce precisely the scenario it seeks to avoid: a militant Islamist movement that serves as a magnet for foreign jihadists and provides a platform for terrorist groups," Bryden wrote in an essay for the Center for Strategic and International Studies in December 2006.

Arguing that since 9/11 Washington has viewed Somalia through a narrow counterterrorism lens, with almost no political engagement and little humanitarian aid, Bryden stated that Washington's new policy of pledging its unconditional support for Somalia's Transitional Federal Government and for longtime rival Ethiopia is "not just self-defeating: it is inflammatory." He wrote: "Washington appears to have designated the Courts as a strategic adversary, elevating Somalia from a simmering regional problem to a global issue. The Courts are now likely to attract support from a far broader range of anti-American and anti-Western interests than they have so far, and the flow of foreign funds and fighters to the [ICU] seems bound to increase dramatically."

Abdullahi Yusuf Ahmed's transitional government had lost credibility among Somalis partly due to the corruption among the government's ranks. But as so often is the case with dizzyingly complicated Somalia, the struggle for power between the Transitional Federal Government and the ICU was oversimplified in the West. The ICU and all its members: terrorists. The TFG: good guys.

Behind the scenes, the Bush administration was focused on three men hiding in Somalia who were wanted in the 1998 bombings of the U.S. embassies in Kenya and Tanzania. According to *New Yorker* journalist Jon Lee Anderson, Michael Ranneberger, U.S. Ambassador to Kenya, had attempted to negotiate with ICU leader Sharif, telling him that if he would eschew terrorism and take action against the three high-value targets, they could work together. "He listened and nodded and seemed to understand. But then he went back to Mogadishu and I never heard from him again. I guess he had no traction there," Ranneberger told Anderson.

Further attempts for diplomatic solutions were abandoned. Ethiopia, Somalia's neighbour, had long been wary of Islamic uprisings, fearing that any movement in Somalia would radicalize Ethiopia's sizable Muslim population. Ethiopian tanks rolled across the border into Somalia on Christmas Eve 2006, with Washington's blessing. No one believed the ICU could withstand Ethiopia's army, but the speed and ease with which it captured Mogadishu was surprising. Within two days, the capital of Somalia belonged once again to the TFG. Back in Toronto, I watched these events unfold and knew that it would be a long time before there would be a peaceful scene at the Peace Hotel again.

THE TAXI DRIVER couldn't believe what he was hearing. Stop the car? *Now?*

It was a few months after Ethiopia's invasion, in March 2007, and the fighting in Mogadishu was at its worst in years. Ethiopian troops were battling a fractured Islamic insurgency, clans warred with clans, and criminals and warlords were fighting everyone. As always, thousands of impoverished civilians with nowhere to go were caught in between. The taxi was speeding away from the chaotic Bakara Market, until the passenger, a bespectacled, gentle forty-seven-year-old Somali-born Canadian named Sahal Abdulle, insisted that they stop. Actually, he was yelling, and Sahal almost never yelled.

Ambling across the street, unaware of the war raging around him, was a massive, crusty tortoise. He was going as fast as he probably could, which wasn't very fast at all.

Sahal had thought he had seen everything in Mogadishu, but spotting a tortoise near the concrete jungle of the market and this far from the city's rocky coastline was like finding a moose striding across Toronto's Bay Street, or a bear ambling across Park Avenue in Manhattan. Sahal knew it was crazy to stop. He also knew he had to. "I just need to protect something," he thought.

Minutes earlier, Sahal had been near the Damey Hotel, reporting on what the mortars and AK-47s and RPGs and bombs had left behind. In military terms, it was called "collateral damage," civilians caught in the fighting. In real terms, it was dead children, women and civilian men, and severed limbs. Sahal was passionate about his duty as a journalist, but sometimes his work just seemed futile. Especially when no one seemed to care. And it often seemed that no one cared about Somalia.

Sahal yelled to the driver, his friend Hussein, "Give me a hand and open the trunk."

"No. We're not doing this," Hussein replied, but he was already out of the car, bobbing and weaving, flinching with every crackle of gunshots.

Together they lifted the tortoise, struggling with its weight despite their adrenalin-fuelled strength. The mighty beast retracted his head and limbs and defecated on them.

The second-oldest of ten children, Sahal was born Abdullahi Abdulle in the Somali town of Galkayo on a Friday in 1962. His mother was in labour for four days giving birth to his older brother, but Sahal was delivered in less than two hours and that's why everyone called him Sahal—Somali for *easy*. Sahal's early childhood, however, was anything but. As a toddler, he developed a condition that doctors could not diagnose but which had similar symptoms to hemophilia, and his nose bled profusely if he was too active. Most of his childhood and teenage years were spent indoors with the elders, drinking tea. His pillow was covered in plastic so his blood wouldn't ruin the fabric.

His only relief was a concoction made by his grandmother, a traditional medicine woman. Every morning, Suban Isman Elmi would rise before dawn and brew a soup made of roots, filling the house with the smells of her magic. Sahal loved his grandmother and admired her grit and otherworldly wisdom. "Whatever I had, I would eat that soup and I would be okay," Sahal said. "I don't know if it was psychological or physiological but that taste, even forty years later, is kindness." When he was seventeen, he went to Nairobi, and the cooler climate cleared up his problem. Two years later, a Somali doctor gave him an injection and miraculously, mysteriously, he was cured.

But those early years shaped Sahal. He was different from other kids his age; perceived as weak, he never learned to ride a bike or play soccer. Other children called him "Sahal Oday," Sahal the Old. He never forgot that feeling of others looking down on him, or worse, not noticing him at all. It was the main reason he became a journalist. He wanted to empower the weak. As he often told others, "I want to speak for the voiceless."

In the late 1980s, with his life's savings—a Nikkormat EL2 camera—hanging around his neck, and his passport stamped with a U.S. visa, Sahal left Africa for the first time, in the hopes of becoming a photographer in San Francisco. He had always expected to return to Somalia, but in 1990, when the fighting that would eventually topple the dictatorship of General Mohamed Siad Barre started, Sahal decided instead to travel north. In November 1990, he drove to Buffalo, crossed the border and asked Canada to accept him as a refugee.

He would not visit his homeland until three years later, with a better camera, a new perspective, and a desire to tell Somalia's story.

Sahal lived the life of many Somali-born Canadians, with one foot in each world, their hearts aching for their homelands, their fingers freezing in Canadian winters. His children were born in Toronto and he loved his adopted home. But as a journalist, he struggled with a need to "fix" Somalia, and after 9/11 he feared his homeland would only be considered as an incubator of terrorism; the underlying basic problems such as poverty, education and government corruption would be overlooked.

I had become friends with Sahal in Toronto, but it was during my trips to Kenya and Somalia that I really got to know him. In Toronto, we often rushed through a meal or coffee, apologizing that we didn't have longer to talk. Yet in Africa we were on Somali time, and one tea led to the next as we apologized for having kept each other so long.

Sahal was working for Reuters while the war with Ethiopian forces was raging in 2007. He had a large home in Mogadishu, across the street from the Shamo Hotel, which was a hub for foreign journalists who were brave or crazy enough to make repeat trips. They liked to tease Sahal about his quirky habits, even though they all had their own ways of coping with war. Sahal had four.

On days when the fighting would wake him before dawn, Sahal, the Constant Gardener (yet another nickname), would seek solace in the cool dirt of his yard, where he had managed to cultivate more than seventy-two different flowers and vegetables. He even grew ginger, which he required for his special brew of Kenyan Ketepa tea. Working in the garden as the sun rose—weeding, watering, caring for these fragile crops—calmed him. At night, he would put on earphones and blast John Coltrane while he smoked a cigar—coping mechanisms two and three. Foreign journalists were his main cigar suppliers and would bring Sahal boxes of Cubans each time they visited.

The rescued tortoise became Sahal's fourth passion. He didn't have a name. He became, simply, "Tortoise." Often when Sahal came home to edit and send photos and articles to his bosses in Nairobi, he was still numb. The lens offered a small measure of detachment in the field, an ability to document but not fully absorb the horrors he was witnessing. But once the fatigue set in and the laptop displayed the reality in full colour, allowing Sahal to zoom in and out and crop . . . well, that's when Tortoise would start his slow walk. "I would be looking at my computer and I would be stressed out," Sahal recalled. "Then out of the corner of my eye, I'd see him on one side of the computer, just slowly, slowly walking." It would take about twenty minutes for Tortoise to make his trek, disappearing for a time behind the laptop screen, before emerging out the other side. "By the time he got there," said Sahal, "whatever you were doing, you would just think of him."

I heard news of the war mostly through Sahal, Ali Sharmarke or local journalists and their reports. Increasingly there was talk of al Shabab. When the ICU was in power, a violent splinter group that called itself the Harakat al-Shabab al-Mujahideen was vying for control. More commonly known as "al Shabab," meaning "the youth," the group's origins likely pre-date 2006, but that was when they became an organized force. Aden Hashi Farah, or "Ayro," was one of the original founders and had reportedly been appointed to this youth militia by Aweys, the Blundstone-boot-loving Red Fox. Shabab were ruthless and had little support among Somalis until Ethiopia's invasion gave them the recruitment pitch they needed, not only among young, impoverished Somalis, but also among neighbouring Kenyans and disenfranchised Somali youth living around the world just as analyst Matt Bryden had predicted. Those giggling cave-dwellers had another gift they could spin endlessly. Christian crusaders were trying to take over Somalia. This was a war against Islam.

The emails I received from Ali Sharmarke during the war sounded more desperate by the week. "You don't know who's attacking you," he would write, since the ICU, al Shabab and the Ethiopian-backed TFG were critical of any negative press. Few foreign journalists covered Somalia that year, but local reporters were dogged and for their efforts they were being targeted and assassinated in record numbers.

ON AUGUST 11, 2007, a large group of Somali journalists, including Sahal and Ali, gathered at the funeral of one of their own. They were burying Mahad Ahmed Elmi, a popular talk-show host on

HornAfrik. Mahad didn't mince words, and, despite death threats, he was relentless in holding the warlords, the Islamists and government officials accountable. Mahad was shot three times in the head on the way to work that morning and was buried the same day, as is customary in the Islamic faith. Before going to the funeral, Ali had called Ahmed Abdisalam Adan, one of his HornAfrik co-founders, who was visiting Canada. "I'm just worried about the young reporters," he told his friend in a weary voice. "The risk is getting so great."

Hours later Ali spoke passionately at the gravesite. He lamented the loss of Mahad, and another blow to journalism in Somalia, and the dwindling hope for peace in the country. "We are in the crossfire—all of us journalists," he said. "The killing was meant to prevent a real voice that described the suffering in Mogadishu to other Somalis and to the world. He was a symbol of neutrality... The perpetrators want to silence our voices in order to commit their crimes." This was uncharacteristic of the usually cautious Ali. But he was mad and feeling guilty. He had inspired a generation of journalists who were now being slaughtered at the rate of one a month.

Ali left the funeral exhausted, and slumped in the front seat of a black Toyota Land Cruiser. Duguf, who had been our fixer, was driving. Sahal sat in the back with Falastine, Ahmed's wife. They were only eight kilometres from Sahal's home near the Shamo Hotel, where they could mourn their colleague behind guarded walls, where the garden and cigars, John Coltrane and Tortoise waited.

Bang. Darkness. Dust.

It was never determined if Shabab had detonated the remote-controlled improvised explosive device or if the Ethiopians or TFG were behind the killing. As Ali had said, everyone wanted journalists dead. The Land Cruiser passengers stumbled out bleeding and deaf. Ali had to be pulled out. He lay motionless on the road. He was fifty.

At first I didn't believe the news when I heard it a day later. I remember the call; I remember that it was my birthday. But I can't remember who called me. There were always rumours from Somalia, and besides, Ali was just one of those guys who didn't die. A picture of his body on the Internet confirmed it and I sat at our kitchen table crying and hating Somalia. Thinking back to the corridors of Horn-Afrik's newsroom, where Ali had proudly hung the international awards his radio station had received, I remembered the dozens of sayings and words of inspiration taped on walls or sitting framed on desks. One hanging near Ali's office read: "Our lives begin to end the day we become silent about things that matter."

Sahal was not sure if he would ever return to Mogadishu after Ali's death. Reuters offered to put him up in a Nairobi hotel after the bombing. He chose a modest one in the town centre and rarely ventured out. When he did, he would see Ali walking the streets. "I knew it was a matter of time before something happened; statistically the chances were there," he told me years later, still tearing up at the thought. "But my sons, Liban and Abdul Aziz, what would they think if anything happened to me? Would they think, 'That son of a gun abandoned us because he was there, selfish, looking after his career and Somalia instead of us?' But I wanted them to have a part of their heritage—the gift of what I had of my father. But now I feel like that gift was taken away," he paused, then repeated, "Now I feel like that gift was taken away."

Liban, Sahal's eleven-year-old son, helped him heal and find the courage to return to Toronto, and then eventually back to Somalia. Liban later conveyed his pride in his father's work to a room packed with Canada's top journalists who had gathered at a gala dinner in Toronto to honour Ali posthumously. Standing on a box to reach the microphone, his voice unwavering, Liban read a speech that reduced the cynical, grizzled crowd to tears. "Reporters have a lot of courage and determination. All they want is to make a difference, to educate people on what's going on in the world. That's exactly what my uncle Ali Imam was trying to do," Liban told the crowd. "Can you believe someone could be killed because they wanted a better world, a more educated society?" After his speech, Liban ran around the ballroom collecting business cards from the journalists, later beaming as he showed me the stack like they were precious and rare hockey cards.

While recovering from his wounds in Toronto, Sahal had left his Mogadishu home, his garden and Tortoise in the care of a trusted cousin, who carefully tended to the plants and animals. But one day in the summer of 2008, cleaners scrubbed the concrete patio out-side Sahal's home with a mixture of chlorine and chemicals. The toxic brew pooled in one of Tortoise's favourite cool afternoon rest-ing places. Tortoise died later that afternoon, and the death of that stubborn reptile felt like Ali's death all over again for Sahal.

Tortoise had somehow survived traffic, the power-hungry war-lords, insurgents, clan warfare, disease, misguided foreign policies, neglect and starvation, only to die a senseless death. Somehow, Tor-toise's death seems like an apt metaphor for Somalia itself.

THE YEAR AFTER Ali died, a young Somali girl named Asho Duhu-low went missing from a refugee camp in Dadaab, Kenya. No one remembers the exact date in August 2008 that Asho disappeared. Her disappearance was barely noticed outside her immediate family, which is not surprising since Dadaab is one of the world's oldest and largest refugee camps, where stories of loss are more plentiful than bread. Alive, young Asho was just one of 230,000 refugees, about 90 per cent Somali, who lived in the United Nations camp in the desert-like northern Kenya region near the border of Somalia. Dead, she would become an international story about Shabab's brutality.

While the details of her disappearance remained murky, the details of her death were not. She died in the Somali port town of Kismayo on October 27, around 4 PM, after she had one last tearful conversation with her father and after her captors buried her legs so she could not escape. A small group of men stoned her to death with large rocks.

Al Shabab had killed Asho as punishment for the crime of "adul-tery." It was a public execution before hundreds, and local reports said some onlookers tried to intervene, running forward in protest until Shabab's militia fired into the crowd. A young boy was report-edly killed. Rock after rock struck Asho's head and chest. A break only came when someone, reportedly a nurse, stepped forward to see if she was dead. Asho had a pulse; the stoning resumed. Pic-tures surreptitiously taken with a cellphone recorded the gruesome aftermath. One blurry shot shows the bloodied face of a girl wearing a soiled pink sweater. On Somalia's Radio Shabelle, a Shabab spokesperson later said that Asho had pleaded guilty and "was happy with the punishment under Islamic law."

I read about Asho in an Amnesty International report and was eager to go to Dadaab to see how other Somali refugees were faring. I had been there before, with Pete Power. The camp was reportedly growing by the day, resources were thin, tension was mounting and Shabab was recruiting amid the disorder.

Around the time I heard about Asho, I also became aware of an Ottawa-based program called World University Service of Canada. Each year, the organization selected refugees living in camps around the world to study in Canadian universities. WUSC had awarded its thousandth scholarship that fall. Of the eighteen students who had been hand-picked from Dadaab, some had come to Toronto, and Muno Osman was one of them. I went to meet Muno in her apartment at the University of Toronto's Mississauga campus, still only thinking of telling Asho's story, wondering if she had known her in Dadaab. When I met Muno, I knew she was a story herself.

With our luggage full of gifts Muno wanted us to give to her sisters and parents at the camp, I went back to Dadaab. This time I worked with Lucas Oleniuk, a Star photographer favoured by editors and reporters alike. Over years of working together, we had developed a sibling-like relationship.

A Prairie high school football star and son of a Saskatchewan prison warden, Lucas was as tough as he was hard-working. In New Orleans, in the chaotic aftermath of Hurricane Katrina, police ripped Lucas's camera off his neck and threw him to the ground after he photographed them beating a handcuffed suspect. He handed over a second camera and then walked the block to cool off before confronting them and demanding back his equipment. They returned the cameras, minus the memory cards. He would continue to find himself in police crosshairs throughout the years, dodging bullets in Bahrain, or following the 2010 earthquake in Haiti, where he captured a wrenching photo of fifteen-year-old Fabienne

Cherisma as she lay dead, clutching three ornamental mirrors. The teenager in the pink skirt, T-shirt and sandals had been running with other looters when police shot at random, striking her in the head.

At Dadaab we tracked down Asho's family, and over the course of a week discovered the sad life of a little girl who had suffered from epilepsy and struggled in school. Her father still carried her prescription for epilepsy medication, folded hard into a little block of paper about the size of a matchbook. He pushed it at us like it was a clue to her disappearance. The story of how she left that camp was impossible to verify, even after interviewing many who saw her on that last day. She may have left willingly for Kismayo, trying to find the Somali town that existed only in her imagination and her grandmother's stories. Or she may have been kidnapped as a bride. One report said she had been gang raped when she got to Somalia and reported the crime, only to be charged with a crime herself.

Jihadi websites justified her killing, purporting that Asho was in fact "over twenty years old, married and practising adultery" and thereby rightfully killed under Sharia law. But we talked to Asho's teacher at the camp's primary school and spent more than an hour in a sweltering, fly-ridden classroom poring over school records to find proof of her age and see her report card. We tracked down someone who was at the Dadaab hospital the day Asho was born. Asho was only thirteen, not that her killing would have been justified had she been any age, but I took delight in debunking the jihadi websites.

A short walk (but what seemed like a world away) from Asho's distraught parents lived Muno's proud mother and father. The whole family had sacrificed to get Muno that coveted scholarship, her sisters taking up chores, her father having to defend his daughter's pursuit of education among some of the traditional Somali elders at the camp who wondered how, at twenty, she could not yet be married. We had brought photos Lucas had taken of Muno on campus, which I'm sure looked to her family like they were taken on Mars. Her sisters handled the photos carefully with expressions that oscillated between pride and fear as we squatted on the ground over plates of cookies and xalwo, a sugary homemade jelly. Mohamed Osman, Muno's father, said he always fought for education for his three girls. "Seeing is believing," he said. "I was always supporting her. Girls are equal beings." Muno's beautiful mother, Safiyo Abdikadir, added quietly, "I just wanted her to be something. I'm illiterate and I know how horrible it is."

They laughed tenderly when describing the day their middle child left. Muno was sobbing. It may have been the happiest day of her life, but that didn't mean leaving was easy. Her parents had to carry their daughter onto the bus, helping her leave the camp the same way they had brought her here as a two-year-old refugee, eighteen years earlier.

Muno took planes—which she had only seen before in the sky—to London and then Toronto. Under the folds of cloth that covered her, she wore new winter boots, jeans and a leather jacket. She almost passed out when she finally arrived at Toronto's Pearson International Airport. Everyone had told her Canada was cold. No one told her, though, that it didn't snow in August. Muno hoped to sponsor her family in Canada one day. Her parents longed for her to return to Somalia and prayed for peace.

In 2006, Dadaab's population was at its limit, staff said. By 2008, it had grown by 30,000 and definitely could take no more. By 2011, more than 300,000 displaced Somalis lived in Dadaab.

Dadaab continues to grow.

ONLY THREE YEARS had passed since Sheikh Sharif met me in Mogadishu and talked about that light at the end of the tunnel; about how he would bring peace so that refugees like those in Dadaab could finally come home. Only three years ago, he was the leader of an Islamic insurgency that some in Washington cited as the next great threat to the West. Only three years ago, he was one of President Bush's evildoers.

I replayed that last meeting as I rode the elevator to his suite at New York's Waldorf Astoria. I made it past the cordon of dozens of NYPD agents standing guard outside, only to be met by a muscular and unsmiling U.S. Secret Service agent. "I have an appointment with President Sharif." *President Sharif.* It was October 2009, and Sharif had just addressed the United Nations. A month earlier, in Nairobi, he made headlines around the world after shaking hands with U.S. Secretary of State Hillary Clinton. She called him the "best hope" in a long time for Somalia. Some feted Sharif as a visionary. New York was his coming-out party.

President Sharif entered the room wearing a blue suit, a white shirt, a delicately embroidered prayer cap and a pin of Somalia's flag on his lapel. His hand was outstretched. Three years ago, we had not shaken hands, and had I tried the gesture would have likely been met with disapproving clucks from his advisors.

The hotel room smelled of roses; large unopened glass bottles of Evian sat nearby. The fruit tray and exotic flower arrangement, with a spiky protea at the centre, probably cost more than most Somalis make in a year. "You're first, Al Jazeera is next," said a jubilant Abdulkareem Jama, Sharif's chief of staff, an American citizen who also acted as our translator. "We have thirty minutes."

Was Sharif the same man I had met three years earlier? Or had he adapted to the times? Some analysts believed he was a chameleon, a politician ready to say what both the United States and the hard-line Islamists wanted to hear. Others just thought he was well meaning, but weak. He laughed when I asked how he had changed, how Somalia was different today.

"The challenges people were facing before were kidnappings, rape, violence, all kinds of problems. No one at the time believed change could come but I had a lot of hope," he said of his 2006 tenure with the ICU. "I find myself in the same spot now where we have a lot of serious challenges and people saying this is not going to work. But I am full of hope."

Same man, different times?

Sharif was among the ICU leadership that fled for safety during Ethiopia's 2007 incursion. According to *New Yorker* journalist Jon Lee Anderson, Sharif was one of the men the United States had contemplated killing. Anderson quoted an unnamed Western official as saying, "Sharif headed south with some bad guys," naming three jihadis who were linked to al Qaeda and were on America's wanted list. "These were people the Americans were keeping a close eye on, and Sheikh Sharif was with them." The United States was planning air strikes to target the men. "In the State Department, there was some back-and-forth over whether or not he was a good guy and could be rescued, or left to die along with the others in the air strikes." One camp believed that "Sharif's attitude made him a bad guy," the official said, while others argued that "diplomacy hadn't really been attempted." Sharif was spared. He fled to Kenya, where he was arrested. After only a few months in custody he was released and moved to Eritrea, where he began a movement against Western "crusaders."

Ethiopia finally conceded defeat in late 2008 and withdrew the last of its troops from war-weary Somalia in January 2009. A temporary government was formed—another Transitional Federal Government—once again with the support of the United Nations. Sharif was welcomed back to Somalia, and the new parliament voted him in as president. The ICU as it existed in 2006 was no more.

Sharif's former ally at the ICU, the wily Hassan Dahir Aweys, opposed the new parliament and formed his own militia, Hizbul Islam. For a while, Aweys's group fought the virulent al Shabab, which had begun to target Somalia's new parliament after Ethiopia was pushed out. But then Aweys flip-flopped and joined forces with Shabab in late 2010.

Professor Addou, the well-respected scholar, had fled to Yemen during the Ethiopian invasion and spoke publicly about the need for negotiations with the TFG. He eventually came back to Mogadishu to work alongside Sharif as dean of Benadir University and minister of higher education. A couple of months after I met Sharif in New York, Addou presided over a graduation ceremony of medical students at the Shamo Hotel, near Sahal's house in an area of Mogadishu thought to be safe. Just as the December 3 ceremony began, a suicide bomber disguised as a woman struck, killing twenty-five and injuring sixty. Addou was among the dead.

"There were hundreds of people in the meeting hall," wrote Mohamed Olad Hassan, a Somali journalist who worked for the BBC and the AP. "The students were all dressed in colourful uniforms for their graduation. The hall had been brightly decorated, and there was a feeling of excitement—such ceremonies rarely happen in Mogadishu. With the conflict raging throughout the capital, the chances to attain academic credentials were limited. This ceremony, perhaps, symbolized a trace of hope: People's lives could continue despite the shelling. Proud parents beamed at their graduating loved ones, who were also sitting in the hall. Journalists, particularly the cameramen, were right in the front for a good view. People were making speeches, and we were taking notes, as usual. Then all this brightness turned to darkness. All I remember is being covered in dust. Some debris apparently from the roof of the hall hit me and there was no light anywhere. I looked across and the young guy sitting next to me was dead. The seat he had been sitting on was mine. We had changed positions for one moment, when I had left momentarily to move my recorder nearer to the speakers. That's when the explosion occurred."

Rather than flee the fighting when Ethiopia invaded, or return to Canada, where he may have been detained or at the very least questioned by authorities, Asparo, our GTA man in Mog, stayed in Mogadishu with his family. In a 2007 phone interview, he told me that the presence of Ethiopian forces had united Somalis, and al Shabab was now seen as the country's saviour. He warned there would be chaos if Ethiopia did not withdraw. Asparo was killed in July 2008, although the circumstances of his death were never clear. Some local reports said he had joined the fight against Ethiopian troops. Others found it hard to believe he was on the front lines.

MY MOGADISHU ALARM clock was a mixture of mortar fire, the morning call to prayer and a persistent Somali cat outside my window. It was January 2010, three months after Sharif addressed the United Nations in New York, and time to test the government's claims that they had a grip on the country.

For the parachute-jumping, hotel-nomad journalists like me who make short visits, rather than live in the region, going into

Mogadishu meant embedding with the African Union (AU) forces responsible for Somalia and known as AMISOM (African Union Mission in Somalia). The 5,300-strong AMISOM force of Ugandan and Burundi soldiers propped up Sharif's administration while thousands of Somali forces underwent training in the country and in nearby Djibouti or Uganda.

When African Express 523 landed at Mogadishu's airport, the first thing I noticed was the new departure terminal. Looked promising. There was a lounge, coffee bar and even a duty-free shop. It had been six months since any mortar attacks had reached the airport, officials boasted. I was given an immigration form to fill out with spaces for Name, Nationality, Date of Birth, Occupation and "Purpose of journey to Somalia." Question 16 asked, "Weapons brought with," and included spaces for the type, serial number, trademark and calibre.

I was warned that journalists could travel only in armoured vehicles, wearing a helmet and flak jacket, and had to be back at the AMISOM base near the airport by nightfall. That meant riding inside behemoth South African–made Casspirs, built to withstand mines and improvised explosive devices. Convoys of these white beasts, looking like deranged caterpillars, slunk through town, commuting between the only AMISOM strongholds—the airport, the AU compound and Villa Somalia, where Sharif and members of parliament worked and lived.

Ugandan Major Ba-Hoku Barigye, whom everyone called "BB," was my AU minder. He had an agenda, which included three meals a day, and he would stick to it no matter the griping or twitching of journalists who were happy to skip meals if it meant getting out on the street during the short visit. BB's two cellphones constantly buzzed with texts. The generator failed one evening, and with the compound lit only by moonlight, BB started scrolling the texts for me to read. "You are going to die today," said one. "Yo are the begest enimy of Somalia so you have too go to the country ergently otherwise you will meet consequence." "Al Shabab very very good." BB chuckled as he read that one.

Mogadishu may not have enough water or food for its people, but it seemed everyone had a cellphone. It was part of the uniform for al

Shabab, and when you are a seventeen-year-old kid who has grown up with war and has no job prospects and maybe no family, I guess texting is pretty cool. Even if some of the threats were laughable, some were chilling.

AMISOM forces did control the airfield and areas around the port, which were essential. But it was pretty hard to see signs of real hope on the streets. Al Mukarama Road, the city's main thoroughfare, looked like a hurricane had swept through, upending buildings and cars and downing power lines. Government soldiers hung off Jeeps with their Kalashnikovs and belts of ammunition. The Associated Press reported that many of the uniformed soldiers, trained thanks to U.S. funding, continued to defect to al Shabab after not being paid their monthly salary of $100. Stories of corruption were still rife.

Perhaps the most jarring sight, however, was the brightly coloured laundry strung between the crumbling facades, or the gaggle of smiling school girls in their matching lime-green uniforms—signs of normalcy, of life. I tried to capture them, firing wildly with a high shutter speed as we roared past in the belly of the angry caterpillar.

AMISOM ran a hospital inside the "safety zone." Somehow, people—women mainly—would find the strength to travel as many as four hundred kilometres, often crossing inhospitable and dangerous terrain, to reach the health centre. The outpatient clinic was open three days a week, and sometimes they would wait eight hours in line, in the punishing heat, holding their limp babies, before doctors could see them. If the clinic couldn't admit all the patients during daylight, they would have to come back the next day and wait all over again. They were beautiful, those elderly patients with deeply creased faces, the slender women and their children. But BB was impatient as I stopped with another photographer to take pictures. The schedule for escorted journalists was tight, but it felt wrong to be banging off frame after frame, without stopping to talk to the women or to play with their children.

Click. The old man with the henna-dyed beard holding his own IV bag barely looked up as I took a photo. A curious little girl with a perfectly round face and almond-shaped eyes peeked from behind her mother's abaya. *Click.* A baby, maybe nine or ten months old, cried hysterically at the sight of me, which made everyone laugh and tut-tut. They were barefoot or wore flimsy sandals. I had my trusty Blundstones, helmet and flak jacket. *Click.*

Two hours after we visited the hospital, an 82-mm mortar shell hit, striking the line of patients. At least five people died, including a Ugandan peacekeeper. Scores were injured. Later, I couldn't stop looking back at the faces in the photographs and wondering if the little girl, the old man or that wailing baby had been among the dead. No names were released, and a Shabab spokesperson later announced that the attack was in retaliation for an earlier fatal assault by AMISOM. I worried that they had heard foreign journalists were in town and were trying to kill us so that the publicity would put them on the front pages of newspapers. Four dead Somalis and a Ugandan peacekeeper didn't merit even a brief mention in most newspapers, including mine. Since Sharif had been president, it had been an endless war of words, a tit-for-tat assault and counter-assault between government forces, AMISOM and al Shabab. They all fought for public support and sometimes it was difficult to see who was pulling ahead. Somalis were fed up with Shabab but equally frustrated by AMISOM assaults. Since the AU forces were mandated as a peacekeeping mission, they were unable to attack until fired upon. But that happened often, when Shabab launched mortar attacks on Villa Somalia—most of which were more of a nuisance than deadly. AMISOM answered those assaults with much higher-grade bombs that would rain down on the Bakara Market or on neighbourhoods where Shabab hid. Most often it was the civilians who were killed.

Somalis even have a word for Shabab's provocation: "flashing." The term normally applies to cellphone calls—flashing is when you call someone's cell once but immediately hang up. Since it costs less to receive a call than to make one, flashing allows the recipient to call you right back if you are low on prepaid minutes. Some believed Shabab was doing the same thing with their attacks—they hoped for AMISOM to "call back" with an attack of their own. A bomb is a bomb, mortars are mortars, a firefight is just a firefight and war helped blur the line between good and bad guys. AMISOM lost support among Somalis when their weapons killed as many as Shabab's.

Al Shabab was also able to offer protection to the average Somali. With nowhere else to turn, market vendors started pledging support or paying a "tax," not unlike the extortion that has helped fund the Mafia for decades. It was a matter of survival.

ISMAIL KHALIF ABDULLE waited in a large empty ballroom inside the government compound known as Villa Somalia. Three glass chandeliers with gold trim hung from the ceiling; outside, a patio overlooked a surprisingly lush Mogadishu. Looking scared, Ismail slouched on a ratty sofa beside two of his friends. He was seventeen, but could pass for thirteen. He had a soft fuzz on his upper lip and wore an oversized pale blue dress shirt with faint pink stripes. His grey dress pants were too big, or missing the top button, so they buckled at the waist and were cinched together with a safety pin.

Abdirashid (Rashid) Hashi, a former Toronto journalist who had recently moved back to Mogadishu to act as a communications director for President Sharif, had been telling me about Ismail for months. Ismail was the main reason I had come back to Mogadishu. "People don't understand how ruthless they are," Rashid had told me in emails about Shabab. He was especially distraught by news that Toronto-born kids were travelling to Somalia to join the group. By that point, at least five had left Canada and gone missing with vague notes or emails later saying they had joined Shabab.

My time with Ismail was short, as I had to get back to the AMISOM compound before dark and could already hear my escort somewhere outside, arguing with Rashid. Through a Somali translator, I asked Ismail if we could go toward the window, where the light was better, and take some pictures before our interview. He immediately jumped up, retrieved a red chair, reached down to remove his prosthetic leg and crossed the stump of his left leg across his right knee. His shirt cuff hung loosely over the raw skin where his right hand used to be. I tried to steady the lens and not tear up as he looked directly into the camera, sweating.

Back on the couch, we hadn't been talking for more than ten minutes when he asked—begged, really—"Can you take me back to Canada?"

About six months before I met Ismail, the Somali teenager was on his way home from school in the Dayniile neighbourhood where he lived, when two members of Shabab came to get him. Al Shabab controlled much of central and southern Somalia by then and this neighbourhood was theirs exclusively. Ismail explained that kids often joined Shabab forces because they were scared. Or they joined because it was a good feeling to belong after growing up with nothing but war. Or they joined for the cellphones. Some joined because they believed that Somalia was part of a global war against the West and felt it was their duty as Muslims. Most just thought that getting onside with the guys with big guns and deep pockets seemed like the smart thing to do.

But Ismail was different. He told them he wanted to continue his education. So the two Shabab members left without a word. A few days later they came back, this time with a truckload of fighters. "They pointed their guns at me and told me I was a thief and I was robbing people, and took me to their prison," Ismail told me, his eyes getting bigger with every detail. In the "prison," which was a heavily guarded house, he discovered that his friend Ali Mohamud Gedi had also been kidnapped, as had two others with similar stories. Two of those boys were sitting beside him as we talked—each of them, like Ismail, was missing a foot and a hand. For twenty-five days, the four were held with little water or food.

On the morning of July 25, 2009, they were driven to a stadium. Ismail asked his captors to loosen their grip. "I'm not running anywhere," he recalled saying to them. They didn't reply. He was pinned down on a dirty mattress in the centre of the stadium as men in white coats and surgical gloves surrounded him. Now he told them to hold him real tight because he didn't want to move as they sawed off his right hand with a knife. He passed out from the pain before they took the left foot. The three other boys underwent the same amputations as a crowd looked on. Their limbs were later hung in the town square as a warning.

Ismail's story didn't end in that stadium. Fifteen days after the amputation, while still captive, Ismail says he was visited by Shabab leader Fuad Shangole, a Somali-born Swedish resident who had returned recently to Mogadishu. Shangole chastised Ismail's captors. "You only cut to here," he said, pointing to Ismail's right ankle. He demanded more be removed and pressed three fingers on Ismail's stump as a guide. Ismail was held down screaming again and this time a saw was needed to cut through the bone.

A few weeks later, Shabab became complacent with their prisoners. Ismail and the others had duped them into believing that they were now willing to join the cause and become suicide bombers. They planned carefully and the first moment they were left alone, they escaped. And here was Ismail, given brief refuge in the president's guarded compound so he could tell his story to a Canadian reporter.

Our time was up. The convoy of armoured vehicles could not wait, and since they would not travel after dark, they threatened to leave me behind, which meant I would probably miss my flight out the next day. Ismail looked at me beseechingly and then his eyes lowered to the Canadian flag pinned to my bag. I fumbled to take it off, clumsily handing it to him as I ran to catch the convoy. It slipped from his fingers, and he dropped it.

As I left the hall, struggling to put on my helmet and flak jacket, I looked over my shoulder to get a last glimpse of Ismail. He was hunched over, digging frantically through the couch cushions with one hand, searching for the damn little pin.

> "For them to perceive the advantage of defeating
> the enemy, they must also have their rewards."
>
> SUN TZU, *THE ART OF WAR*

3 Karachi

KHALID KHAWAJA WAS about as hard to figure
out as Pakistan itself. The tall, slightly stooped former associate of
Osama bin Laden had been an air force pilot during the 1970s and
80s before joining Pakistan's spy service, the Inter-Services Intelligence, or ISI. He was kicked out of the ISI in 1988 after criticizing
then-president Muhammad Zia-ul-Haq for failing to "Islamize" Pakistan, which was like attacking WikiLeaks founder Julian Assange
for failing to share information.

In "retirement," Khawaja was an enigma. He stayed close to
people in power but was thrown in jail periodically on unspeci-
fied security charges. He waxed fondly of bin Laden ("the man like
an angel") and boasted that he could still contact the world's most
wanted fugitive. In July 2001, he told CBS: "Your White House is the
most vulnerable target. It's very simple to just get it." After 9/11, Khawaja created an organization called Defence of Human Rights and
represented families of the "disappeared," citizens who vanished off
Pakistan's streets and were presumed dead, or held incommunicado
in ISI dungeons.

Khawaja did not mince words when criticizing the West or defending his quest for Islamic law in Pakistan, but his allegiance to bin Laden did not preclude him from taking unlikely bedfellows. In late 2001, he negotiated with the Taliban as part of a delegation that reportedly included former CIA director James Woolsey. He often met with foreign journalists—even female or American Jewish ones, such as *Wall Street Journal* reporter Daniel Pearl. In fact, when Pearl disappeared in 2002 on his way to an interview in Karachi, police first went to Khawaja.

Khawaja was one of the reasons I wanted to go to Pakistan in 2006. Aside from hoping to talk to him about his well-known connections, I knew that Khawaja was also tied to various Canadians, including the family of Guantanamo Bay detainee Omar Khadr. I had been covering the story of the Toronto-born teenager since 2002, when U.S. Special Forces shot and captured the fifteen-year-old in Afghanistan. Khadr was on trial for war crimes and accused of throwing a grenade that killed a U.S. Delta Force commando. Khawaja had been close to Omar's father, Ahmed Said Khadr (who was killed by Pakistani forces in 2003), and I had been researching the senior Khadr and trying to situate him in al Qaeda's hierarchy for years.

Khawaja had also known Amer El-Maati, a Canadian with alleged al Qaeda connections who was wanted by the FBI. Authorities believed he was hiding in Pakistan, and I had a hunch Khawaja knew El-Maati's whereabouts. I harboured fantasies that Khawaja would put me in touch with the elusive Canadian.

At the time, I was working for a *Star* editor named David Walmsley, a bouncy Irishman with blue eyes and a big smile, who liked to discuss stories over "a pot o' tea," which was his code for consuming as many pints as possible after work before taking the train back to his suburban home. David was a reporter's editor, someone adept at managing both up and down. He was no doubt ambitious and had little trouble climbing the ranks at Toronto's big papers. He was also not a details man, more of a big-picture guy, which annoyed some of my colleagues. But he made decisions without worrying about the politics of the *Star* and put a lot of trust in his reporters. He would randomly refer to me as the "Future," or respond to emails with just a "Zoop Wheee Boing." His enthusiasm was contagious. Once I understood his exuberant lexicon, I loved working for him. I especially loved him that day when he asked, "Where do you need to go for this beat?"

"Pakistan," I told him.

"Then go."

There was no country more important to understanding al Qaeda, the war in Afghanistan or the roots of 9/11 than Pakistan; and there was likely no country more difficult to decipher. After 9/11, President Pervez Musharraf quickly became one of Bush's most important allies and vowed to crack down on jihadi elements fuelling the insurgency in Afghanistan. But that meant fighting from within, and tackling an American enemy that both Pakistan and the United States had helped create.

In 1979, at the height of the Cold War, Pakistani-supported jihadist groups were part of Team Good Guys. The Soviets had invaded Afghanistan, and then Pakistani president Zia-ul-Haq used the occupation by the Americans' communist foe as an opportunity to gain the international standing he had sought since seizing power from Zulfikar Ali Bhutto in a 1977 coup. With substantial financial help from Saudi Arabia, and covert CIA backing, Pakistan became the launching pad for the mujahideen in Afghanistan. Muslim fighters from around the world raced to the region to join the legions of Afghan warriors. These were the glory days of the jihad, as fondly remembered by Khawaja and other former fighters. Pakistan, and in particular the border city of Peshawar, became host in the 1980s to a ragtag gaggle of spies, politicians, contractors, journalists, adrenalin junkies and jihadist-wannabes, all itching to get across the border.

Since President Zia-ul-Haq would not permit foreign funding to go directly to the seven main jihadi groups, the ISI became the trusted conduit. The agency essentially became a state within a state, as Pakistanis often say, and it was during this decade that the much-feared spy service cemented its position as Pakistan's great puppeteer.

The war against the Soviet occupation of Afghanistan is now well known, even part of Hollywood history—a tale of the noble fighters and their CIA friends conquering the great communist infidels. The movie *Charlie Wilson's War*, adapted from journalist George Crile's book of the same name, portrays these heroics through the story of U.S. congressman Charlie Wilson (Tom Hanks), the cocaine-snorting ladies' man who pulled the political strings for the CIA's covert war. In the movie, Wilson also enlists Maryland congressman Clarence Dickinson Long (known as "Doc Long"), who is so moved by the plight of Afghan refugees during a visit to Peshawar that he dramatically declares: "This is good against evil, and I want you to know that America is always going to be on the side of the good. *Allahu Akbar.*"

Being on the side of good, however, really depends on where you're standing.

With the eventual defeat of the Soviets (and in the absence of other international players who largely left with them), the ISI played a pivotal role financially, politically and militaristically in supporting the rise of Mullah Omar's Taliban from the chaos. Pakistan needed a friendly Afghanistan, fearful as it was of the threat of its other neighbour, nuclear-armed archrival India.

Pakistan formally cut all ties with the Taliban in 2001, but switching gears and heeding Bush's ultimatum of "either you are with us, or you are with the terrorists" did not sit well, especially within the ISI. On September 10, 2001, the Taliban was not considered a terrorist organization. There was an ambassador for the Taliban in Pakistan. Moreover, there was fear about what would happen when NATO forces and the United States withdrew from Afghanistan. Where would that leave Pakistan? The landscape had been dramatically altered by the time I visited five years later, but the mindset within Pakistan's establishment had not.

When I arrived in Pakistan with photographer Pete in 2006, our driver, of course, loved Pete's name. "Mr. Power!" The sign he had brought to the airport read: "Mr. Peter Power and Mr. Michassa Haphart." I think I confused him but he took us to the hotel anyway.

We had three goals for our trip: meet Khawaja to discuss his Canadian and ISI connections; get inside the Red Mosque, a bustling and militant Islamic centre in the heart of Islamabad; and visit the restive tribal Waziristan region that bordered Afghanistan. As I later discovered, the three stories that resulted would help me contextualize the country in the tumultuous years ahead.

KHAWAJA WAS IN Karachi and urged us to meet him there. We agreed, reluctantly, and after a series of phone calls and discussions through intermediaries, were given directions to a half-built triplex not far from a Karachi slum. Perfect.

In a 2002 *Vanity Fair* piece after Daniel Pearl's gruesome death, writer Robert Sam Anson wrote about reporting in Karachi:

> The reporter who comes to Karachi, Pakistan is given certain cautions.
>
> Do not take a taxi from the airport; arrange for the hotel to send a car and confirm the driver's identity before getting in.
>
> Do not stay in a room that faces the street.
>
> Do not interview sources over the phone.
>
> Do not discuss subjects such as Islam or the Pakistani nuclear program in the presence of hotel staff.
>
> Do not leave notes or tape recordings in your room.
>
> Do not discard work papers in the waste basket; flush them down the toilet.
>
> Do not use public transportation or accept rides from strangers.
>
> Do not go into markets, movie theaters, parks, or crowds.
>
> Do not go anywhere without telling a trustworthy someone the destination and expected time of return.
>
> And, above all, do not go alone. Ever.

Well, there were two of us. We had a driver we trusted and editors in Toronto, as well as some reliable contacts in Pakistan, who knew when our interview with Khawaja would take place and when we were due back. Many local journalists believed Khawaja's importance was overstated and that he was merely a mouthpiece who enjoyed publicity. Probably. But Karachi, a chaotic seaside city of 15 million where many al Qaeda leaders came to hide after being ousted from Afghanistan in 2001, was unpredictable, and it was wise to take basic precautions.

Parking beside a massive abandoned construction site, we were sure we had the wrong place. Then a slight boy with a droopy eye and limp ushered us into the dusty ground floor of the building and to Khalid Khawaja, who sat uneasily on a broken, three-wheeled office chair. Looking up briefly, he pointed to another wobbly seat.

There was no doubt Khawaja seemed to have a knack for knowing people in the news, so it came as no surprise when he told us by way of introduction that the half-built building belonged to millionaire Saifullah Paracha. Paracha, Guantanamo Bay prisoner 1094, was born in 1947 and is the detention centre's oldest remaining captive.

Paracha's case was intriguing. Unlike many of the other Guantanamo detainees who were picked up in Afghanistan or Pakistan (often for a sizable U.S. bounty), Paracha was picked up by the CIA in Bangkok, Thailand, on July 8, 2003. He was transferred to Gitmo fourteen months later. The Pentagon alleged that the prominent Pakistani businessman, who studied in New York in the 1970s and spent thirteen years living there and working as a travel agent, had ties to Osama bin Laden and KSM, al Qaeda's number three, and had offered al Qaeda leaders his textile export business as a means to smuggle explosives into the United States. His son was serving a thirty-year sentence in the United States for providing material support to terrorism.

Paracha denied all allegations and told a hearing at Guantanamo that his interest in Afghanistan had always been charitable—which, before 9/11, meant negotiating with the Taliban. Paracha told the military panelists that when the Northern Alliance took over he talked to them as well.

"My purpose was not to help the Taliban, the Northern Alliance, or the transitional government," he said at a hearing known as a

Combatant Status Review Tribunal, where he addressed the military board members in English, referring to each one of them as "sir."

My purpose was this: Afghanistan is a poor country and we should help wherever we can, whenever we can. I had no inclination toward the Taliban, the Taliban government, or the Northern Alliance. I am not a political man. I just wanted to help people. I am not an extremist. I mentioned in my write-up that my children go to Christian missionary schools. Fundamentalists do not send their children to schools like that. You can see from the interrogation reports, the report that is classified, that they [U.S. interrogators] have done a lot of investigation about me and put it on the record.

The session got heated when board members questioned Paracha about meeting bin Laden.

BOARD MEMBER: Do you believe Osama bin Laden is a man of peace? Do you think that by producing a program about Islam and the Qur'an, that would make Osama bin Laden a peaceful man?

PARACHA: Sir, I do not know if he is a peaceful man or not.

PRESIDING OFFICER: Osama bin Laden has issued a fatwa against the United States and he is not even a Muslim cleric. The man issued a fatwa!

PARACHA: Sir, Osama bin Laden is not entitled to issue a fatwa.

PRESIDING OFFICER: But he did anyway.

PARACHA: I know he did.

PRESIDING OFFICER: And people believe him!

PARACHA: I know sir, but I don't believe that.

PRESIDING OFFICER: I know you say that you don't believe in him. But you are saying that Osama bin Laden is a peaceful man.

PARACHA: Sir, I am not saying that Osama bin Laden is a peaceful man. What I am saying is *my message* according to the Qur'an would be one of peace. That is what we wanted him to talk about.

BOARD MEMBER: What are your feelings concerning the attack on the World Trade Center on 11 September, 2001?
PARACHA: Sir, I have been to the World Trade Center many times. I have taken my children to the World Trade Center. I thought it was one of the many wonders of the world. My own nephew was there. My own blood, they were there! . . . I was just as concerned as anyone could be.

And on the hearing went. The transcript provides an excellent glimpse into Paracha's personality (and those of the presiding officer and board members) but gives little evidence to help determine his guilt or innocence. What is clear is that if guilt by association were a war crime, then Paracha would be convicted. He admitted at his hearing that he met KSM nearly a year after 9/11. And he said he needed proof that al Qaeda was responsible for the attacks.

BOARD MEMBER: Do you believe Osama bin Laden would still like to do great harm to the United States?
PARACHA: I do not know, sir.

If guilt by association were also a crime in Pakistan, then Khawaja also would be kept in jail.

As we sat talking in Paracha's building, Khawaja recalled his friendship with Ahmed Said Khadr. He confirmed that Khadr had been in close contact with al Qaeda's elite, in particular the Egyptian faction led by the group's number two, Ayman al-Zawahiri. But he said Khadr's importance in al Qaeda was often overstated, as there was great mistrust of his travels back to Canada and many members of the paranoid organization believed the Egyptian-born Canadian was a spy. As for Amer El-Maati, the Canadian who according to the FBI was "wanted for questioning in connection with possible terrorist threats against the United States," Khawaja was more circumspect. He held the FBI flyer I had brought for him and stared at El-Maati's photo. I explained that U.S. Attorney General John Ashcroft had once called El-Maati "a clear and present danger." That seemed to amuse Khawaja. He hinted that he might know where

El-Maati was living with his wife and child, and we agreed to talk further—conversations that never materialized.

Our interview lasted more than an hour and at times Khawaja would stand to make a point, but he always spoke softly. He quickly became bored with questioning about Canadians and wanted to talk instead about foreign policy. Like leaders in Mogadishu, he liked to answer questions with questions and needed little provocation to launch into a rant. "Almost all the governments of this world are the terrorist governments," he said, moving closer to stress his point, but looking somewhere in the distance, over my shoulder. "They are responsible for the terrorism and for only their victims they cry."

When conversation turned to Daniel Pearl, he again waved his hand, clearly tired of this topic. "I knew him like I know you," he said, shrugging his shoulders, and then steered the discussion back to 9/11 and the wars in Iraq and Afghanistan. "After those people were killed, over 100,000 people have been killed by Americans—and that is proven. Killed. And we know who has killed them," he said. "Until now you have not charged anybody for that, which means up until now Americans have killed all these innocent people. They have abducted thousands of people and their families, like the family of the project here [Paracha]. They have just tortured and butchered them and there is no justice, no way in the world we can get any justice. See, Islam allows us to take revenge, equal revenge," he continued. "You break my tooth, I can break your tooth back."

History was repeating itself, Khawaja said, but this time the West was not happy. "We fought jihad in Afghanistan [in the 1980s]. The whole world said it was jihad. The Canadian government said it was jihad. The American government said it was jihad. The Pakistani government said it was jihad. So, it was a well-known thing that we are fighting a noble war in Afghanistan against the Russians. If killing Russians was permitted because of our faith, then the faith is the same. Why, after all, today the same faith does not allow us to do the same things to the Americans?"

Khawaja predicted that NATO forces would eventually be defeated in Afghanistan and forced to retreat like the Soviets. "The world is like a cage for us. We want to get out of this. So whether we stay here, we win. If we don't stay here, we die; we win. For us, life starts after this death. We do not believe in all these comforts. For this life is like a toilet. It's a necessity. You have to use it but you want to get out very fast. We play only a win-win game. For this reason, you cannot win from us. You fight to live, live a comfortable life. We fight to die. You love to live. We love to die."

Khawaja was always good for a sensational sound bite, and the *Star* story that followed my interview would highlight the quote: "*You love to live. We love to die.*" But take away his grandiose rhetoric and life-is-a-toilet view of the world, and some of his messages seemed mainstream by 2006. The majority of Pakistanis despised the Taliban, but there was widespread anger over historical amnesia as the war in Afghanistan dragged on. As the death toll rose, so did anti-American sentiment. Places like Guantanamo or the CIA's black sites angered Pakistanis as much as their own government's practice of holding terrorism suspects without charges or trial. Pakistani forces were dying for a war that most Pakistanis felt was not theirs to wage.

A Pew Global Attitudes Project poll found that in 2004, 51 per cent of Pakistanis surveyed believed that the real purpose of the "war on terror" was to wage war on unfriendly Muslim governments and groups. Two years later, the majority polled said the war had made the world a more dangerous place. Although inconceivable in the West, polls also showed that nearly a quarter of the Pakistani population had a favourable view of Osama bin Laden. In most quarters, he was held in higher esteem than President George W. Bush.

Then came the drone attacks. In 2006, two U.S. predator drones killed nearly eighty people in Pakistan's tribal region, further eroding support for the Musharraf-Bush alliance and sparking protests about the American incursion into Pakistan. Both strikes were meant to kill Zawahiri. News reports in the West covered the fact that he was not among the dead, but quoted Pakistani and U.S. officials as saying the mission was a success since the second strike destroyed a training camp. News reports in Pakistan showed the bodies of madrassa students, and quoted villagers saying there had been no camp, just a religious school for the poor.

During our interview, Khawaja warned repeatedly that the West still perilously overlooked the significance of Pakistan's connections to the Taliban and would never be able to conquer them in Afghanistan. The term "AfPak," used to emphasize the importance of considering both countries (and regarded as a derogatory phrase in Pakistan), was later popularized by the U.S. special representative to Afghanistan and Pakistan, Richard Holbrooke, but in 2006 it was not yet a foreign policy buzzword.

For almost four years after our Karachi interview, Khawaja would call or text me, often in the middle of the night in Toronto, asking me to write about cases of the "disappeared" and still promising information on El-Maati. Sometimes we would talk about the war and his views on why Pakistan was imploding. "You'll lose this war. You'll see," was his refrain, as if it were my personal war to lose.

In early 2010, the phone calls stopped.

THERE IS NO better way to understand Pakistan's connection to the war in Afghanistan than to travel to the Federally Administered Tribal Areas (FATA) and stand on a spot along the 1,600-mile border, which cuts through the heart of the region's Pashtun tribal belt. Because it isn't a border at all. Pakistan may have gained independence from India in 1947, but in the FATA, being Pashtun took precedence over citizenship. The FATA is often referred to as Pakistan's Wild West, since, despite its name, most control is in the hands of tribal elders, not the federal government. The female literacy rate is about 3 per cent. The fiercely conservative tribesmen live by a strict code of honour—Pashtunwali—that above all else dictates that guests must be provided with warm hospitality and protection. That, combined with the fact that the FATA was the jihadi epicentre in the 1980s, made it the perfect place for the Taliban and al Qaeda to find refuge.

But getting to the border in 2006 was going to require some serious help. This meant tagging along with experienced journalists, or enlisting the aid of the army. In the end, Pete and I were fortunate enough to get both.

"You're in luck!" army spokesman Major General Shaukat Sultan Khan told me as we sat in his office in Islamabad. The military was organizing a junket to a remote outpost in Kundi Gar, on the Afghan border, which would give us an excellent view from ten thousand feet—even if it was a view controlled entirely by the Pakistani army. It was going to be hard, Major General Sultan said, shaking his head, but he would do his best to secure us a spot. We drank more tea and talked of Canada.

Days later, we were in the company of a handful of journalists, including the BBC's Barbara Plett and the *Guardian's* Declan Walsh, one of the most respected foreign reporters in the region. Declan had the unassuming and easy-going nature of a foreign correspondent who had talked his way out of more than one precarious situation. Only when he darted around Islamabad in his battleship grey Volkswagen bug he had named Betsy, driving like a true Pakistani, did you see his aggressive side.

With brief stops at staging areas, ostensibly to have a tea—but in fact, we later learned, to repair our helicopter—we eventually arrived at a desolate Shawal Valley post that consisted of little more than well-worn goat paths and stone compounds that looked like they were constructed in the days of Ghengis Khan. The military outnumbered the journalists about five to one.

Major General Sultan, an officious and compact major general who had been educated in the United States and had served as the public face of Pakistan's army since 2003, strode up the hill toward the base while some of the cameramen wheezed under the weight of their equipment at such an altitude. "You're the first women up here," he said, delighted. In our honour, an English sign that read "Ladies Urinal" had been erected with an arrow that pointed to a hilltop khaki tent. I went inside, to be polite and show that I appreciated the effort, but changed my mind as I was about to drop my pants over the dugout hole and a fierce wind shook the tent. I feared that I would not be remembered as one of the first women to visit the base, but rather the Canadian reporter who mooned the troops.

The purpose of the trip was clear. The army wanted us to visit the tranquil base and report that its troops had the region under control.

"This border is sealed," army Brigadier Imtiaz Wyne pronounced dramatically at a makeshift podium erected for the occasion. As if on cue, thunder began to rumble and the sky turned an angry shade of grey. "We stop any movement across the border from rear to front or front to rear," Wyne continued over the noise, adding that since operations were launched in the area, 325 "miscreants" had been killed, while the army had lost 56 of their own troops.

The visit was cut short as the weather rolled in. Although our group had arrived in two khaki Mi-171 helicopters, we all crammed into one for the quick descent. We rocked horribly as the helicopter struggled with the weight, slowly rising like an obese man attempting to stand after sitting cross-legged on the floor for too long. Looking out the windows we could see that the troops below were running, fast. It took a few minutes to realize that they thought we were going to crash, and as we clipped a tree before clearing the ridge, Pete and I thought we would too.

In Rawalpindi at the end of the day, we drank more tea and Major General Sultan presented each of us with a small plastic trophy bearing the words "Gold Army Division." Although this type of formality may have been common in Pakistan, it still felt strange to have soldiers clapping for us, especially since I knew our stories would be unlike the glowing tales of military dominance that some of the local press would write.

The problem was that it was almost impossible to verify the army's claims that they had the upper hand in the area. Foreign journalists were forbidden from going alone, and many local journalists had been killed when they tried. We had been unable to talk to area residents during our escorted visit. We would find out later that in nearby Miran Shah, the capital of North Waziristan, a convoy of paratroopers had been ambushed by Taliban-linked fighters on the outskirts of the city just after we left.

There were other telling and ominous signs. A few months earlier, another attack in Miran Shah had shown just how brutal the frontier had become and how ineffective the army had been in protecting its residents. A local gangster named Hakeem Khan had ruthlessly ruled the region for months, but had made a fatal mistake when he killed four members of the local Taliban who refused to pay his required "tax." Vengeance was swift. Truckloads of black-turbaned Talibs arrived and not only was Khan beheaded for the murders, so were his relatives. Their bodies were hung in the centre of town and their houses were burned to the ground. A twenty-eight-minute video recording of the executions spread quickly throughout Pakistan, and a few days after our visit to Waziristan I watched the film at Declan's house. Men shouted, "Long live the Taliban of Waziristan," as the corpses were dragged behind a truck. Hundreds looked on with a mix of disgust and bemusement. The video ended with the words: "This is not drama. This is reality." The reality was that the Taliban was now firmly entrenched in the region.

Despite their claims otherwise, the Pakistani army was breathing its last gasps during our visit. A few months later, in September, the army pulled out of the area after a negotiated settlement with tribal elders known as the "North Waziristan Accord." The agreement amounted to a ceasefire, on the theory that if the army withdrew, the locals would have no trouble cracking down on foreign militants. Without having to worry about attacks from the Pakistani army—which was ill equipped to fight in the region and all too often killed civilians in the crossfire—the old order could resume and fight cross-border Taliban traffic. President Musharraf celebrated the deal during a trip to Washington, even though within Pakistan the Waziristan Accord was widely regarded as an admission of defeat. After a White House meeting President Bush told reporters: "When the president looks me in the eye and says, the tribal deal is intended to reject the Talibanization of the people, and that there won't be a Taliban and won't be al Qaeda, I believe him."

Gaining a foothold in the FATA region was critical and the Waziristan Accord would ultimately fail. Soon, that wouldn't be the only region of Pakistan in peril.

THE RED MOSQUE was fascinating for its level of militancy and its location, smack in the middle of the country's capital, scarcely a mile from the compound that housed the Pakistani president, parliament, and headquarters of the ISI. Beside the mosque there was a madrassa whose students consisted mainly of impoverished youths from FATA or outside tribal agencies. While they studied and lived under the instructions of an outspoken leader who extolled the virtues of fighting the jihad, President Musharraf was just a few blocks away wining, dining and assuring Western leaders that Pakistan was a committed partner in fighting jihadists. The Red Mosque seemed like the embarrassing and persistent drug dealer hanging out on the corner of the rehab clinic. In many ways, the fight for the Red Mosque exemplified the struggle for the soul of Pakistan itself.

Abdul Rashid Ghazi was the religious leader of the Lal Masjid (Red Mosque) and his older brother, Maulana Abdul Aziz, was the mosque's respected chief cleric. Their father, Maulana Abdullah, had founded the sprawling compound in 1965, shortly after Islamabad became Pakistan's capital. In the days of the Soviet occupation of Afghanistan, the senior Ghazi's Friday sermons were renowned for their passionate glorification of the jihad, and the school was praised for educating the country's poor. President Zia-ul-Haq and other senior government officials frequented the mosque.

In 1998, just weeks before al Qaeda bombed the U.S. embassies in Kenya and Tanzania, Ghazi travelled with his father to Afghanistan to meet Osama bin Laden. He was impressed by the tall, soft-spoken orator. Two months after that meeting, in October, Ghazi's father was assassinated while walking through the Red Mosque's courtyard, a bag of groceries in each hand. Ghazi and his brother took control of the Red Mosque and vowed to see their father's vision of Pakistan as an Islamic state become a reality.

Ghazi was well educated, articulate and, unlike his older brother, fluent in English. Although he was by 2006 considered one of Pakistan's most militant religious leaders, he had never thought he would follow in his father's footsteps. In his youth, Ghazi had rebelled against a traditional Islamic education, refusing to grow a beard and insisting on wearing Western clothing. He attended Islamabad's secular Quaid-i-Azam University, and after graduating with a master's degree in international relations, he got a job with the Ministry of Education. For a brief time, he worked with the United Nations cultural organization, UNESCO.

But the death of Ghazi's father affected him profoundly. His father had left the mosque to Ghazi's devout brother, but Ghazi eventually gave up his career to run the madrassa and over the years became increasingly political. In 2001, he emerged as one of the leaders of a religious alliance opposing the invasion of Afghanistan. Three years later, he gave impassioned speeches condemning the Pakistan government's military action against pro-Taliban militants in the tribal region, from which many of his students hailed. His signature was included on a fatwa demanding that all Pakistani soldiers who died should be described as "killed," whereas slain militants were considered "martyrs."

I wanted to go inside the Red Mosque and felt listening to Ghazi would help me understand the divide between moderates and militants in Pakistan. Could Ghazi and his followers become the greatest threat to Musharraf and the U.S.-Pakistan alliance yet?

Before talking with Ghazi, I had met the principal of the Jamia Hafsa, the mosque's girls' school. Umme Hassan was married to Ghazi's brother Maulana Abdul Aziz. As we talked, young girls lounged on mattresses in classrooms, reciting the Qur'an, rocking as they read verses in Arabic, looking up shyly at me.

The summer before, the girls' school had been thrust into the news following a devastating attack in the United Kingdom. On July 7, bombs had exploded in London's Underground and on a double-decker bus, in a plot that became known as "7/7." Attention quickly turned to Pakistan when it was revealed that one of the bombers had spent two months studying at a madrassa near Lahore. British Prime Minister Tony Blair demanded to know what was being taught in these religious seminaries. Musharraf immediately banned all new admissions of foreign students to madrassas. Twelve days later, police raided the Red Mosque compound, but as they stormed the girls' madrassa they were met with fierce resistance. Police commandos bursting through the entrance found female students who were horrified they had been caught without their *niqabs* and fought back with whatever weapons they could find. Clouds of tear gas sent the women and girls staggering blindly onto the street, where police continued the battle with batons, sending sixty to hospital. Images of the confrontation were broadcast across Pakistan. The raid was a public relations disaster for Musharraf. Already considered a Bush lackey, Musharraf was criticized for attacking the mosque only to placate the British government.

Umme Hassan shook her head and closed her eyes when she recounted the storming of her school, saying security forces had threatened to kidnap her if her husband did not turn himself in. Her school's popularity, she said, only increased after the botched raid.

A short walk away, I was ushered with Pete into Abdul Rashid Ghazi's office. He sat on the floor as a rusty fan pushed around sweaty, stale air, and he motioned for me to sit nearby. Since an assassination attempt, Ghazi was said to always have his AK-47 within reach, and so I felt slightly unnerved as we spoke; I could not see it resting against the wall anywhere in his office.

Ghazi was defensive as we began our interview, perhaps anticipating questions about his support for the Taliban. "America should not expect from us that we will give them flowers," he said before I raised the question of Afghanistan. "When defending ourselves, we can sometimes make an offensive defence."

Like his father and brother, Ghazi believed both Afghanistan and Pakistan should be ruled by Sharia law and, like his sister-in-law, denounced the raid as an unnecessary show. He was determined to unseat Musharraf, although he would not specify how, and insisted that he was a reasonable man and willing to negotiate. The morning before police stormed the compound, he said, he had met cordially with the police commissioner. "They could have arrested me then," he told me. "[But] they wanted to communicate a message to the West."

His parting comment as we left the mosque was to warn that the next time the sovereignty of the Red Mosque was challenged, the consequences would be far greater.

IN THE SPRING of 2007, about six months after we left Pakistan, a female brigade from Umme Hassan's madrassa (along with a few men), most cloaked entirely in black and armed with religious righteousness and bamboo batons, became Islamabad's street vigilantes. In March, the group kidnapped women they accused of running a brothel and dragged them back to the Red Mosque. The alleged madam, "Aunty Shamim," was held with her daughter, daughter-in-law and granddaughter for three days. A brief standoff with police followed, but ended when Aunty Shamim was released with a purported signed confession concerning her illicit brothel. While the kidnapping should have horrified neighbours, in some circles the women were hailed as heroes for clamping down on a brothel when Musharraf would not.

Emboldened by their newfound fame, the group began threatening merchants who sold DVDs and CDs that they considered un-Islamic. They burned stacks of the contraband at the mosque, sending thick plumes of black smoke over Islamabad. The dark cloud would have hung over the nearby governmental confines, but Musharraf hardly needed the smoke signal to realize trouble was brewing inside the Red Mosque.

One June evening, around midnight, the Red Mosque gang pushed their luck, raiding a massage parlour and abducting five Chinese masseuses. By now they had the full attention of the government, and after tremendous pressure (including angry reprimands from a perturbed Beijing), they released the women less than twenty-four hours later. But the glove had been dropped. If Musharraf would not enforce Islamic law, then the students of the Red Mosque would. "It is the duty of the government to stop the massage parlours," Ghazi told journalists at a press conference. "Since the government is not doing it, it is the responsibility of society to do it. We have no other choice." Later, in an interview with the New York Times, Ghazi said that while he did not believe suicide bombings could be justified within Pakistan's borders or in a civilian setting, such as a supermarket, he continued to support the killing of American soldiers in Iraq or Afghanistan. He believed this was their "mission."

The massage parlour raid sparked a police crackdown and stand-off that quickly spiralled out of control that summer. The siege of the mosque and madrassas by government forces was known as "Operation Silence," and what was expected to be a quick and decisive operation by Pakistan's elite commando force turned into a week-long battle against a well-armed militia in bulletproof vests hiding inside the mosque and madrassa. The number of dead, which included civilians, Pakistani forces shot or killed in booby traps, and the madrassa's militants, is disputed, but most accounts put the toll at more than one hundred. Ghazi's brother, Maulana Abdul Aziz, was caught in an embarrassing escape attempt, dressed as a woman.

One of the last holdouts killed was Ghazi. A few hours before the final raid, Ghazi predicted his death in a telephone interview with local television station ARY. "I know I am about to be martyred. But I do believe my blood will bring about an Islamic revolution. My last message to those fighting for the glory of Islam is that they should avenge my murder, besides waging jihad against Musharraf, to get rid of this illegitimate American stooge who has taken hostage the entire Pakistani nation at gunpoint."

Musharraf's government declared victory and Washington congratulated its ally on its tough stance. "Wherever there is fundamentalism and extremism, we have to finish that, destroy that," Musharraf said in a television address.

But the raid proved a flash point in Pakistan, criticized by the country's militant Islamists, who praised Ghazi as a martyr, and those alarmed by the level of violence and force. It was the turning point that would divide Musharraf's government and the country's moderate and fundamentalist forces.

The siege would ultimately embolden those fundamentalist forces, the "fundos" as they're known in Pakistan, who would portray the attack on the mosque as part of the West's war on Islam. Just as the Ethiopian invasion in Somalia had bolstered the ranks of Shabab, the Red Mosque raid would prove to be disastrously counterproductive. I wondered if this is not what Ghazi meant by launching an "offensive defence."

KHALID KHAWAJA HAD longstanding ties to the Red Mosque and its leaders. He held demonstrations after the siege calling for a police investigation into the killings and criminal charges against Musharraf. For the next few years he remained one of those characters in Pakistan who had contacts in all the wrong places and kept popping up in news reports, which I thought made him invincible.

My curiosity over why he had stopped calling by 2010 ended when I read a local report about his kidnapping. On March 26, 2010, Khawaja, along with another well-known former ISI colonel known as Colonel Imam and a British journalist, were abducted while travelling in North Waziristan, in Pakistan's FATA region. Colonel Imam was known as the "godfather of the Taliban" for his role in nurturing Mullah Omar's group in the 1990s, and presumably could easily negotiate the dangerous Waziristan region. Khawaja had promised Asad Qureshi, who was making a documentary on the Taliban, an interview with a Taliban leader. A previously unknown group calling themselves the Asian Tigers claimed responsibility for the kidnapping and demanded the release from custody of three key Afghan Taliban leaders. A few weeks after their demands were not met, they executed Khawaja, shooting him in the chest and head and dumping his body on the roadside near Mir Ali with a note that warned that other "American spies" would meet the same fate. Before his murder, Khawaja had been forced to make a videotaped statement confessing that he still worked for the ISI and had links to the CIA, and, curiously, that he had set up Ghazi's brother, Maulana Abdul Aziz, convincing him to escape the Red Mosque in women's clothing, only to have arranged to have agents waiting to arrest him. Declan Walsh received an email at his *Guardian* address, purportedly from the Asian Tigers, titled "khalid khawaja (episode is over)." It read: "Khalid Khawaja is no more . . . We have given the deadline in order to approve our demands. The ISI and government didn't take it serious. This is the last warning to set your minds. What would be next?"

But who were the Asian Tigers?

In the three years since the Red Mosque raid, the complicated tapestry of Pakistan's militant groups had become almost impossible to untangle. The "Talibanization" that began in the FATA had spread into the cities. Pakistan had become the suicide bombing capital of the world, surpassing both Afghanistan and Iraq. In 2007, Pakistan suffered fifty-six suicide bombings that killed 640, compared to just six bombings the previous year. A devastating attack on December 27, 2007, killed Benazir Bhutto, the popular chairperson of the Pakistan Peoples Party who had recently returned from exile. The following year, in September 2008, a bombing at Islamabad's Marriott Hotel killed at least 53 people and injured more than 260. Like many foreigners, I had stayed at the Marriott, and as I watched the television footage of the hotel burning to the ground I couldn't help thinking of the Pakistani doormen resplendent in their traditional headdress and uniforms dripping with tassels. They would have been among the first to die when a tarpaulin-covered truck, laden with rounds of ammunition, six hundred kilograms of high-grade TNT and RDX explosives, broke through the security gates at the hotel entrance. Local press dubbed the bombing "Pakistan's 9/11."

Anger over the Red Mosque raid brought together a new generation of fighters—many of them survivors of the raid, or relatives of the deceased—who aligned themselves with militants fighting in Afghanistan or Kashmir, but were intent on hitting home. A powerful new umbrella group for Pakistani fighters called the Tehrik-i-Taliban Pakistan (commonly referred to as the TTP or Pakistani Taliban) had formed in December 2007 under the leadership of Baitullah Mehsud and his deputy, Hakimullah Mehsud. Khawaja, Colonel Iman and Qureshi were reportedly going to interview Hakimullah when they were kidnapped.

Khawaja's murder was more than the story of a former spy with murky connections whose luck ran out. His killing revealed the complicated world of Taliban splinter groups that had risen out of the ashes of the Red Mosque. These new organizations involved younger and more vitriolic members whose ideological goals were broad (and therefore harder to combat). The Asian Tigers were believed to be a cover for a small cell of Punjabi sectarian militants that normally targeted Pakistan's Shia Muslim minority. The previously unknown group demanded the release of high-profile prisoners in Afghanistan, suggesting they had links to the Taliban. Yet Colonel Imam was the "godfather of the Taliban," and local reports purported that even Mullah Omar had pressed for his release.

Much of the case remains a mystery today. Qureshi was released in September 2010 after a ransom was reportedly paid. Colonel Imam died in custody in January 2011. Local newspapers at first reported that militants killed him. Government officials said he died of a heart attack. A video of his execution later surfaced, confirming he was shot.

IN THE EARLY fall of 2010, I went back to Islamabad and was amazed during the drive from the airport to my guesthouse to see how it had been transformed into a military zone. The sophisticated capital once had a reputation as one of the most boring cities in the world because it was so tranquil, with its wide, austere boulevards for strolling, its leafy parks, posh government buildings and the lush Margalla Hills as a backdrop. Now, boring would have been a good thing. Trying to navigate blocked off streets and checkpoints made you feel like a frustrated mouse in a maze. Marketplaces and anything "Western" started to look like targets and were treated as such.

There was little optimism in 2010. Asif Ali Zardari had replaced Musharraf as Pakistan's president two years earlier, following the assassination of Zardari's wife, Benazir Bhutto. The Red Mosque siege was just the start of a series of political blunders that had pushed Musharraf from power. Eventually, Washington tired of propping up the unpopular dictator and his seemingly half-hearted, or ineffective attempts to curb militancy and backed Bhutto and then her husband in supporting Pakistan's return to civilian rule. Zardari, one of Pakistan's most controversial political figures, nicknamed "Mr. Ten Percent," for his reputation of taking kickbacks from the government coffers, may have won over two-thirds of the country's voters, but his popularity plummeted almost immediately after his election. He was regarded almost unanimously in Pakistan as corrupt and out of touch.

I arrived a couple of months after the data dump of 92,000 Pentagon documents, released through Julian Assange's whistleblower website, WikiLeaks. Reports concerning Pakistan again ignited the debate over whether the country was America's friend or foe. The thrust of classified U.S. State Department reports essentially blamed Pakistan, and in particular the ISI, for the faltering Afghan war. The cables contained raw field data and would not be considered "intelligence" until the veracity of the information and sources could be confirmed. At worst, the documents were titillating diplomatic gossip, fly-on-the-wall information from meetings with world leaders and junior bureaucrats. At best, the cables provided proof of the dark, dirty and duplicitous world of realpolitik.

If international pressure over the war in Afghanistan and domestic political and economic woes weren't enough, floods of biblical proportions cemented Pakistan's reputation as a cursed country. Impacting the devastation of the August 2010 floods was the fact that little international aid followed. After Haiti's earthquake in January 2010, $31 million in donations poured into the Red Cross due to a successful campaign in which 3.1 million Americans used their mobile phones to donate $10 each. The same campaign for the floods in Pakistan? About $10,000 was collected, despite the fact that the loss caused by the floods affected more people than were affected by the Haitian earthquake, the 2005 earthquake in Pakistan and the 2004 tsunami in South Asia, combined. There were a variety of reasons for the apathy: donor fatigue; Mr. Ten Percent being president (he visited his father's chateau in France as his nation suffered); lack of access to affected areas and therefore lack of crucial media footage; timing (the flood happened during the slow summer months when journalists are on vacation); the flood's devastation by nature being more insidious than the immediacy of an earthquake, tsunami or tornado; or perhaps because Pakistan was simply considered the bad boy on the block and, sadly, there was little international sympathy.

Before I arrived, the White House had just pledged another couple of billion to Pakistan over the next five years in its fight against al Qaeda and the Taliban. But of course the fighting was no longer against the traditional concepts of al Qaeda and Taliban that had existed ten years earlier, nor was it limited to the border region. The WikiLeaks cables underscored Pakistan's deceitful role in fighting the war in Afghanistan. The documents alleged that certain players within the ISI had never stopped supporting groups like the Afghan Taliban, the warlords (such as those belonging to the notorious Haqqani network), the border bandits from Waziristan, or local jihadi groups, including Lashkar-e-Taiba (LeT). LeT had been officially designated a terrorist entity in Pakistan in 2002 but continued to operate freely under various names and charities. Even after the group was implicated in the 2008 Mumbai attack, in which Pakistani militants killed more than 160 during a sixty-hour siege of luxury hotels, a train station and Jewish centre, many of the group's members roamed free. LeT originally was formed to fight for the independence of the disputed Kashmir region, and there were factions within Pakistan's military and the ISI that regarded the group as an important reserve force for future conflicts with India—much to the ire of Pakistan's nuclear-armed neighbour, and of the United States.

In Islamabad, I decided to track down one of the most notorious characters named in the WikiLeaks files—Hamid Gul, a former ISI chief who embodied the contradictions of Pakistan's military thinking and its suspicion of the United States. Gul headed the ISI in the crucial years at the end of the Soviet occupation of Afghanistan and was credited as the architect of the Red Army's defeat. But the former ally had become an embarrassment to Western leaders when he later accused the United States of abandoning Afghanistan and blamed the administration for a variety of conspiracies, including the 9/11 attacks, which he believed was an "inside job." When accusing fingers pointed back, he challenged the United States to charge him, offering to appear in any American court. A proposal to place him on the UN terrorism list failed only when China reportedly came to his defence. He was once labelled "Pakistan's most dangerous man."

Gul was a well-known figure inside Pakistan, but he acquired international recognition when the WikiLeaks documents fingered him as an important player in coordinating attacks against U.S. forces in Afghanistan. Most damning was a report that stated he had met senior Taliban members in Pakistan in mid-2006 and instructed the insurgents to conduct attacks using improvised explosive devices in Kabul during the Muslim holiday of Eid. "Gul instructed two of the individuals to plant IEDs along the roads frequently utilized by Government of Afghanistan and ISAF [International Security Assistance Force] vehicles," the report stated. A suicide bomber was to hit NATO or Afghan government targets. "Make the snow warm in Kabul. Set Kabul aflame," he reportedly told the bombers.

Under the headline "The Audacity of Hamid Gul," the *Washington Post*'s Jeff Stein had written of Gul's alleged duplicity on his *SpyTalk* blog. "Given Gul's longtime, vocal animosity for Washington, it's not inconceivable that he would get his hands dirty with the insurgents at such a primitive tactical level, planning car bombs like a Pakistani Tony Soprano."

I visited Gul in his Rawalpindi office, where he sat behind a large wooden table, bare except for a photocopied *Economist* article upon which his eyeglasses sat. He smiled warmly as his son ushered me to a chair across from him. We talked about Canada (his son was a fan of *Star* national affairs columnist Thomas Walkom and was delighted that I sat near him in my newsroom). "It's nonsense," Gul told me when I asked about the WikiLeaks allegations. "If that is the quality of the intelligence on which this war is being fought, I can only lament the paucity of wisdom as well as expertise." A few long minutes passed in uncomfortable silence before he resumed talking. "The fact is that I support the Afghan resistance. I continue to support that. Wherever you go and occupy without sufficient reason." He did not believe 9/11 was cause to go to war, because he did not believe 9/11 was the work of al Qaeda, but rather, a U.S. conspiracy. "Nine-eleven has still not been proved. You have turned the world upside down without holding a proper inquiry. Has Osama bin Laden been charge sheeted, indicted? Why [not]?" he continued. "Why have there been no trials in absentia?"

After ten years of emails, phone calls, letters and countless discussions not just held in foreign locales, but in Ottawa, New York, Florida and elsewhere, I was tired of debates and conspiracy theories about 9/11. Apparently, Gul was not.

"Have you formed an opinion?" he smiled at me.

"I'm a journalist, so I don't have opinions," I replied, eager not to spark a lecture on how the World Trade Center could have only collapsed from a controlled demolition, or that a missile, not a plane, destroyed the Pentagon, or any of the other popular theories.

"If you want to be neutral I will not accept that," he countered, laughing, but apparently serious.

Treading cautiously, I said, "Well, I read the 9/11 Commission Report and I found the evidence convincing. But I won't deny there are some outstanding questions." He was satisfied.

The seventy-three-year-old Gul denied the direct involvement the WikiLeaks documents alleged he'd had with senior Taliban or al Qaeda members, and it was hard not to believe him, if only because it would have been difficult for such a high-profile figure, so long out of the game, to go undetected. Imtiaz Gul (no relation), a respected Pakistani analyst and author, said he suspected much of the information in the Pentagon files came from questionable Afghan intelligence sources, and Gul's name was included in an attempt to make the information appear more valuable. "Trust me. I have covered Afghanistan for decades. I'm a Pashtun myself. I know Persian. I can talk to these people," Imtiaz Gul told me over lattes in an Islamabad café in 2010. "[Gul] has an image there that is larger than life because he had good relations with the Taliban. People still look at him in that light."

Gul may not have had the direct hand in fighting NATO forces that the documents state, but he certainly supported the goals of the Afghan Taliban. He told me he admired the Pakistani-based Haqqani group and its leader. "When the United Nations Security Council tried to put me on the list, I categorically said, 'I respect Haqqani. He is a great mujahid. He is an honourable man, so are my friends in the Northern Alliance.' More than half of the governors in Afghanistan are my friends ... That doesn't mean that I have the ability to help them. As you can see, I'm sitting here."

"As Tony Soprano," I responded, and a quizzical look came over Gul's face.

"Tony Soprano?" I tried again, describing the popular American television series and explaining he had been compared to the main character in a *Washington Post* blog.

"Tony Soprano, what did he do? Is he a villain or a hero?" he asked.

How do you explain a mob boss who runs a strip club and orders hits, but who was painfully human, had panic attacks and cried to his shrink?

"I would say he's a sympathetic villain."

Without missing a beat Gul replied, "Ah, or an unsympathetic hero."

It seemed as good a time as any to wrap up the interview. I wasn't convinced Gul had any of the links the documents purported, but there was no doubt he was still one of Washington's problems, representative of the Pakistani old guard that supported groups such as Haqqani, or LeT.

As I got up to leave, he offered: "Listen, I have all my sympathies for the American people, for the Western people. They want to live in peace. We do appreciate the science and technology and what they have given. Much of what we have today is due to the contribution of the West and no one can deny that. But the policy makers? They do the wrong things at the wrong times. The Afghanistan war? Wrong war, for a wrong cause, at the wrong time, with the wrong people, at the wrong place. Everything is wrong."

I turned to leave and he startled me with a paternalistic pat on the cheek before a more formal handshake. "When the war in Afghanistan is over," he laughed, "you'll have to come back and meet the most dangerous man again."

THE RED MOSQUE had faded from the news but I was curious to see what had become of the place where I once sat with Abdul Rashid Ghazi. Maulana Abdul Aziz, Ghazi's brother and the chief cleric of the Red Mosque, first said he was too busy to be interviewed but later agreed to meet at a rented home in an area popular with Afghan refugees, not far from the mosque.

After trying to escape the 2007 siege dressed as a woman, Abdul Aziz spent two years in custody on terrorism charges before his release in April 2009. He returned to the Red Mosque under a shower of rose petals and surrounded by the rousing cheers of supporters. During his first sermon he vowed to continue his mission to bring Islamic rule to Pakistan. Local media hinted that he had been released only after striking a deal with the Zardari government to help curb the record number of suicide bombings inside Pakistan. He denied any deal-making.

"As we predicted, there would be a severe reaction. Our struggle was very peaceful. No fingers were cut, no houses were burned, no shelves were looted before [the raid]. Nothing took place in the wrong manner," he began as we sat on the floor of one of the bedrooms in the home.

When I protested that the vigilante actions of his students such as the kidnappings, extortion and threats were indeed criminal, he retorted that he respects only religious law. Then he accused the Zardari government of its own crimes. "Corruption, nepotism, bribing, all the country's institutions have sunk to the worst levels... there's a great gap, increasing day by day, between the common man and the government."

Abdul Aziz was proud of his brother and pleased with the response his death had generated, and if he was embarrassed by the nature of his escape, he showed no signs of regret. "At that time I thought I would have been martyred there, rather than escaping," he said. "If today when I recall the escape, I think it was God's will. No doubt, if I were not here, someone else would be looking after the schools and campaign. But I think it was a better decision to keep me alive."

Some of the recent violence in Pakistan was being traced back to yet another group that had emerged following the raid and called itself the "Ghazi Force." Most of its members were relatives of his deceased students, and the group was believed to have links to Pakistan's Taliban, the TTP. Abdul Aziz denied any contact with members of the group named for his brother and said that although he understood their actions, he did not condone the violence. "But," he said, "we should remember the atrocities committed by the Pakistani regime at that time against the women and children. The majority of those students were from those tribal areas. People are unarmed in this area, but those tribesmen, they're not unarmed."

Abdul Aziz was preaching the same message he had before his arrest, albeit now to a much scaled-down congregation in a smaller mosque. "I still feel the solution for the troubles of Pakistan is the implementation of Islamic law. If we don't implement Islamic law, what is happening in the tribal area will engulf the whole country."

Before leaving his home, Abdul Aziz disappeared briefly and came back cradling two large hardcover books wrapped in a white sheet. "A gift," he said unwrapping the English translations of the Qur'an. Then he signed his name on the inside cover and told me to get reading.

PAKISTAN IS A multifarious country to explain. But despite its complexity, there certainly are many "experts," as Mosharraf Zaidi, a columnist for the News and former advisor on international aid to Pakistan for the United Nations and European Union bemoaned in his August 2010 Foreign Policy piece: "Pakistan is a country that no one quite gets completely, but apparently everybody knows enough about to be an expert. If you're a nuclear proliferation expert, suddenly you're an expert on Pakistan. If you're a terrorism expert, ditto: expert on Pakistan. India expert? Pakistan too, then. Of South Asian origin of any kind at a think tank, university, or newspaper? Expert on Pakistan. Angry that your parents sent you to the wrong madrassa when you were young? Expert on Pakistan." I am not an expert on Pakistan, but have been lucky that my job as a journalist has entitled me to knock on some pretty interesting doors.

Despite how the country is often portrayed, Pakistan is not on the verge of collapse as a failed state, nor is it populated by millions of raving mad jihadis. One night, as I sat on a patio of an Islamabad restaurant with Tom Hussain, a friend from the United Arab Emirates–based newspaper the *National*, we puffed apple-flavoured *shisha* after our dinner and before the pistachio gelato, and he described the country he had grown up in, left, and then returned to and tried to make sense of through his writing. All around us were teenagers and young couples wearing everything from tight jeans or cleavage-bearing tops to full coverage. "This is Pakistan," Tom said, looking around at the giggly, eclectic mix. Unfortunately it's this Pakistan that is complicated by the fundos and corrupt politicians. The mullah-military nexus that was created during the Soviet occupation has not been overcome, which means that somehow people like Hamid Gul, Khalid Khawaja and Abdul Aziz are still relevant, even if they aren't.

Entire books are devoted to understanding Pakistan, and in the past decade there have been many. One of the best is by respected Pakistani journalist Ahmed Rashid. Rashid writes in *Descent Into Chaos* that the U.S. and NATO forces failed to understand that the Taliban is not a monolithic body but a "lumpen population, the product of refugee camps, militarized madrassas, and the lack of opportunities in the borderland of Pakistan and Afghanistan."

The West's failure to understand the Taliban or its distinction from al Qaeda, coupled with Pakistan's ill-advised military actions, such as the raid on the Red Mosque, only fuelled a new generation of hate and distrust for both local and foreign governments, and gave rise to a new Taliban bent on attacking Pakistan. There was no doubt by 2011 that the propaganda war had been lost in the region, and the United States had failed in its purported battle for the hearts and minds of its populace. Pakistanis were fed up by the level of violence in their country and by their government's corruption, but equally hated the Taliban. The failure to follow through with promises of nation building in both Afghanistan and Pakistan, however, did lead to disillusionment and easy pickings for al Qaeda and the Taliban.

By the spring of 2011, the CIA's drone attacks in the border region were stirring incredible controversy. Unmanned predator aircraft that fired hellfire missiles and were piloted half a world away were a terrifying presence in the sky. Peter Bergen and Katherine

Tiedemann of the New America Foundation had been vigilantly tracking the drone strikes and estimated that from 2004 until April 2011, between 1,439 and 2,290 people had been killed. At this rate, it was conceivable that by the ten-year anniversary of 9/11, the drone attacks in Pakistan alone may have killed as many as those who died on September 11, 2001.

The drone program substantially increased under the Obama administration. In 2009 alone, there were fifty-one U.S. attacks, while there were only fifty-four during Bush's eight years in power. There were militants among the dead—most famously, TTP leader Baitullah Mehsud (believed to have been the mastermind of Benazir Bhutto's killing). Mehsud was getting a massage on the roof of his compound in South Waziristan when a drone smashed his hideout in August 2009, also killing one of his wives. But more often it was civilians who were killed. According to Bergen and Tiedemann's analysis, only a dozen of the more than one hundred drone attacks in 2010, which killed between six hundred and one thousand people, hit the intended targets.

Drone attacks may be preferred over foreign boots on the ground, but when they are based on shoddy intelligence, the effect can be devastating. A joint poll between the New America Foundation and Terror Free Tomorrow (funded by the United States Institute of Peace) in the FATA region in 2010 showed that nine out of every ten people opposed the U.S. pursuit of al Qaeda and Taliban. Only 16 per cent said they believed the drone strikes accurately targeted militants.

The beginning of this decade was a delicate time in Pakistan's history. Religious extremists killed two high-profile politicians who dared to speak out against the country's blasphemy laws, and President Zindari was criticized for his apathetic reaction. U.S. troops were scheduled to begin withdrawing from Afghanistan in July 2011. Mistrust between the United States and Pakistan was at an all-time high, as was the world's cynicism and rhetoric.

There was a shortage of easy solutions and an abundance of complex problems. Then a May 2011 raid on a high-walled compound, in a quiet military town near Islamabad, would make things even more complicated in Pakistan.

"The results would have been catastrophic. What this case revealed was spine chilling. The potential for loss of life existed on a scale never before seen in Canada. It was almost unthinkable."

ONTARIO SUPERIOR COURT JUSTICE BRUCE DURNO

4 Toronto

THE PLOT WENT LIKE THIS: Two U-Haul trucks would be parked at busy Toronto intersections during the morning rush hour. One would be at King and Bay Streets, the heart of the city's financial district, where downtown roads are clogged with streetcars and cabs, and sidewalks are packed with waves of zombie-like workers lost in their iPods and morning routines, startled only by the odd pedestrian trying to walk the wrong way like a salmon struggling against the current. The other truck would be a few blocks south and west, on Front Street, in the shadow of the CN Tower, close to the headquarters of the government-funded Canadian Broadcasting Corporation and the Toronto detachment for CSIS, Canada's spy service. It is a similar rush-hour scene here, but in the mix are a few early-rising panhandlers and tourists. Each truck would contain a one-ton fertilizer bomb, embedded with metal chips to maximize damage. A third bomb would simultaneously hit a Canadian military base.

The "Battle of Toronto," as its plotters called it, would cause glass and debris to rain from the sky as buildings collapsed and vehicles flew through the air from the shock waves, like toy cars in the hands of a tantrum-prone toddler. Those who died would have paid for Canada's involvement in Afghanistan since 2002 and the country's cozy relationship with the United States. They had elected a government that sent troops into that war, so there was blood on their hands and on those of every tax-paying Canadian. What if some of those pedestrians were children, or immigrants, or among the many Canadians against the war? Collateral damage, the plotters justified.

The group's two ringleaders were seduced by radicals online, and romanced by the notion that they were fighting for a greater religious and political purpose. Certainly that was a more attractive life than the mundane existences they led as young fathers and husbands, barely out of high school and toiling at dead-end jobs. More than a dozen misguided Muslims became their faithful followers. The Battle of Toronto would give them the fame and glory they sought in this life and the next.

Then came the evening of June 2, 2006.

OUR BACKYARD WAS filled with Star staff. More than sixty photographers, reporters, summer interns and editors stood with beers and burgers, crammed together behind our hundred-year-old downtown home. My husband Jimmie was tending the barbeque beside the paper's photo editor, Ken Faught. Little Christmas lights were strung along the fence and candles flickered on side tables and floated in the pond. Under the backyard canopy of trees, it was easy to feel you were anywhere but in the heart of Canada's biggest city. It was around 8 PM, a perfect early summer evening, warm and slightly humid in that pre-thunderstorm calm.

My cellphone rang.

"It's going down."

The scene, as I recall it, proceeds in slow motion. The voices and music fade into a warped soundtrack, and friends continue to mill about laughing, but the only people in focus now are Ken and Jimmie, barbeque flippers in hand, looking into the kitchen, where I stand alternately nodding and shaking my head.

Then the scene goes into hyper drive.

I mouth to Ken, *"It's happening now,"* which sends him running around shouting at the photographers to meet him in the front yard away from the party noise.

We had prepared at the *Star* for this moment. Although we kept the secret tight, Ken had told a handful of photographers that a major terrorist bust would happen soon. A few editors knew too. Of course, Jimmie was in. The poor guy had been living with the stress of this story and providing vital advice for weeks.

But, stupidly, I just never imagined it would go down on a Friday night. *Pre-dawn raids.* That was always what happened, and not just in the movies. Almost every large gang or drug bust I covered as a crime reporter started before the morning's first light, when cops burst through the doors banking on the fact that their targets were home and groggy with sleep. "Pre-dawn raids" was as much a crime cliché as murders on "quiet, tree-lined streets." Surely, the arrest of a Toronto terrorist cell would follow the same pattern?

Ken was better prepared and had already designated photographers "on call" and given them a "one-beer rule" for our party. After a brief front yard huddle, his team jumped into their cars, some with reporters in tow, and blanketed the city and municipalities, heading east, west and north of Toronto. We didn't know at that point where anything was happening, just that it was *going down.*

Ken drove me, with one hand on the wheel, the other cradling a burger, straight to the newsroom, where he would coordinate his shooters. I already had about three thousand words of a rough story and notes on my work computer, but there were many unknown details I had still to piece together. It was ninety minutes to the first deadline. Throughout the night, as word spread, a succession of *Star* editors would come into the newsroom to gather at desks, bark into phones and then huddle around the front page before it was sent to print. I called my former editor Lynn McAuley, who has an encyclopedic knowledge of national security issues (actually, she is the human Google—someone you want as your Trivial Pursuit partner). Aside from knowing the background to the case, she also happened to be one of the hardest working and best line editors in the business. She was walking along the boardwalk enjoying Friday night with her son Conor. Mere minutes later, they were both in the newsroom.

By 9 PM, we had a bare-bones version of the story online. At 9:16 PM, the RCMP sent out a cryptic release saying there would be a press conference the next morning, to announce a major arrest. No details were given.

That night, our editor-in-chief, Giles Gherson, made a rare decision in our age of instant news. We would not post our full account of the terror investigation (which ended up totalling more than 5,500 words) online until 5 AM, in case our competitors tried to catch up before their deadlines. The gamble paid off and gave us a good head start. And as is often the case with a major news story, over the weekend the media began covering the media. NBC came to our newsroom and then our media columnist wrote about our coverage, including a photo of the NBC interview. The Star was covering the coverage of our coverage.

On what had to be a slow news day, the New York Times published a story that Monday about the Star to accompany a front-page story about the case, with the headline, "In Bomb Plot News Coverage, A Toronto Newspaper Shines." The Star then immodestly ran a full-page ad of that article. It was classic Star chest-thumping, and though done with the best of boastful intentions, it made some of us cringe as if we were once again ten years old and being paraded in front of our parents' dinner party guests to perform. Toronto is home to one of the fiercest newspaper wars in North America, with three daily broadsheets and one tabloid, the Toronto Sun. The rivalry with the Globe and Mail was always vicious and the Star was not going to miss taking an in-your-face bow—as the Times noted. "The competition between Toronto's four major daily newspapers is often intense, particularly over crime news. But its results are rarely as one-sided as the coverage that followed the arrests of seventeen Ontario residents in what police call a terrorist bomb plot," wrote Ian Austen (one more suspect was later arrested and the group subsequently dubbed "the Toronto 18"). "Nor did The Star, Canada's largest newspaper by circulation, make any attempt at modesty. Underneath a main headline in type several inches high, another headline boasted that 'The Star takes you inside the spy game that led to last night's dramatic arrests.'"

Others weren't so keen to pat us on our back. In fact, a blog post on the website of the American right-wing *National Review* seemed downright pissed at our reporting: "*The Toronto Star* is easily the most left-wing major media outlet in a country full of left-wing media," the post stated. "It could be argued that their constant support for multiculturalism and their soft-on-terror-and-crime views provided conditions favorable for these homegrown terrorists to develop. It is therefore highly ironic that their strong crime beat is leading the coverage on this story, as there is not a more politically correct media outlet in the country."

It was a relief to finally get the news out. For months, I had been poking around on the case, trying to piece together tips that started with an August 2005 arrest at the Fort Erie Peace Bridge. Two young Somalia-born Canadians were caught trying to smuggle guns into the country, but I had heard from a prominent member of Toronto's Muslim community that it was at the behest of someone named Fahim Ahmad. He had apparently rented the car for them. People were talking. I was curious about Fahim's involvement, but at first had no idea what I was investigating. Over a matter of months, as I casually pursued the case when not working on other stories, I was inadvertently picked up on police wiretaps, I knocked on the door of one of the armed suspects, and I set off alarm bells by asking an old police contact about a northern Ontario training camp for jihadi wannabes (which I thought sounded too ridiculous to be true).

A few weeks before the June bust, I had received a friendly warning; nothing official, nothing on paper, but a phone call from someone I knew in the federal government who said the RCMP was not happy with some of my probing. In fact, I was told: "You are making a lot of asses clench in Ottawa." There was no ultimatum or threat of criminal sanctions and, of course, we were free to publish what we saw fit. But if the *Star* wrote about the investigation before the arrests and as a result the suspects went underground and "the CN Tower went boom," then the RCMP would happily hold a press conference to blame the Star for the terrorist attack.

Funny thing is, at the time I got that warning I was still uncertain how big the investigation was. Now I knew. In the weeks that followed, we took the warning seriously and huddled in Giles's office. Senior editors needed to know what/if/when we would go to print. We joked that I must have freshly laundered, frilly underwear in my drawers, lest the RCMP come snooping.

I liked to laugh at paranoid reporters after learning the embarrassing way not to become one myself. My lesson came in 2004 during an investigation into an alleged Algerian cell of al Qaeda–inspired terrorists belonging to a faction called the Salafist Group for Call and Combat. I had met a man who professed to be a former police mole, along with his lawyer, at a noisy Italian restaurant in Toronto. We were all jittery. It was hard to figure out if this self-confessed police agent was who he said he was or simply an excellent con. He was trying to figure out if he could trust me. The lawyer, a contact from my crime-reporting days, was just trying to figure out what the hell was going on. There was no doubt the mole had been in contact with both a national security cop and a spy, and there was a good chance that, whether con or not, the RCMP and CSIS would not want him talking to a journalist. As we lowered our voices over pasta, I suspiciously eyed a scruffy blond guy sitting a few tables away as he leaned in closer to listen to us. He was drinking a Coke, but didn't seem to order any food. A short time later, my blond Bond threw some money on the table and disappeared. *How obvious!* Surely Canada must train its spies better than this? The lawyer asked the waitress: "That gentleman? Does he come here often?"

The waitress looked at the back of the broad-shouldered man making a hasty retreat.

"You mean Gregg Zaun? Yeah, he's here a lot. A lot of the players come in."

We had just spooked our supposed spook. Gregg Zaun, catcher for the Toronto Blue Jays, was undoubtedly freaked out by the gawking trio of baseball fans.

Paranoia aside, it was not inconceivable that journalists in Canada would be watched when the stakes were high. In 2004, the Mounties had raided the house of *Ottawa Citizen* reporter Juliet O'Neill in an attempt to identify the source who had leaked information concerning Maher Arar, the Syrian-born Canadian rendered by the United States to Syria. I couldn't imagine the RCMP would make the same mistake twice (the backlash against the raid of Juliet's house had been fast and fierce), yet still, every time an unmarked van was parked near our house after the warning, I did wonder.

In the end, it was Jimmie and Lynn (neither of whom would shy away from a story, especially at the request of police) who asked the crucial question. *"What would the story say?"* We were riding so high on the adrenalin of being in-the-know and grappling with mighty ethical questions of being an independent, free press that we had forgotten the journalism. Before the arrests, I had only pieces of a story. I knew a few names, details, and now the scope of the investigation, but there were dozens of other leads I couldn't substantiate. What could we write? Police were investigating a terrorism plot? Hardly front-page news. So I continued to chip away (full-time now) on the story, not knowing if we would pull the trigger before the cops.

In the end, they went first. But we got a tip.

The barbeque continued that June evening minus "Team Terror," as we later called ourselves.

By 2 AM, eight very full hours later, we returned to the barbeque with printouts of our front page with the screaming headline, "Terror Cops Swoop." But the story was just beginning.

FAHIM AHMAD WAS the type of guy who always looked like he was sneering. His high-school yearbook photo shows a kid in glasses with a straggly beard and a long mullet that could pass for hockey hair. His right eyebrow is raised and slight frown lines crease his forehead in an expression that seems to say, *"Yeah, what are you looking at?"*

By all accounts, Fahim had comfortably assimilated into Canadian life when he first moved to Canada at the age of ten. He was born in Kabul, Afghanistan, an only child, and his parents fled with him to Pakistan when he was just one. His father, who had worked as a civil engineer with Afghanistan's Ministry of Irrigation, hadn't yet served his two years of mandatory military service. In Pakistan, he continued to work as an engineer while his wife taught and Fahim attended a prestigious private school.

One of Fahim's aunts living in Canada eventually sponsored his family, and they moved to Toronto in October 1994. Canada's social services and diversity made the country a favoured destination for immigrants. "Toronto the Good," as it is known, is the fifth-largest city in North America and among the most multicultural in the world. But the transition for Fahim's well-educated parents was difficult. They became citizens (along with Fahim), but they had to work double shifts in menial jobs, taking home minimum wage even as they balanced work with English courses. Fahim was often left home alone and while he was still fairly popular at school and enjoyed typical teenage pursuits of girls and soccer, he missed his parents during those early years.

The 9/11 attacks occurred a month after Fahim's seventeenth birthday, and as he would later tell a court, "everything changed." Fahim struggled with the backlash toward Muslims after 9/11. His family had never been particularly devout, but now he found himself defined by his religion. Taunts from other kids started to sting. He sought solace and guidance at a mosque near his home in Mississauga, a suburb about a twenty-minute drive west of Toronto. He grew disdainful of his secular parents and sought father figures at the mosque instead. "I would go to those having the longest beards and largest turbans and would take this as a sign of knowledge and devotion," Fahim later said.

And he spent hours online. One website led to the next as he travelled deeper and deeper into the labyrinth of extremist chat groups denouncing the West's "war on Islam" and calling Muslims to arms. Confusion turned to anger. While Fahim remembered little of his youth in Afghanistan, he soon became fiercely patriotic about the country where he was born and furious with the war waged by his adoptive home.

Fahim's obsession led him to an Islamic Internet forum called Clear Guidance, which had been started by a tech specialist from Houston and had become a place where young Muslims essentially talked among themselves. Over a period of about two years, Fahim left more than 750 posts. He was addicted, living a second life that he called his "fantasy world." In early 2003, he wrote: "come on bros, i need some jihad talks, anything! its like so dead my sources for videos is no more either," he continued. "i know u guys can hook me up." A link to a ninety-minute al Qaeda recruitment video was later posted.

On Clear Guidance, Fahim met his future wife, Mariya Mohammed. Mariya had also immigrated to Canada, moving with her family from Saudi Arabia just months earlier when she was fifteen. As she would later write to the court: "Coming from a country where the face veil was a norm (and believe it or not a fashion statement) and having gone to a public school that was totally segregated—the transition for me in a Canadian society was very difficult. I spent most of my days at home and frequented Internet websites. I came across an Islamic forum called 'Clear Guidance'—it should have been called clear misguidance. Because that is exactly what it did. It had extremist adults pretending to be Islamic scholars—manipulating Quranic verses and Islamic texts and contained numerous audios and videos of the sufferings of Muslims around the world."

Fahim and Mariya became engaged before they had ever met in person and, encouraged by others at his mosque, but over the objections of their parents, soon got married. Fahim was just eighteen, Mariya sixteen. Struggling to make ends meet, they lived with her parents and siblings. Fahim got a job at Walmart, and since they didn't have a car, he would walk an hour back and forth to work each day. After Mariya experienced crippling postpartum depression following the birth of their first child, Fahim would get up at night to feed and look after their daughter. The young couple was miserable. They wanted to live what they believed was the true Islamic life, one that was glorified by their online friends and acquaintances at the mosque. They did not tell their devout buddies that most nights they watched movies and would often indulge their cravings for Kentucky

Fried Chicken sandwiches, which would have been considered *haraam* (forbidden) because of the non-halal meat.

During his years at Mississauga's Meadowvale Secondary School, Fahim had become friends with another struggling Muslim youth named Zakaria Amara, or Zak. Zak had spent his childhood bouncing between homes, countries and faiths. A middle child, with a brother two years older and a sister two years younger, Zak was born in Jordan and baptized as Orthodox Christian during a visit with his mother's family in Cyprus. When he was four, the Greek-speaking youth moved to Saudi Arabia, where his father was an oil worker. Six years later, Zak's mother took him to Cyprus, where he attended an Arabic school and converted to Islam. He immigrated to Canada with this family a couple of years later. As with Fahim, Zak's hardworking parents (his mother at a beauty salon, his father in his dry cleaning business) were rarely at home, and Zak would spend many hours at the Ar-Rahman Islamic Learning Centre, located in a Mississauga strip mall and also attended by Fahim.

After 9/11, the outside walls of the centre were vandalized with scrawled messages of hate, so guards were hired to protect the prayer room. A *Star* reporter interviewed a sixteen-year-old Zak at Ar-Rahman as the bombs began to fall in Afghanistan in October 2001. "I'm just worried that if American soldiers start to die, the backlash will start all over again," he said.

As the Muslim community rallied together against the backlash, Zak's parents were fighting and their marriage was falling apart. Like Fahim, Zak sought solace online, starting an Internet site called "The Brothers of Meadowvale," where he led discussions about the city's best halal meat at fast-food joints and posted his own rambling raps. His classmates may have been pining over untouchable females, but Zak was writing in "Wake Up" about the *deen* (way of life) and the peace he finds in hearing the *Iqama* (second call to prayer).

I am filled with peace when at the masjid I hear the Iqama.
But when I show more interest they call me Osama.
Just trying to practice my deen so they call me extreme
They tell me I am too young, I am only sixteen.

In the summer after Grade 12, in 2003, Zak travelled to Saudi Arabia to interview for a position studying at the University of Medina. He was desperate to become an Islamic scholar, and when his application was denied he returned devastated. A year later, his father moved out, gave him the car keys and left for Saudi Arabia, never to return. Around the same time, Zak proposed to Nada Farooq, an outspoken, devout Muslim girl he had met at high school. She quickly became pregnant, and the young couple was thrust into a world of financial and parental responsibilities. Zak worked at a gas station.

MUBIN SHAIKH ALSO struggled after 9/11. As someone who defied stereotypes, he was hard to describe. Mubin drank Tim Hortons coffee (if it could still be called coffee after four creams and four sugars) and said things like, "I'm from the T-Dot" (Toronto). He believed Sharia law should be practised in Ontario and would not touch alcohol, but hugged female friends and did coke, sometimes lots of it. He was charged in 2007 and pleaded guilty to "threatening bodily harm" after freaking out on two twelve-year-old girls who called him "Taliban boy." He was a former Canadian army cadet who flirted with the idea of becoming a jihadi in Chechnya. He had a black belt and tattoos, and for a time wore his beard and garments long. Mubin was born at Toronto's St. Michael's Hospital, played one of the wise men in his grade school Christmas pageant, studied Arabic in Syria, toured Pakistan, taught religious studies and married a blond, blue-eyed Polish-Canadian convert to Islam. All this before he turned thirty-five.

Shaikh was endlessly charming when he wanted to be—interesting, articulate and self-assured. His openness and unabashed conviction bordered on arrogance (as did his habit of referring to himself in the third person), but somehow that also made him likeable. Even his name was intriguing—Mubin, meaning distinct or perspicuous (clearly expressed and therefore easily understood). He was one of those characters a fiction writer would dismiss as unrealistic. Which is probably just what CSIS thought when Mubin called the spy service in 2004.

As with Fahim, Zak and other young Muslims, 9/11 was a wake-up call for Mubin. "I was a spoiled, naive, idealistic Canadian boy going through an identity crisis," he would later say. Suddenly his long beard and devout Muslim ways made his neighbours and co-workers wary. Instead of confronting the newfound racism, an angry Mubin fled, leaving Canada in search of a true Islamic life and education. He landed in Syria and for two years studied Islam, taught English and lived modestly. But instead of finding the religious comfort he craved, he discovered something else: he missed Canada. "I went there and that's when I really realized how good we have it here. That's what it did for me." In March 2004, he returned home. His brother met him at Toronto's Pearson International Airport arrivals gate with a Tim Hortons coffee and chocolate-glazed Timbits.

Not long after Mubin returned, one of his childhood friends was arrested in Ottawa and became the first person charged under the anti-terrorism laws that Canada introduced after 9/11. Mohammad Momin Khawaja was a twenty-seven-year-old computer software developer who worked on contract for Canada's Foreign Affairs department. He was arrested in connection with a British case involving nine others. They had planned to bomb London nightclubs and other crowded targets. Khawaja was found guilty four years later, in October 2008, of financing and facilitating terrorism. A judge ruled he was "a willing and eager participant," while Khawaja maintained that the British crew had duped him into designing and building an electronic trigger for their bombs, a device nicknamed the Hi-Fi Digimonster. A 2010 appeal of his sentence was turned down and he was given a life sentence.

But when Mubin heard about his friend's arrest, he was sure they had the wrong guy and decided to let CSIS know of their mistake. It wasn't the first time he had called the service. In 1997, indignant over a pamphlet he had received at a mosque that called for the creation of an Islamic state through jihad, he alerted Canada's spy agency.

Mubin had grown up with Khawaja and knew his family from the days when they lived in a west-end Toronto neighbourhood. He wanted to help Khawaja. He met a CSIS agent and relayed his fond memories of the Khawaja family to a doubting officer. Mubin also enquired about working for the service.

In the months that followed, Mubin did not convince CSIS of his friend's innocence, but was put through a series of polygraphs and interviews as the spy service tested his reliability as an informant. He told his handlers that his motives were simple. He wanted to root out terrorism and his travels had been a wake-up call. "I had this utopian Islamist world view, like a lot of these young kids have. They think there's like this perfect Islamist state out there, somewhere in the Middle East. Well, it ain't in the Middle East, buddy," he would later say. "It was simply realizing how good we have it here. So I signed right up, man. I had no qualms about it."

Mubin later told me espionage was in his genes. His grandfather had been a member of the Indian police force's Criminal Intelligence Bureau during the days of British rule. Before his death, he told Mubin a story about once going undercover for six months as a sadhu, one of India's yoga-practising Hindu mystics, and obtaining a murder confession from a priest.

By 2005, CSIS had started using Mubin on fact-finding assignments. For his first foreign trip, they sent him to Yemen to follow a group of Canadian youths who had gone there for religious studies and whom CSIS wanted to keep tabs on. But Mubin never made it out of the Sanaa airport, as suspicious Yemeni authorities denied him entry. Returning dejected, he would get a second chance just a few months later. CSIS instructed him to go to a banquet hall north of Toronto and meet some guys named Fahim and Zak.

THAT FATEFUL NOVEMBER 27, 2005, meeting at the Taj Banquet Hall marked the beginning of Canada's largest terrorism investigation.

CSIS had started watching Fahim in cyberspace as early as 2002, when the Toronto teenager, who called himself the "Soldier of Allah," was chatting with other like-minded radicals on Clear Guidance and another site called At-Tibyan Publications. Agents read as Fahim discussed plans with "Mr. Fix It" (aka: Aabid Khan, a British resident) about paramilitary training in Pakistan. Khan purported to have connections to the outlawed Pakistani groups Lashkar-e-Taiba and Jaish-e-Mohammed. Two other young men from Atlanta were also interested, and the group decided to meet in Toronto in March 2005. Before the meeting, CSIS agents knocked on Fahim's door.

Canada's spy service will at times attempt to disrupt plans in nascent stages. That was apparently what happened to the alleged leader of the Algerian group I was probing in 2004, when I discovered my Blue-Jays-catcher/spy Gregg Zaun. It was later reported that he fled Toronto for Algeria, unable to cope with the incessant surveillance and pressure (the alleged leader, not Zaun).

In 2010, the Security Intelligence Review Committee, the government agency that oversees CSIS, raised concern about these "disruptions" and encouraged the government to keep close tabs on the agency's practices. CSIS, the watchdog body warned, could not step outside legal means to infringe on civil rights in the name of fighting terror. (The committee had been created in 1984 after CSIS's predecessor had scandalously done just that. The RCMP's security services had handled the country's terrorism investigations until it was revealed that their renegade unit had conducted illegal break-ins, fake letter campaigns and even burned down a Quebec barn to prevent a meeting between Black Panther radicals and Front de libération du Québec separatists.) CSIS defended its disruption tactics and invited the scrutiny, saying they were part of community public outreach, and sometimes alerting parents or an individual that CSIS was watching them proved enough to dissuade people from going further with illegal activity.

Apparently not Fahim, however. The first time agents visited he told them that yes he was visiting websites, but had no interest in taking his activity further. When they came back a few weeks later, prior to the visit from two Atlanta men, again Fahim brushed them away. (The two Atlanta men would go on to film surveillance tapes of possible Washington, D.C., targets and send them to Khan in Britain. They were both convicted in 2009 and given sentences of thirteen and seventeen years.)

CSIS continued to monitor Fahim. When he rented a car for two gun-smuggling accomplices, they were watching, which is why border guards pulled the car over at the Peace Bridge in August 2005.

Only when CSIS transferred the case to the RCMP, in November 2005, ten days before the meeting at the Taj Banquet Hall, did it become a criminal investigation. The RCMP-led security unit that took on the case dubbed it Project OSAGE. Mubin swapped his CSIS handlers for RCMP counterparts and was sent to infiltrate the group (CSIS continued to conduct its own parallel probe).

FAHIM AND ZAK were at the Taj Banquet Hall that night, attending a fundraising event for five Muslim men Canada was trying to deport for terrorism connections. The introduction to Mubin seemed almost too easy. Mubin may have been an outsider but his long beard and religious aura drew the others to him. It was Zak who first approached. "Peace be upon you," he said, pulling down the red checked kaffiyeh that covered his face. They introduced themselves using their kunyas (Arabic nicknames) and soon afterward, Fahim joined the pair. Mubin's religious and military background easily impressed the jihadi wannabes. He had studied in the Middle East and undergone weapons and survival training during his six years as a member of the Royal Canadian Army Cadets. He told them everything they wanted to hear, including a bogus story about his travels to Yemen, and complained that CSIS had grilled him upon his return. The big talker Fahim retorted: "If CSIS comes to my house, they'll know what I'll do," and then he made a gun with his fingers. Mubin could one up that, and showed them his firearms licence. Then it was Zak's turn. He hugged Mubin, the weight of his 9-mm handgun in his jacket pocket pressing against Mubin, who laughed, "Bro, are you happy to see me?" He was in.

During the next seven months, the Toronto 18 plot and Project OSAGE would develop. In December 2005, Mubin went north with Fahim, Zak and ten of the recruits to the small town of Washago, Ontario, to lead a "training camp." They wanted to mimic the al Qaeda camps in Afghanistan and live primitively in tents, surviving the elements. The younger members were told only that it was a religious retreat and later said they had no idea of the scope of Fahim's plot.

Mubin was given the *kunya* of Abu Jendel (Father of Soldiers) and led the drills along with Zak, Fahim, a nineteen-year-old aspiring engineer named Amin Mohamed Durrani and Steven Chand, the twenty-five-year-old son of Fiji immigrants who had converted from Hinduism to Islam and had once been in Canada's military reserves. Over twelve cold days, the crew pretended to be fighting in Chechnya as they marched and ran through the snowy Ontario woods. If a group of brown-skinned campers in the predominantly white town of Washago was not enough to draw attention, the green-and-brown "camouflage" uniforms they wore in the snow certainly did the trick.

Exercises that started with paintball games gave way to firearms training as Mubin showed them how to use the 9-mm Zak had brought. Fahim had brought the bullets in a sock. Mubin supplied more bullets and the targets. He later told me he felt sorry for the younger members, who were clearly in over their heads. A couple fell asleep during Fahim's lectures, and couldn't be motivated to march, let alone run through the woods. Mubin would tell a court that Fahim once whined to him: "They don't want to jog. They don't want to do anything!" One of the youths admitted after his arrest that when he heard howling one night he thought wolves were going to attack and had trouble not peeing himself out of fear. Mubin later quipped to his RCMP handler that it should have been called Operation Potty Training.

But despite the haplessness of some members, Fahim and Zak were serious and committed. Fahim made grandiose speeches, telling the group they were training to kill the *kuffar* (non-believers). At one point, he played a series of videos on his laptop by American preacher Anwar al Awlaki called "The Constants of Jihad." Awlaki spoke in flawless English and used contemporary examples to make his argument that the world was turning against Islam and that it was the duty of good Muslims to battle back. As the group watched, Mubin watched them. "Guys like Anwar al Awlaki provide do-it-yourself Islam," Mubin later said when trying to explain the popularity of the preacher who was living in Yemen. "He's building a fantasy and then pushing them over the edge. It appeals at a very basic level. It's like sheep food and they gobble it up."

Fahim videotaped the training camp for posterity. "If we don't [get] a victory, God willing, our kids will get it," Fahim said during one of his speeches, as freezing rain pummelled the group. "This has to get done, Rome has to be defeated," he said.

But the Rome speeches started to irritate Zak, who dismissed Fahim as all-talk-no-action. By March 2006, Zak began to build his own crew and distanced himself from Fahim and the younger members. One plot now became two. Zak pushed ahead with the plan to park truck bombs on Toronto's busy streets and began trying to acquire the ammonium nitrate he needed and purchase enough fertilizer and bleach to produce his own bombs. But CSIS was one step ahead, grooming a second informant to tap into Zak's group, while Mubin maintained close ties with Fahim.

Shaher Elsohemy was the perfect plant. An Arab entrepreneur in his early thirties, he had been friends with one of Zak's confidants and had a university degree in science. Two of his uncles were chemists. He also ran a travel agency and had once worked as an Air Canada flight attendant. When CSIS first called him, he assumed it had something to do with a flight he had taken to Miami earlier that year, during which he was inexplicably questioned by U.S. authorities. But the spy service wasn't interested in helping him clear that up. He would later testify that CSIS had encouraged him to "dangle that you are an agriculture engineer" before members of Zak's group.

By the late spring of 2006, Zak's "Battle of Toronto" plot was falling into place. He had built a remote-controlled detonator, and Elsohemy would become his chemical supplier. The RCMP became his landlord, surreptitiously entering his apartment at will. During one of ten covert entries, agents found a circuit board, a black box, a battery pack and a video that showed how he had managed to make his homemade detonator work. Another time, they found a black binder with the title "Bomb Making Manual" and ammunition for a

9-mm pistol. Zak was picked up on wiretap bragging to a cohort that his attack is "gonna be kicking ass like never before."

Fahim, meanwhile, was still playing GI Jihadi on camping trips and talking about the fall of Rome. He told Mubin he wanted to storm Parliament Hill and personally behead Canadian Prime Minister Stephen Harper. Zak wasn't the only one wary of Fahim. Jahmaal James, a Jamaican convert who tried unsuccessfully to go to Pakistan for training, told Mubin that Fahim had become a liability. He was a little too "obvious," Jahmaal complained to Fahim. Wearing a camouflage outfit to the mosque like he had just returned from fighting in Tora Bora certainly didn't help him keep a low profile.

The parallel plots continued, and what Fahim may have lacked in skill, he made up in determination. Police continued to watch, listen and document, both from the outside, and with Mubin and Elsohemy right in the middle of it all. Hundreds of officers were seconded to Project OSAGE.

Police had waited for the final sting before making the arrests that Friday night in June. They swooped in after an undercover officer delivered what the suspects believed was three tonnes of ammonium nitrate fertilizer.

In total, fourteen Muslim adults and four youths were charged and Fahim and Zak were fingered as the groups' leaders. The youngest accused was fifteen; the eldest was a forty-three-year-old bus driver and janitor at the mosque where Fahim and Zak prayed. The Toronto 18 defied a single profile. They ranged from a high school flunky to a computer programmer who brought home a six-figure salary. There were more than 82,000 intercepted calls included among the volumes of evidence disclosed to the phalanx of defence lawyers, who also ranged in profile from the experienced criminal and constitutional lawyers to the rookies.

WHEN THE CASE went to trial, prosecutors were understandably concerned about Mubin, their star witness. Since the arrests, he had had a public spat with the RCMP over his salary. He had been paid $297,000 for turning his life upside down. Elsohemy had been paid more than \$4 million. Then there was his relapse with cocaine. He had a breakdown after the arrests and spent more than \$30,000 in a five-month binge of cocaine, cabs and hotel rooms before he got clean again. His attack on the school girls in 2007 also made for ugly headlines. While Elsohemy disappeared into a witness protection program, Mubin seemed to be everywhere and talked openly about his work with CSIS and the RCMP. When I first contacted him after the arrests, but before his name had been made public, he answered the phone saying, "What took you so long?" Later, he would update his Facebook profile to list the RCMP and CSIS as his employers.

POSITION: Intelligence Consultant Type
DESCRIPTION: If I told you—I'd have to kill you :I
For the record I am/was not, nor do I claim to be an Intelligence Officer of CSIS. Nor do I want to be cuz they're unarmed and underpaid. Sucks to have to stay in the loop, eh? ;).

The prosecution's fears played out during some of the trials of the younger members when Mubin became more effective as a witness for the defence. He was particularly sympathetic to the younger accused, a fifteen-year-old convert and a sixteen-year-old who seemed to like weed and partying and was more interested in chasing girls than infidels.

At a brief preliminary hearing for the fifteen-year-old, his lawyer, Nadir Sachak, presented a convincing and rather humorous defence that the teenager had been duped into joining the camp. Mubin helped.

Q: "Boys-will-be-boys activity?"
A: Yes.
Q: It's—it's something like when you were a kid, probably. You probably played Cowboys and Indians, right?
A: I was the Indian.
Q: You were the Indian, so you were the bad guy; right?
A: Because I was brown.

Q: Okay, but you played cops and robbers?

A: Cops and robbers, yes.

Q: You were the robber?

A: Not always.

Q: All right, okay, but I mean basically what I'm trying to suggest is ...

A: Yeah.

Q: ... this is an extension of—of a game that could be played innocently?

A: Innocently, yes.

Q: Right.

A: Right.

Tim Hortons loomed large in the courtroom too.

Q: It appeared that you guys were going to Tim Hortons or a donut shop on a regular basis?

A: Tim Hortons, yes.

Q: Tim Hortons, and this—to what, drink coffee?

A: Yes.

Q: And what, to use ...

A: To use the ...

Q: ... the washroom?

A: ... facilities, yeah.

Q: What, number one and number two?

A: Oh, yeah.

Q: So like where would you guys go to do a number one at the camp?

A: Anywhere really. I mean there were general areas where you would go and it was known that people would, you know, use facilities accordingly over there.

Q: Okay, number two?

A: No, you had to go to the Timmy's.

Q: So you had to basically ...

A: Wait.

Q: ... hold it until the evening every night?

A: Oh, yeah, two, three days even. Depending. There were, I don't want to say shifts, but …

Q: All right, so basically the trips to Tim Hortons were to take a dump and to eat some food?

A: Yeah.

Mubin was integral in unravelling the government's prosecution of three of the four youths by admitting that Fahim had asked him to keep the real purpose of the camp "on the down low."

Q: On the down low. And so conceal the real objective?

A: Yes.

Q: Manipulate these boys …

A: Yes.

Q: … as it turned out?

A: Yes.

Q: Deceive these boys?

A: Yes.

Q: Trick these boys?

A: Yes.

Q: And as a result of some of the trickery, manipulation and deception, these boys are here today?

A: That's right.

Frequent references to Tim Hortons and downplaying the plot as merely a fantasy of young, angry kids were at the core of the defence's arguments in the cases against Zak, Fahim and some of the other main players too. But in those trials Mubin was solid on the stand and withstood days of cross-examination. Defence continued to paint Mubin as an *agent provocateur* who had entrapped the fantasy-prone youths, but it didn't seem like the judge was buying it.

For four years, the case crawled through Canada's courts and largely fell off the media's radar due to a publication ban that restricted the reporting of pretrial proceedings. My friend and colleague Isabel Teotonio sat through every day of those hearings, studiously taking notes and patiently waiting until the bitter end to reveal all she had discovered. But in the meantime, the public's initial shock and fear turned to skepticism. I privately worried that maybe we had been too sensational in our coverage and it was a bad investigation after all. Perhaps the case wasn't as big as our headlines had first declared. There had been dozens of examples in the panic after 9/11 in which screaming arrests gave way to whimpering court cases as charges were thrown out and no apologies given for reputations left in tatters.

Some of the fiercest criticism about the RCMP's investigation came from within Toronto's Muslim community. Yes, some of the men had been caught in the act, but would they have ever reached that stage had the police moles not pushed them?

If Mubin had expected widespread praise for his service he was sorely mistaken. In his blog, he later wrote: "When these targets were then arrested—I realized I had to go public otherwise the Muslim community would be lost and confused as to what happened. I thought (foolishly) that due to my background, the Muslim community would understand that this was not a conspiracy—not a setup. Big mistake. The community fell into denial and dreamed up all sorts of scenarios—not one of them suggesting guilt of the accused. They had rallies, brought busloads of people, opined passionately about this and that—expressing a new found interest in the presumption of innocence but one that could not afford to admit wrongdoing even to this day."

Later he updated his blog bitterly: "OH—a word to my fellow Muslims who have judged me so harshly: please come and see/hear the evidence for yourself. Please read the agreed statement of facts. I know you do not accept anything from a lying spy like me but how about hearing it from their own mouths? Will you STILL not believe?"

In the end, the net had been cast a little too wide. Some of the accused were held for months but never went to trial. Charges against three of the four youths and four of the adult suspects were stayed. Abdul Qayyum Jamal, the forty-three-year-old janitor at the mosque and father of four young boys, had been identified as a leader of the group by some media outlets based on his age, and spent seventeen months in solitary confinement before charges were dropped. He later said that his life—and that of his wife and sons—had been ruined by the publicity.

But five of the accused pleaded guilty and were sentenced or released after receiving credit for the time served in pre-trial custody. Four of the accused fought their charges and lost.

As their trials were underway, Fahim and Zak made surprise guilty pleas and confessed to their roles as leaders. Fahim was sentenced to sixteen years, which meant he could apply for parole in 2014. Zak received a life sentence, which in Canada translated to a minimum of twenty-five years behind bars before being eligible for parole (followed by a lifetime of monitoring). After being given two-for-one credit for the years he was held before his trial, Zak would be eligible for parole by 2016.

The Canadian government hailed the convictions as a successful test of the country's new anti-terror laws.

TERRORISM, OF COURSE, is not funny. Suicide bombing wannabes are not funny. But Chris Morris's film *Four Lions* about a group of young British Muslim men who want to become martyrs, is darkly funny. Really uncomfortably, sadly witty, and about the best example I've seen of why "homegrown terrorism" is such a tragicomedy. (Since 9/11, "homegrown terrorism" has come to denote Western-raised youths radicalized locally, by the Internet or religious leaders who fight in the name of al Qaeda, but who, in most cases, do not have any formal links to the group.)

The plot of *Four Lions* follows a wretched group of young struggling jihadists as they devise a plan to attack London. They devote an inordinate amount of time to making the martyr video with a toy gun. They attempt to train crows to become suicide bombers. They argue about appropriate targets. Boots drugstore? "They sell condoms that make you want to bang white girls." One character randomly shouts offscreen, "Fuck Mini Babybels," as if the little wheels of cheese encased in red wax were an affront to Muslims worldwide. When one member says his father could be praying in the mosque they considered bombing, crazed leader wannabe Barry (who also goes by Azzam al Britani) retorts: "Has your dad ever bought a Jaffa orange?"

"Once or twice."

"Right. He's buying nukes for Israel, bro. He's a Jew."

In another scene, one member raps like Zak:

I'm a mujahideen and I'm making a scene.
Now youz gonna feel what the boom boom means
It's like Tupac said when I die I'm not dead
We are the martyrs, you're just smashed tomatoes

(The rhyme works with a British accent, which makes it sound more like to-ma-ters.)

The movie brought back memories of the many times we had laughed in our newsroom, darkly marvelling at terrorism's theatre of the absurd. One of the suspects in a 2010 Ottawa terrorism case had auditioned for *Canadian Idol*, singing an extremely off-tune version of Avril Lavigne's "Complicated." Resplendent in a traditional shalwar kameez and *pakul* hat, he did the robot dance and moonwalked across the stage and spoke in a fake Pakistani accent (not surprisingly, the *Star* had a record number of hits once we dug up the clip and posted it on our website). The arresting RCMP officers found it quite funny too and joked that they should moonwalk during the bust, or, when reading the suspects his rights, add, "Well, it's *complicated*." But the laughs could also be had at the Mounties' expense. They called their investigation Operation Samossa (yes they spelled it with two *s*'s).

Four Lions was made before the arrests of the Toronto 18 but could have easily been based on Canada's pathetic crew. Mubin told me that after running around "training" at the Washago camp, the jihadists would warm up at the Tim Hortons with French vanilla coffees (although no one suggested calling them "Freedom Vanilla").

Even though they were apparently ready to be hardcore, no one except Mubin had brought proper winter camp gear. The vicious fighters had to sleep in their cars with portable heaters. A few squealed when they saw a mouse.

Yet clearly, as the evidence and sentences demonstrate, some of the group's members were determined and capable of causing mayhem, and none of this would seem funny had they succeeded. Blowing yourself up or taking a gun into a crowded shopping mall does not require sophistication. That's one of the problems with homegrown terrorists: even the ridiculous cannot be dismissed. Yet sometimes "equally dangerous" is an overreaction that not only ruins reputations, but causes a backlash that inspires the next group, or feeds into al Qaeda's narrative of the West's war on Muslims.

There is considerable debate among intelligence analysts about what constitutes the greatest terrorism threat to the West today— Afghanistan's al Qaeda and its affiliates, or the seventeen-year-old on a mission who plots from his Ohio basement.

After the invasion of Afghanistan, al Qaeda as it existed before 9/11 was no more. Many of the group's senior members were killed or captured and the rest were on the run. But as attention shifted to the war in Iraq, al Qaeda managed to rebuild in Pakistan's tribal region, and what was reconstituted under the leadership of Osama bin Laden and his Egyptian lieutenant Ayman al-Zawahiri is often referred to as "al Qaeda central" or the "core." Regional factions that developed around the world, such as Somalia's al Shabab or Yemen's al Qaeda in the Arab Peninsula (AQAP), may have pledged allegiance to al Qaeda but were not directly tied to the core. These are often called "al Qaeda-affiliated" groups. The final category is the "home-grown" groups, or individuals who are "inspired" by al Qaeda. Some may try to reach out to al Qaeda's core or affiliates, such as failed Times Square bomber Faisal Shahzad, but most can find the tools and direction they need without leaving home.

The majority of failed plots and successful attacks on Western soil, including London's 7/7 bombings, have been the result of locally driven plans, suggesting that al Qaeda central no longer has the capacity to launch an assault on the scale of 9/11 and that home-grown terrorism is a pressing issue. But since the majority of plots have been foiled, it also indicates that the suspects possess more fervour than skill. And no one believes al Qaeda is impotent. Brit-ain's foiled liquid bombing plot in 2006, which intended to bring down ten transatlantic flights, including two bound for Canada, did reportedly have guidance from al Qaeda's core.

Forensic psychiatrist Marc Sageman was one of the first to research the homegrown phenomenon. Sageman's background makes him unique among academics; he once served as a U.S. Navy flight surgeon, has a doctorate in political sociology and in the late 1980s, during the Soviet occupation of Afghanistan, worked for the CIA in Islamabad, where he had access to the Afghan mujahi-deen. Those were the pre-9/11 days, when Afghan's religious fighters were Hollywood heroes. (The 1988 movie *Rambo III* ends with the line: "This film is dedicated to the gallant people of Afghanistan.") In 2008, Sageman published *Leaderless Jihad*, which describes how a disjointed force of local al Qaeda groups has created something like Facebook terrorists. "These homegrown wannabes form a scattered global network, a leaderless jihad," he wrote.

Sageman's study was important in debunking assumptions that homegrown terrorists were all brainwashed by charismatic lead-ers (although there are some examples of this) or suffered from economic depression or familial or sexual issues. Many were well educated and from stable homes. Sageman believes the threat they pose outweighs that of a reconfigured al Qaeda. In October 2009, he took this view to the U.S. Senate Committee on Foreign Relations: "The paucity of actual al Qaeda and other transnational terrorist organization plots compared to the number of autonomous plots refutes the claims by some heads of the Intelligence Community that all Islamist plots in the West can be traced back to the Afghan Pakistani border. Far from being the 'epicenter of terrorism,' this Pakistani region is more like the finishing school of global neo-jihadi terrorism where a few amateur wannabes are transformed into dangerous terrorists."

Sageman identified four stages to the homegrown radicalization process (not necessarily linear): a sense of moral outrage; belief that Islam is under siege; a personal moment that pushes them to action; and a connection to networks or others. Leaderless jihad, as the name suggests, is a bottom-up social mobilization that does not need a leader to call the shots. The question then is: if this is the problem, how can it be countered? Michael King, a Montreal researcher and PhD student, and researchers Jamie Bartlett and Jonathan Birdwell conducted a 2010 study that tried to answer that question by looking into the root causes of radicalization. They studied sixty-two homegrown terrorists, including members of the Toronto 18 and others from the United Kingdom, Denmark, France and the Netherlands. Because of the sample size, they concluded the study was "illustrative rather than predictive." The authors made a distinction between radicals who simply rejected the status quo and those who were violent. "Differentiating between these types of radicalizations is extremely important because targeting the wrong people can breed resentment and alienation, and erode the very freedoms Western governments want to preserve," they wrote. "Violent radicals are clearly enemies of liberal democracies; but non-violent radicals might sometimes be powerful allies."

The thrust of their suggestions came down to three overriding principles: encourage positive activism; demystify and deglamorize al Qaeda; and engage the community. "Al-Qaeda inspired terrorism in the West shares much in common with other counter cultural, subversive groups of predominantly angry young men," they wrote. "Young people need space to be radical: bold, different, awkward and dissenting," they continued. "This can be an important antidote to radicalisation that leads to violence. Engaging in political and social protest is a good—not a bad—sign and must be encouraged."

As for community involvement, the authors suggested a social, street-level approach, similar to those used to tackle street gangs. While they would also recommend religious counselling for those who had adopted al Qaeda's perversion of Islam, the authors stressed that religious re-education alone would not work.

"(M)ission drift must be avoided," they wrote. "Prevention work must import multi-agency approaches from successful counter-gang techniques ... There is some common ground, at least for some individuals, with gangster lifestyles, both in the nature of group or gang recruitment, and also in inter- and intra-group dynamics." The gang comparison had been discounted in some police and security circles, but thinking back to Toronto or Compton gang members I had interviewed in the late 1990s, I saw many parallels. Many talked about the need to belong to something bigger, the feelings of alienation, and a seething anger that had just been channelled dangerously. Some of the best gang rehab programs used former gang members who worked with police to educate them on gang recruitment, while also helping kids get off the streets.

My favourite recommendation in the study was deglamorizing or poking fun at terrorism. The Pentagon scored one of its best public relations coups in 2006 when they released a video of the feared Iraqi insurgent Abu Musab al-Zarqawi having some serious problems with his machine gun. The clip shows the brawny leader wearing New Balance tennis shoes under his black flowing robe and looking rather flummoxed when he can get his automatic machine gun to fire only one shot. He has to call over one of his men when he is unable to fix it as it jams. Another fighter later grabs the gun by its smouldering barrel, burning his hand. The tape was far different from the edited version posted online by Zarqawi's group, where the burly and fierce-looking leader is pumping gunfire into the air and pledging his allegiance to al Qaeda.

This really seems to be the crux of the issue with homegrown terrorism: figuring out how to control the narrative. It had to be made clear that killing thousands in Toronto was not part of a holy war waged against unjust infidels, as savvy orators like Anwar al Awlaki could eloquently preach. It was about killing innocent people and fuelling a cycle where violence only begets more violence.

"DEAR JUSTICE DAWSON, I want to begin by telling you how deeply sorry I am for the horrible things that I have said and how much I regret the actions that have led to me standing before you today,"

Fahim Ahmad began a letter to the judge determining his sentence. "I understand that simply saying sorry is not enough and no excuse can ever be good enough for all I have said and done. I write this not as an excuse, but rather an explanation as to how someone, no different than any other 17-year-old whose [sic] into sports and movies, can end up in a situation like this."

Across six handwritten pages, Fahim described how he had lost his way.

I would vent and say foolish things to get attention. The void of having a mentor was filled by religious elders whom I would take from without questioning. And the void of having friends, another set of "friends" who were only names on a computer screen... I was advised to get married in order to avoid free-mixing with the opposite sex. Therefore I was married at age 18... I was told that it was unlawful to live in a house on mortgage and so, I moved out at 19. I was told that contraceptives were unlawful to use, so I became a father at age 20....

There is no way for me to describe the feeling of sitting there in court, with my family sitting behind me and hearing all those wiretaps being played at trial. I couldn't believe that that was my own voice saying all those terribly hurtful things... I have failed as a son to my parents who had so much hope and expectations from me. I have failed as a husband to my [wife] who sacrificed so much for me. As a father to my kids, on whose entire childhood I've missed out and whose only memory of me is being behind glass. I have failed as a son to my in-laws who have done so much for me and supported me. Most of all, I have failed as a citizen of this country that has given me so much to be grateful for. Yet after all this, my wife still stands by me, helping me and supporting me every step of the way. My parents still pick up my calls and we've never been closer. My kids still call me daddy and ask everytime when I'm coming out of the glass. My in-laws still support me in every way possible. I am undeserving of such love, that I have always had, yet only after incarceration, have come to appreciate.

In a separate sentencing hearing, Zak also tried to explain his actions to Superior Court Justice Bruce Durno. "Everyone found it difficult to reconcile between my charges and my humble and kind personality, thus leading the way to many discussions about the justification of terrorist acts. At first, I vigorously defended my positions but every time I walked away, I walked away with doubt in my heart. Despite their lack of education and expertise, their moral and logical arguments were like pickaxes that chiseled away at my ideological walls," he read from his letter to the court. "Your Honour, I spent days upon days trying to summon words appropriate, meaningful and deep enough to express my regret and seek forgiveness for my actions. At the end, I realized that only promises and actions could suffice. Therefore, I would like to promise you and my fellow Canadians that I will use my sentence to build myself from a man of destruction to a man of construction... I will embrace whatever sentence you give, since in reality I deserve much more than a mere sentence, but at the same time I hope that you do not deprive me of a chance to pay for the moral debt that I still owe."

It is difficult to know the sincerity of either apology or the tears that followed. These were the same men who had sat through weeks of hearings rolling their eyes or smirking. On wiretapped conversations, they had talked about deceiving the infidels. But the psychiatric assessments of Zak and Fahim were fairly optimistic about the likelihood of rehabilitation. Psychiatrist Arif Syed wrote that Zak "was looking for the right answers through the lens of anti-establishment glasses." Dr. Syed wrote:

> The spiritual ideal of jihad (fighting oneself) stagnated, hardened, and sank into self-aggrandizing bravado. The daily drudgery of working in dead-end, low-paying jobs helped to create an intellectually stunted environment. Internet jihad videos became more exciting and their causes became more urgent. In their gatherings and conversations, the group would 'just want to talk about grievances.' Zakaria's wife felt that the motivation of much of the early conversations her husband had was that 'it's not really about

doing jihad; it's about being a man'... He did not have the intellectual and scholarly tools to debate against the isolating extremist ideology he left himself open to.

In assessing Fahim, Toronto psychiatrist Julian Gojer concluded that Fahim did not suffer from a personality disorder and was at low risk for engaging in terrorist activity again.

> My overall clinical impression is that he (is) an intelligent young man who has considerable potential to complete a university education. He is a non-psychopathic individual, has no mental illness, is very remorseful, and but for his prior religious and political views had no conflict with the law... He appears to recognize how he allowed his mind to be influenced by religious individuals and that he failed to examine carefully how religious texts were misinterpreted for him. He takes responsibility for his actions, and wishes to make amends for his actions by counseling youth who may be misled like him.

According to both Zak and Fahim, their apparent enlightenment came from the school of hard knocks. Both said they felt they had changed their outlooks during their time at Toronto's Don Jail, one of the country's oldest and toughest prisons. As a young and still-naive crime reporter I had spent some time reporting from the jail, where a couple of inmates tried to spit on me and grab me as I passed. Whenever I walked through the prison's front doors, blinking back into the daylight, I was tempted to kiss the ground.

For Fahim, it was meeting two Muslim volunteers who offered a different interpretation of the Qur'an. He claimed he grew close to one man, identified in the psychiatric report as "Mr. Hakim," despite the fact that he at first doubted his commitment to Islam since he was not bearded. "He recalls that Mr. Hakim then asked if he was any better or any worse for not having the facial hair and this made Mr. Ahmad realize that the right answer was 'no,'" Dr. Gojer wrote. "This motivated him to shave off his own beard. Since then,

Mr. Hakim has had a hand [in] inspiring Mr. Ahmad to re-evaluate his beliefs and prioritize them." More apparent epiphanies came for Fahim when other inmates were quiet and muted the televisions out of respect for him as he prayed, and when he forged a friendship with a Jewish inmate; they poked fun at each other's cultural stereotypes, even swapping their kosher and halal meals.

Zak told his psychiatrist he also had conversations with non-Muslims that affected him, including an inmate who had apparently served with the Canadian military in Afghanistan but was happy to listen to Zak talk about the injustices committed on the Muslim world. As Dr. Arif Syed wrote: "Zakaria's emotional life may have become (paradoxically) liberated while confined in jail."

"HI MICHELLE, I hope this finds you in good health and spirits," begins a jailhouse letter from Fahim Ahmad. He was sent to a Quebec prison to serve his sentence, and although I wanted to interview him in person, he claimed the facility had strict rules on visiting journalists, so a letter would be better. I wanted to know what his thoughts were following his conviction, to gauge if there was real remorse. Did he recall that I had tried to interview him five years earlier?

"I do remember your phone call prior to my arrest," Fahim wrote. "I recall I wasn't having a good day and it wasn't really a pleasant exchange. I didn't, at the time, know who you were, as I never read the paper...

"When one locks himself out from the outside world and takes a tunnel vision path to how he sees everything around him, it's easy to fall into some deep holes and develop a mentality not based in reality. A lot has changed since June 2nd of '06, and I will talk about that a bit later."

Over both sides of two lined pages, singled-spaced, Fahim tried to explain, saying he hoped to help others not make the mistakes he had. "This isn't some school project where you get a bad mark, feel bad for a day and move on to the next assignment and life goes on as usual," he wrote. His major regret—and motivation for pleading guilty—was the pain he had caused his family. His major realization was that his misguided mentality was "one-sided, isolated, black and white, we're right and everyone else is wrong."

It is not a letter of remorse, and he begins by complaining about the legal system and claiming that allegations against him were exaggerated, that he was never a leader of the plot.

But he took the blame for his own actions. "To pretend that I'm completely innocent and this whole case is a lie and so on, well, I would only be fooling myself."

above The post-9/11 mood captured in the face of Genetta Giudice as she watches over a prayer service in the streets of Boston's Little Italy on September 14, 2001. The U.S. flag, which has 48 stars and is from the mast of the uss *Sims*, belongs to her brother, Nick Giudice, who served in the navy in World War II. Jim Rankin / *Toronto Star*

top Sheikh Hassan Dahir Aweys in October 2006 in his Mogadishu home during an interview with the author. Aweys was a leader of the Islamic Courts Union and, following Ethiopia's invasion, joined forces with the outlawed Shabab. Peter Power / Toronto Star

bottom Patients wait at the medical clinic protected by African Union peacekeepers in Mogadishu, Somalia, in January 2010. Two hours after this photo was taken, an 82-mm mortar shell hit the clinic, killing at least five and injuring dozens more. Michelle Shephard / Toronto Star

above Ismail Khalif Abdulle inside Mogadishu's Villa Somalia in January 2010.
Shabab fighters kidnapped the seventeen-year-old and cut off his hand and
foot in a public amputation. He had refused to join the al Qaeda–linked group.
Michelle Shephard / *Toronto Star*

top Author in Mogadishu in 2010 when security demanded that journalists travel with African Union forces. The Ugandan and Burundi peacekeepers provided protection for Somalia's embattled Transitional Federal Government. Yasuyoshi Chiba

bottom Author interviewing Pakistan's former ISI director Khalid Khawaja in Karachi, April 2006. Khawaja was kidnapped and executed four years later by a group calling themselves the Asian Tigers. Peter Power / *Toronto Star*

top A detainee runs the track at Camp 4 inside Guantanamo's detention centre. The Pentagon forbids photos that identify prisoners. Michelle Shephard / Toronto Star

bottom Nasser al Bahri, known as Abu Jandal, during an August 2009 interview in Sanaa, Yemen. Abu Jandal was once a chief bodyguard for Osama bin Laden. Lucas Oleniuk / Toronto Star

top About two hundred kilometres north of the Arctic Circle in Harstad, Norway, Ismail sees snow for the first time in January 2011. Norway accepted the Somali teenager on an emergency basis as a refugee in need.
Michelle Shephard / *Toronto Star*

bottom Civil rights activist Tawakkol Karman greets admirers on the streets of Sanaa in February 2011. The director of Women Journalists Without Chains was at the forefront of the early revolutionary protests in Yemen.
Michelle Shephard / *Toronto Star*

top A young protester calls for President Saleh to end his three-decade rule. Saleh was forced to leave Yemen in June 2011 to seek medical attention in Saudi Arabia after an explosion at his presidential palace. Michelle Shephard / *Toronto Star*

bottom An effigy of Yemeni President Ali Abdullah Saleh flaps in the wind in February 2011 above Sanaa's "Change Square." Michelle Shephard / *Toronto Star*

top Influential cleric Shaikh Abdul Majeed al Zindani holds a press conference February 17, 2011, calling for the end of street protests in Sanaa. Zindani is designated a "global terrorist" in the United States but is also a long-time supporter of American ally President Saleh. Michelle Shephard / *Toronto Star*

bottom U.S. President Barack Obama observes a moment of silence at a memorial site at lower Manhattan's Ground Zero on May 5, 2011, four days after Osama bin Laden was killed in Pakistan by a team of elite U.S. Navy SEALS. Michelle Shephard / *Toronto Star*

5 U.S. Naval Base, Guantanamo Bay

SURREAL. IT WAS the overused descriptor for journalists trying to explain the place. But really, there is no better word.

Consider the fact that the notorious U.S. Navy base had a gift shop that sold "Kisses from Guantanamo" magnets with big red lips, snow globes, stuffed iguanas, and camouflage beer cozies that read, "It don't GTMO' better than this." There once were pink baby onesies for sale emblazoned with the words "Future Behavior Modification Specialist" and T-shirts of prison guard towers draped in American flags that read: "The Taliban Towers at Guantanamo Bay, the Caribbean's Newest 5-star Resort."

Surrounded by U.S. servicemen and women, I sat at the base's outdoor movie theatre one night, eating a $1 tub of popcorn and drinking a Red Stripe, watching Matt Damon run around Iraq in *Green Zone*. On another night, I attempted to show a downloaded copy of *Harold & Kumar Escape from Guantanamo Bay* on our media room video screen. During the very colourful opening scene, someone from the Miami-based United States Southern Command called to say a foreign computer had been detected and must be immediately disconnected.

I have a Starbucks card "Good for all GTMO locations," even though there is just one. On my twenty-third trip to the base, passengers on a ferry ride included Madonna and Cher impersonators. They had entertained the troops at the Tiki Bar two nights earlier.

Photographing detainees from the shadows of a guard tower for three hours one November dawn, I wondered how these men had survived years in legal limbo, in a place Amnesty International called "the gulag of our times."

In June 2008, Khalid Sheikh Mohammed, aka KSM, al Qaeda's number three and the alleged mastermind of the September 11 attacks, laughed, preened, stroked his long, grey-flecked beard and proclaimed "death to America" as we watched him through a double Plexiglas window in a Guantanamo courthouse. His arrogance was palpable and made the 9/11 victims' relatives whom the Pentagon had flown to the base sob. I thought of Toronto widow Cindy Barkway and how her husband David had become a victim of KSM's war. I also wondered how the CIA's 183 waterboarding sessions of KSM would taint the possibility of a fair trial. Writer Christopher Hitchens was waterboarded for a story and he lasted mere seconds before activating the "dead man's handle," the predetermined signal to make his tormentors stop. Hitchens wrote in a 2008 *Vanity Fair* article, "If waterboarding does not constitute torture, then there is no such thing as torture." It was frustrating that KSM's mistreatment could cloud what should otherwise be a straightforward prosecution to lock up a madman for life.

I've been to Guantanamo spinning classes with Marines, watched karaoke on humid, salty Cuban nights, and debated into the wee hours of the morning with a military public affairs officer (PAO) about why he should not delete a photo I took of the prison camp with a blue sliver of ocean in the background. Included among the pages of Pentagon Ground Rules we had to sign in order to get access to the island base was a list of photo restrictions. Every frame had to undergo a painful censorship process known as OPSEC (Operational Security). Photographing the coastline was a no-no.

"But al Qaeda knows Cuba is an island," I tried more than once.

"Those are the rules, ma'am."

"But anyone can see the entire base on Google Earth?"

"Sorry. It's the rule."

Ah, the rules. Some made sense—we were after all working on a military base where KSM was housed. Some, however, were nonsensical edicts from Washington that had to be enforced by hapless PAOs and prompted spectacular fights between the media and military. It didn't help that there was already a clash of cultures. The antithesis of a journalist is probably a soldier. They follow orders, defer to rank and learn not to test the rules. It is our job, if not our nature, to challenge authority and ask questions. So when we were told only one pen was permitted in the war crimes court (since two were considered a national security risk), we naturally asked why. What if we ran out of ink? And while we're at it, please tell us why we cannot take photos that show the plastic orange barriers? Why are three tents in a frame allowed, but not four? Why does that picture you just deleted look a lot like one a PAO posted on the Department of Defense website?

Why can't we talk to detainees or photograph their faces when they give their consent?

"Geneva Conventions."

But wasn't that the whole point of Guantanamo? It was why the Bush administration chose Cuba—to circumvent the Geneva Conventions and traditional rights afforded prisoners of war.

"These are detainees, not prisoners."

"Exactly."

"Exactly."

"Huh?"

In the spring of 2010, I was one of four journalists the Pentagon banned from future visits to Guantanamo. Our offence was that we named a former army interrogator who had been convicted of detainee abuse and been given a sentence of five months in return for his cooperation in another case. Two years earlier, I had tracked the interrogator down and he had given me an on-the-record phone interview, professing his innocence. He even told me he was looking forward to testifying, "to clear my name."

After nearly ten years and two dozen visits to the prison, it is hard to pick one story—one surreal moment—that best demonstrates the insanity of covering this sad chapter of history.

So here is just one: On my thirty-sixth birthday, a Filipino waiter presented me with a McDonald's iced cake in the base's Irish pub, O'Kelly's, as journalists, lawyers, marines, sailors, coastguards, soldiers and who-knows-who-else, sang "Happy Birthday" and laughed as I tried to blow out a trick candle protruding from Ronald McDonald's crotch.

Welcome to Gitmo.

THE JOURNALISTS WERE running. Some wore pajamas. Some still clutched beer bottles and struggled to move quickly in their flip-flops. Looking like frantic cockroaches scurrying from the light, Guantanamo's press corps was fleeing the floodlights of the tent city, where we slept, for the dark aircraft hangar that housed the media centre and our connection to the outside world.

It was January 21, 2009, just past midnight, twelve hours after Barack Hussein Obama was inaugurated as the forty-fourth president of the United States. Nearly three dozen journalists had come from all over the world to cover the ongoing war crimes hearings that week and watch Obama's inauguration from the island prison he had long criticized. As I emerged from the shower tent, I stood for a few moments blinking uncomprehendingly at my colleagues as they scampered toward the hangar. Then it dawned on me. There was news. So I ran too.

Minutes earlier, *Washington Post* reporter Peter Finn had broken the story many of us had expected, but not necessarily that night. Obama was suspending Guantanamo's trials. Finn had acquired a draft of the executive order that would be signed later that day.

Obama's 120-day suspension of all military commissions would give Pentagon prosecutors time to review the law and would halt the handful of war crimes trials underway. As his first act in office, this was a clear signal that this administration was breaking from the one that came before. A day later, Obama would go one step further and order Gitmo closed, shuttering the place that had become a powerful symbol of U.S. hypocrisy and arrogance. How could indefinite detentions be okay for the United States, but not Egypt or Syria? America, Obama said, would regain the "moral high ground." He gave a deadline of one year—three hundred and sixty-five days—to either transfer, release or prosecute the remaining 245 detainees and shut down the prison. His executive order also banned the use of harsh interrogation practices and the CIA's overseas black sites. Obama said the United States would confront global violence without sacrificing "our values and our ideals."

Keeping in the theme of Gitmo's tragicomedy, *Saturday Night Live* spoofed the closure with a skit about the prison's going-out-of-business sale. "Hoods! Blindfolds! Shackles! Chains! Dog bowls for people!" shouted the mock guard, holding up the prison paraphernalia. "If it's used to humanely detain or interrogate prisoners, we've got it! We're passing the savings on to you!" In Washington, a spokesperson for Defense Secretary Robert Gates was questioned about the NBC comedy. He declined to comment. He hadn't seen it, he told reporters.

Although public sentiment would later sway, Obama's decision to shut down Guantanamo was cautiously supported in the United States. At the time, it seemed that only former vice president Dick Cheney was publicly clamouring for Guantanamo's continued existence, urging that the prison camp stay open until "the end of the war on terror." Whenever that would be. Maybe around the same time there was victory in the war on drugs.

Perhaps I was just among those swept up by Obamamania and was deluded into thinking that this man who came in on the wings of CHANGE was actually capable of delivering all he promised. I had seen what a powerful symbol Guantanamo had become abroad and how terrorists had used it in their propaganda. While I understood the uphill legal and political challenges Obama faced and that he was rather busy with pressing domestic issues, I still somehow believed the prison would close by 2010.

Peter Finn was more skeptical, and his story announcing Guantanamo's closure proved rather prophetic. "The Obama administration faces a host of legal, logistical and diplomatic challenges in its plan to close the military prison here, and if the effort stumbles, it could bring steep political costs," he wrote.

> As the outlines of President Obama's intentions surfaced in a draft executive order Wednesday—pledging the humane treatment of detainees and an end to torture, along with closure of the prison—the difficulties ahead became equally clear. Among them is the risk of politically explosive acquittals: Transferring cases out of Guantanamo raises the prospect that some may not stand up in court because of evidence tainted by torture or based on intelligence material that is inadequate in court. If the administration were to create a new system of indefinite detention for some prisoners—those considered too dangerous to release or impossible to prosecute, for example—Obama could alienate part of his core constituency.

"Hotel California" was a song that played often on Radio GTMO, the military station with the slogan "Rockin' in Fidel's Backyard." Bobble-heads of Fidel Castro smoking a cigar and standing on a Radio GTMO boom box were popular souvenirs among journalists and lawyers. The station was fun to listen to mainly because of the public service announcements, not the music. "Hi. I'm a banana rat. I may not survive the hurricane season. But you can," began one. (Seen most often as road kill, the indigenous possum-like rodents were of great fascination on the base. You could buy stuffed toy banana rats wearing black op T-shirts and Banana Rat breath mints at the gift shop.) Even though the music wasn't exactly *au courant*, I still wondered every time the Eagles tune played if it wasn't some DJ's joke.

Obama, among others, would soon become only too aware of how Gitmo seemed "programmed to receive." *You can check out any time you like. But you can never leave.*

WHEN THE HIJACKED planes crashed into the Pentagon, the Twin Towers and a field in Pennsylvania, the U.S. Naval Base at Guantanamo Bay was a sleepy Cold War relic that existed more as a geographical marker than an essential American post. Spread out over forty-five square miles of land and water (roughly the size of Manhattan), the base population consisted of iguanas, banana rats, snakes, a family of snowy-white barn owls and about 750 active duty personnel. Another 2,000 family members and contract labourers, mainly from Jamaica and the Philippines, also resided in barrack-style housing. Being posted to Gitmo was either a plum assignment for sailors looking to kick back in the Caribbean or a sentence in Alcatraz for adrenalin junkies. The base had one main function by 2001: it served as a centre for "migrant ops," where refugees picked up by the U.S. Coast Guard could be processed.

For Cuba, the base was the unwanted house guest who had over-stayed her welcome, and no matter how much clattering of dishes went on in the kitchen, she just wasn't leaving. When a miffed Castro complained about the use of water and power on the base, the U.S. military began producing its own electricity and built a desalination plant in 1964. Huge barges came from Florida laden with supplies.

The problem for Castro was that there was a perpetual rental con-tract with the United States that predated revolutionary Cuba. After Christopher Columbus discovered Guantanamo Bay in 1494, the land remained in Spanish hands for more than four hundred years. The first U.S. Marines landed in Gitmo in 1898, at the start of the Spanish-American war. With the defeat of the Spanish, a grateful Cuba gave the United States the prime port and plot of land.

Five years later, U.S. President Theodore Roosevelt signed an agreement with Cuba's first president to lease the land. Roosevelt later renegotiated the terms and the annual rent was set at $4,085. The 1934 treaty stipulated that both parties would have to agree to break the contract—in other words, unless the United States agreed to leave, Cuba could not force it. And why would the United States give up a strategic spot where the Caribbean Sea, Atlantic Ocean and Gulf of Mexico meet? Since Castro refused to cash the U.S. Treasury Department rental cheques after he took power in 1959 (except once, by mistake, he says), there wasn't even a fee.

After the Cuban Revolution, the United States found itself occupying hostile land, and American troops were forbidden from using what's known as the northeast gate, which led from the base into Cuba. The land on either side of the 17.4 miles of fence was mined and U.S. Marines kept a close eye on Castro's Frontier Brigade and vice versa.

During the Cuban Missile Crisis in 1962, the Caribbean base was smack in the centre of a potential nuclear Armageddon as the Soviet government began building Cuban bases for ballistic nuclear missiles with the ability to reach most of the continental United States.

Before Guantanamo became what it is today, most people probably recognized its name as the setting for Rob Reiner's film *A Few Good Men*. In one of Hollywood's most famous courtroom dramas, a U.S. Marine colonel played by Jack Nicholson spars with Tom Cruise, a young Navy JAG:

"You want answers?" Nicholson sneers from the witness box.

"I think I'm entitled."

"You want answers?!"

"I want the truth!" Cruise shouts.

"You can't handle the truth! Son, we live in a world that has walls and those walls have to be guarded by men with guns . . . You don't want the truth because deep down in places you don't talk about at parties, you want me on that wall, you need me on that wall. We use words like honour, code, loyalty. We use these words as the backbone of a life spent defending something. You use them as a punch line. I have neither the time nor the inclination to explain myself to a man who rises and sleeps under the blanket of the very freedom that I provide and then questions the manner in which I provide it. I would rather you just said, 'Thank you,' and went on your way.

Otherwise, I suggest you pick up a weapon and stand a post. Either way, I don't give a damn what you think you are entitled to."

The movie was set at a time when the Soviets and a communist Cuba were the enemy, not the Taliban and al Qaeda. But even though post-9/11 the enemy was no longer on the other side of the fence line, the movie dialogue seemed fitting nonetheless. Concerns about detainee treatment or the application of Geneva Conventions were all too often met with derisive comments about not understanding the new reality, exemplified in Cheney's famous post-9/11 quote of now having to work through "the dark side." It was easy to imagine the modern-day court scene, Cheney on the stand, as some young, earnest lawyer from the American Civil Liberties Union demanded that he justify waterboarding.

As for Cuba, Castro may still have been seething over the U.S. presence, but the animosity between the countries had diminished by the start of the twenty-first century. Disputes over Gitmo just seemed like posturing between traditional rivals, half-hearted punches thrown at each other because the other kids were chanting, "Fight, fight, fight."

TWO DAYS AFTER Christmas 2001 and two months into the war in Afghanistan, U.S. Defense Secretary Donald Rumsfeld announced that the U.S. base at Guantanamo Bay, Cuba, would house suspected al Qaeda and Taliban captives. For weeks, an interagency group in Washington had laboriously debated about what to do with the captives, and early suggestions had included sending the men to Guam, to a brig in South Carolina, or even to a prison in Manhattan. When the idea of Guantanamo was raised, all other possibilities were dismissed. It was about as secure and isolated a spot as you could find to hold prisoners considered the "worst of the worst." Moreover, Guantanamo was attractive to the Bush administration because it was outside the reach of the U.S. courts and the rights afforded prisoners on American soil.

Rumsfeld's endorsement in announcing the new prison, however, was rather tepid. "I would characterize Guantanamo Bay, Cuba, as the least worst place we could have selected," he told reporters. "Its disadvantages seem to be modest relative to the alternatives." The base whose welcome sign greeted visitors as "The Pearl of the Antilles" had just become "The Least Worst Place."

In just a matter of weeks the dozy Gitmo was besieged by sailors, soldiers, Marines, coast guards, and airmen and women who would make up the military joint task force known as JTF-GTMO. At its height, the base population would number as many as 9,500 servicemen and women.

On January 11, 2002, the first prisoners arrived and were placed in outdoor pens that resembled large dog kennels. The primitive conditions of Camp X-Ray, where detainees were crammed together in 320 cells, exposed to the punishing Cuban sun and given only a bucket as a toilet, sparked outrage worldwide. Four months later, they were moved to a newly constructed permanent facility called Camp Delta, built along the coast with parts and equipment shipped from the United States. Camp Delta was about a ten-minute drive from the main base, over rolling, cactus-strewn hills. Delta included Camps 1, 2 and 3, and consisted of 720 mesh steel cells built along two corridors in a boxcar-like arrangement. By early 2003, construction of Camp 4 was completed and the most cooperative—or, in Gitmo parlance, "highly compliant"—detainees moved in. Camp 4 was geared more toward communal living and detainees slept in ten-cot bunkhouses and had a common recreation area. Next came Camps 5 and 6, which were two-storey indoor prisons modelled after facilities in the United States. At first detainees were held there in segregation, where they could only yell through the corridors to one another. In later years, detainees in Camp 6 were permitted to socialize and attend classes together in a common area. The only facility whose location was a mystery and remained off limits for journalists was Camp 7. That was where KSM and other "high-value" CIA captives were detained.

When the prison camp's population was at its peak, in 2003, there were nearly 660 detainees. By early 2011, eight detainees had died in prison: six apparent suicides (although the circumstances in some of the deaths remain suspicious), one who died of colon cancer and another who collapsed while exercising.

As detention facilities expanded, so did the base. And like U.S. bases around the world, Guantanamo became a military Pleasantville that tried to replicate Middle America for homesick troops. There was the trifecta of fast-food joints—McDonald's, Taco Bell and KFC. There was a parched golf course and a pottery and ceramic studio. You could buy iPods at the large grocery/department store known as the Navy Exchange, or NEX. You could visit the beauty salon, get a tattoo or become scuba-certified.

The troops had a saying that there were only three ways to leave your Gitmo tour: Hunk, Drunk or Chunk. "Hunk" if you decided that PT (physical training) was the best use for your downtime (spinning classes at 6 AM Mondays, Wednesdays, Fridays and 6 PM Tuesdays and Thursdays). "Drunk"—well, the opportunities were endless. Grab a couple of six-packs and a twenty-sixer at the NEX and take them to your trailer. The thatched Tiki Bar had good Bob Marley tunes, karaoke some nights, and a Jamaican bartender and beer. Or, there was the popular O'Kelly's, the Irish pub with fried pickle appetizers and draft beer. "Chunk"? See aforementioned fried pickles and fast-food mecca.

Journalists covering Gitmo's trials initially stayed on the leeward side of the island, which consisted only of an airstrip, cafeteria and lodgings known as the Combined Bachelor Quarters, or CBQ. Journalists slept either two or four to a room with a shared kitchen and bathroom; the CBQ was akin to a Motel 6. The luxury of staying there was the freedom we enjoyed walking unaccompanied to the beach, going for a run or grabbing meals without a military escort. Logistics is what made it difficult, as each day we had to be bused, ferried and bused again to the court and media centre on the other side of the bay. That sometimes meant a 4 AM wake-up call for a 9 AM court hearing and headaches for television crews trying to do live hits. But when our accommodations later moved to the other side of the base, I would miss those nights when we were ferried back across the bay under the stars in low-slung boats, sometimes as late as midnight. Most of us were too tired to talk and would just listen to whatever music our captain was playing; and if you put your head back, felt the Caribbean breeze and closed your eyes, you could escape briefly, if only in your mind.

The geographical beauty was so incongruous with the place. Poor Miss Universe 2008 found that out the hard way. Dayana Mendoza was obviously struck by Cuba's splendour when she blogged about her Gitmo visit:

> This week, Guantanamo!!! It was an incredible experience... All the guys from the Army were amazing with us. We visited the Detainees camps and we saw the jails, where they shower, how they recreate themselves with movies, classes of art, books. It was very interesting. We took a ride with the Marines around the land to see the division of Gitmo and Cuba while they informed us with a little bit of history.
>
> The water in Guantanamo Bay is soooo beautiful! It was unbelievable, we were able to enjoy it for at least an hour. We went to the glass beach, and realized the name of it comes from the little pieces of broken glass from hundred of years ago. It is pretty to see all the colors shining with the sun. That day we met a beautiful lady named Rebecca who does wonders with the glasses from the beach. She creates jewelry with it and of course I bought a necklace from her that will remind me of Guantanamo Bay :) I didn't want to leave, it was such a relaxing place, so calm and beautiful.

Could someone not have saved Dayana from herself and told her about the whole Amnesty-International-Gulag-of-Our-Time part, or that "recreate" is not a verb to describe how one engages in recreation? The *New York Times* discovered her blog, and within hours the story went viral. I had to laugh when I read it, because I knew the artisan Rebecca and had spent many mornings myself picking up that gorgeous sea glass from the beaches.

Rebecca Bayless, mother of two, wife of Major Kyle Bayless and president of Guantanamo's Spouse Association, was indeed beautiful, as Miss Universe said, and perhaps one of the sweetest people I had ever met. She left Guantanamo in May 2010 after three and a half years of living there, where she had discovered she had a talent for making jewellery from the sea glass that washed up on Gitmo's shores. There were a few stories of how it ended up on Glass Beach, including one about pirates and rum bottles. Another tale traced the glass back to an old men's club for enlisted sailors, known as the "White Hat Club" (presumably because enlisted men wore white headgear in the early part of the twentieth century), which was perched decades ago on the cliff above the beach. Sailors would simply chuck their empty bottles over the rocks after imbibing, and the broken glass, worn smooth by years churning in the ocean, washed back up on shore a century later as brilliant little chunks. But the most likely, and least romantic, explanation for the sea glass was that the base's trash used to be dumped directly into the ocean. Yesterday's garbage had become today's treasures.

GITMO WAS NEVER going to be a "good news" story. *The Least Worst Place.* And yet it was startling how the Pentagon rarely missed a chance for bad publicity. I often pictured the Pentagon as a cat prancing with tail held high, dropping a near-dead mouse from her mouth and then recoiling in confusion when the precious gift elicits shrieks and scolding. That bafflement started on day one.

Navy Petty Officer Shane McCoy was a twenty-seven-year-old sailor with a military unit called Combat Camera when he arrived at Guantanamo as one of three military photographers to shoot the January 11, 2002, arrival of Guantanamo's first detainees. Although a handful of journalists were on the base reporting on their arrival, cameras were forbidden. Shane was told that three events needed to be documented: the airport arrival, the transport from the leeward side of the base across the bay to the prison, and then finally, the "in-processing" of detainees inside Camp X-Ray. Shane tossed a coin with his friend Mike Pendergrass to determine who would go inside Camp X-Ray, the coveted position. Shane got the inside job.

"Before they even drove in the gate I was shooting everything that happened. I was covering as best I could within their restrictions of how close I was able to get," Shane later told me. He wasn't even sure what he had, because he was shooting blindly. He just moved quickly on an adrenalin high, alternating between his two Pentax cameras. Shane wasn't allowed close to the detainees, so he had to shoot from a distance. At one point he hoisted his camera affixed to a monopod high above the prison fence and, with the timer set, managed to bang off three or four frames. "We weren't shooting for release," Shane said, believing his photos were for internal, historical purposes only. "I sent my first batch of images immediately after shooting. I went and picked my top five images and sent them out. Then I started doing a bigger edit and it was probably an hour later it was all over the news. Somebody in the Pentagon had seen them and released them immediately. They were marked for 'Official Use Only.' Whoever it was thought, 'Hey this is really newsworthy, we need to get this out quick.'"

Shane's images of the detainees kneeling in orange jumpsuits, blindfolded, shackled, with dogs and military guards barking at them, sparked condemnation worldwide. Even some of those who supported Guantanamo were aghast at the photos. The damage was irreparable. Years later, tours of the facilities included a visit to the overgrown and abandoned Camp X-Ray in the hopes that journalists would stress that these conditions no longer applied. Public affairs officers had even marked the exact location where Shane had stood to take his photos and encouraged journalists to do before-and-after shots.

As time went on, Gitmo stories were often reduced to briefs and sound bites, heavy on rhetoric and light on context. My connection to Guantanamo was the story of Omar Khadr, the Toronto-born detainee whose case polarized Canadians and who was the subject of my first book. I found the story fascinating not just because he had grown up in an "al Qaeda family," but also because of the wider implications of his case. Under international law he was considered a child soldier since he was captured at fifteen. His case tested whether justice could be blind, since traditionally child soldiers are rehabilitated, not prosecuted for war crimes. It was easy to sympathize with a kidnapped and drugged child soldier from Africa, but what about one who was indoctrinated by his family and killed an American? He was also the only detainee facing a murder charge, even though by 2010, more than five thousand American service members had been killed in Afghanistan and Iraq. In Canada, Khadr's story was heavily influenced by the country's disdain of his mother, sister and brothers, who had been dubbed "Canadians of convenience" when they returned to Toronto after 9/11.

Over the years, my stories about Khadr prompted death threats, dozens of obscene emails, letters and calls, a lawsuit for defamation, a complaint to the provincial press council, reprimands from high-ranking government officials and the racist I liked to picture in boxer shorts with a can of Molson Canadian balancing on his gut as he called from his basement to tell me I was a bitch. Some readers accused me of being a "terrorist-lover" for questioning Gitmo's legal process, while others called me a Bush stooge for interviewing the U.S. soldiers injured the day Khadr was captured. If one article prompted both responses, then I felt I had done my job that day.

I watched Khadr grow up in Gitmo. He was a pimply, scrawny fifteen-year-old when shot and captured in Afghanistan in 2002, and he was a broad-shouldered, bearded twenty-four-year-old man when he pleaded guilty to five war crimes, including murder. The plea deal gave him one more year in Gitmo and a ticket home to spend the remainder of an eight-year sentence in Canada.

Like all Gitmo cases, Khadr's prosecution limped through the process, and the logistics meant I had to fly to Washington, then take a military flight from Andrews Air Force Base to Guantanamo (where pilots took a sharp turn just before landing, to avoid Cuban airspace), spend a day or two before the hearing and then make the trek home. Sometimes you could spend a week in Guantanamo for what amounted to a two-hour hearing and adjournment. But you never knew what would happen, so it was essential to go each time— an argument I made often to each of the six editors I worked with over the years of my Guantanamo coverage. The extra time spent in Gitmo also allowed me to cover much more than Khadr.

The problem was that the meat of the Gitmo stories—the crucial debate about what Guantanamo represented in a post-9/11 world—was complicated and legalistic, and therefore many reporters and editors considered it boring. It was sexier to write about the Starbucks. I understood that. I wrote about the Starbucks. Then eventually Gitmo fatigue set in. The prison became like that crack in the wall you just learn to live with because fixing it seems like too much bother. I also understood that. I had Gitmo fatigue too.

But Guantanamo is the sore that festers—the name itself became synonymous with human rights abuses. "Gitmoize" became a verb to describe how to toughen up a facility. It wasn't uncommon at demonstrations around the world to hear handcuffed protesters scream, "This is not Guantanamo" as police dragged them away.

There were really two fundamental issues: the conditions of confinement and the law. Holding men in the outdoor pens of Camp X-Ray for four months was inhumane. When new facilities were built they complied with U.S. federal standards and, in the case of Camp 4, offered living conditions superior to many maximum-security prisons I had visited in the United States or Canada. But some detainees in Camps 5 and 6 were still confined to small cells with almost no human contact. Many were held like that for more than nine years. I remember one day in 2006 just staring at what seemed like a choreographed dance between detainees and guards as the prisoners paced like caged cheetahs, taking about five steps before hitting a wall or cell door and swinging back. Guards paced side to side too, looking like captives themselves as they peered into the cell windows every three seconds. Even the most heinous of convicted criminals in Western prisons are granted basic rights sometimes denied Guantanamo prisoners, such as blankets, appropriate footwear and toiletries (not to mention books, televisions, access to phones).

Then there were the interrogation methods, which again, in the early years, fell short of any international standards. Aside from the moral repugnancy of those practices, most experienced interrogators would later agree that those methods just didn't work. Having a female soldier reach into her pants and pretend to smear menstrual blood on the face of a devout Muslim detainee will elicit screaming, not cooperation. The intelligence community remains divided on the effectiveness of the other techniques colloquially called "torture lite," but most whom I have interviewed over the years believe that depriving prisoners of days, or weeks, of sleep will make them largely incoherent and anything they say unreliable. In Guantanamo, keeping prisoners awake by forcing them to stand in painful positions was common, and moving them from cell to cell for days on end was known as the "frequent flyer program."

But as the prison conditions improved over the years, the general news coverage didn't. Critics of Gitmo would run shots of Camp X-Ray's outdoor pens when describing Guantanamo's facilities, or include complaints about the prison that had long since been rectified. On the other end of the spectrum, some would dine out on details about the improvements. THEY GET TASTY FOOD AND HEALTHCARE! THEY GET ART CLASSES! SOME DETAINEES DON'T WANT TO LEAVE! These were the screaming headlines about the caloric count of prison meals, details about the top-notch medical facilities and classes.

The truth was somewhere in between. Detainees were well fed and did get better health care than most Americans (or Canadians). But those military doctors providing superior health care had also helped devise interrogation plans to exploit a detainee's vulnerabilities and sanctioned the force-feeding of hunger-striking prisoners—both considered by many in the medical community as violations of a doctor's Hippocratic Oath. I was always skeptical about the military's claims that some detainees didn't want to leave.

Conditions were easier to write about but ignored the main overriding issue: these men had not been convicted of any crimes. Most hadn't even been charged. By 2011, only six detainees had trials or pleaded guilty before military commissions. That meant that less than 1 per cent of the more than 770 men who had been at Guantanamo had had their guilt assessed in court. For the first few years, the U.S. administration had also flouted international treaties that grant detained foreign citizens the right to consular access, putting the United States on par with other regimes that routinely hold prisoners incommunicado, such as Iran, Egypt and Syria. In wartime, international law does permit the detention of battlefield captives. Many of Guantanamo's detainees, however, were not caught fighting NATO troops in Afghanistan, but were handed over by Pakistani forces in return for lucrative bounties. Besides, the Bush administration had declared that these were not POWs entitled to Geneva Convention rights. POWs should be released at the end of "active hostilities." When would the "war on terror" end?

There were indeed terrorists in Guantanamo. There were mass murderers who celebrated 9/11 and people I hope are never released. That is what made it so surreal. I have no doubt that some of the "worst of the worst" detained on the other side of the island were still hoping to slaughter us non-believers while we played Scrabble and drank Scotch. Not everyone was a wrongly captured goat farmer. One of the detainees was allegedly part of a group that threw a grenade in Afghanistan at friends of mine, Star photographer Bernard Weil and former Star correspondent Kathleen Kenna. Kathleen barely survived the attack and Bernie has never forgotten it. But in the ten years since 9/11, since only a handful of detainees had gone on trial and hundreds were swept up in this decade of fear, it was the stories of the goat farmers that resounded around the world.

GEORGE ORWELL WROTE in his 1946 essay "Politics and the English Language" that "political language—and with variations this is true of all political parties, from Conservatives to Anarchists—is designed to make lies sound truthful and murder respectable, and to give an appearance of solidity to pure wind."

In our time, political speech and writing are largely the defence of the indefensible... Thus political language has to consist largely of euphemism, question-begging and sheer cloudy vagueness. Defenceless villages are bombarded from the air, the inhabitants driven out into the countryside, the cattle machine-gunned, the huts set on fire with incendiary bullets: this is called *pacification*. Millions of peasants are robbed of their farms and sent trudging along the roads with no more than they can carry: this is called *transfer of population* or *rectification of frontiers*. People are imprisoned for years without trial, or shot in the back of the neck or sent to die of scurvy in Arctic lumber camps: this is called *elimination of unreliable elements*.

Lieutenant-Colonel Ed Bush, head of Guantanamo's public affairs unit in the second half of 2008, was the master of Gitmo gobbledygook. I liked Ed, and the fact that he'd allow me to call him Ed or Bush while snarling at others who didn't address him as Lieutenant-Colonel Bush. I think he actually found it funny when I would start questions with "Yo, Bush." We didn't agree on much, but I respected the fact that he fully believed the views he espoused, rather than acting as a Pentagon puppet. In the rare moments when he was not providing pithy quotes, we talked about exercise, writing, and if the conversation turned to his children, his macho demeanour melted. Ed was also loud, demanding and probably a nightmare to work under, but like so many of the public affairs officers, he was endlessly fascinating.

Bush, who had no relation to the president but once told me he "sure wished he did," didn't really walk through the prison camps as much as he strutted, chest thrust out, chin held jauntily. Over the years I had been on more than a dozen scripted tours of Gitmo with other commanders but the Bush tour was one of the more memorable. If a journalist asked a question that used the word "prison," Ed would quickly reprimand. Guantanamo was not a "prison" but a "detention centre." Interrogations? No such thing at Guantanamo, Bush insisted to our confused crew. Detainees were brought for "reservations." We couldn't help but snicker at the term. A shackled, blindfolded detainee, known only by his internment serial number and forced into a windowless room where he would answer questions, was not going for a three-course candlelit meal.

"There is no punishment at Guantanamo," decreed Bush at one point. But what do you call it when some prisoners had their "comfort items," like blankets or toothbrushes, taken away if they were "non-compliant"? Or the fact that some got to live in Camp 4, while others languished in the solitary confinement of Camp 5? These were "rewards of compliancy." Suicides were "asymmetric warfare." Detainees who were hunger-striking were also not "force-fed," but "enterally fed." Enteral feeding meant being strapped to a chair while a tube was inserted in your nose and snaked into your stomach. The prison nurse always noted brightly during tours that butter pecan Ensure was the favourite flavour. How do they taste it? Apparently when they later burp.

Bush led the Louisiana Army National Guard 241st Mobile Public Affairs Detachment. When they came to Guantanamo in April 2008, the unit was known as "Katrina-tested." In other words, these soldiers had handled press briefings following the U.S. government's bungled relief effort of Hurricane Katrina in New Orleans. Since they withstood that pressure, it was presumed they could manage Gitmo. "I could not ask for two better things on my resumé in terms of crisis management and crisis communication than Katrina and here," Ed told me, adding a rare glib comment: "I'm going to have the mother of job offers when I go home."

Wrestling semantics may seem like an insignificant activity, but really it came down to crucial questions of law. In redrafting the laws of war, the Bush administration referred to Guantanamo detainees not as POWs but as "enemy combatants." Rather than hold traditional military hearings for the captives or charge them criminally, a new set of laws for military commissions was drafted (and later amended after the U.S. Supreme Court struck it down as illegal). Attorney and law professor Muneer Ahmad, who was one of the first lawyers to represent Omar Khadr, called the term "enemy combatant" the "granddaddy of all the doublespeak that followed."

"It's an invented term that the government has attempted to legitimize through repetition. Once they invented that term, they had to invent a whole language to go along with it," Muneer said of the Gitmo gab. When the first detainees were charged in 2004,

Muneer made a point of challenging the use of "court proceedings" to describe the military commissions. "I would always ask, 'What court? What courtroom?' In order to make the point that the made-up military commission system, which had no rules and permitted evidence obtained through torture, was not a court. They were trying to linguistically dress up the commission in the same way that they physically dressed it up with pretty, blue-velvet curtains and nice mahogany furniture."

Ed Bush never seemed to let the negative press get to him, although he once admitted that it was "disheartening." "I don't have any false hopes that after all this I'm going to go out and Google 'Guantanamo' on Monday morning and see all these great things on Guantanamo. It's not going to happen. It is what it is," he said during one of my trips.

Every night, after a day of delivering his message, Ed would work out, and then retire to his room to write fairy tales about princes and dragons and wizards for his young kids at home. He hoped one day to publish these fantasies—stories he wrote while on duty, far, far away in a place called Guantanamo Bay.

A couple of years after Ed's unit left, written rules were drafted to help PAOs talk to journalists. The overall message in the pocket-sized "JTF-GTMO Guide to Speaking with the Media" warned the PAOs to "stay in your lane."

"Always maintain control of your emotions with the media," was one tip. "Maintain a professional attitude during the interview; remain in control even when the media seem aggressive or questions seem silly."

Some points in the guide seemed obvious, but I guess needed stressing. "Make sure your facts are correct the first time. Never lie or cover something up. The media may already know the truth. If you don't know, say, 'I don't know.'"

My favourite tip was to "not provide enemy with propaganda material by grumbling and thoughtless complaining."

"Remember," the guidebook concluded, "When you are talking to the media, you are talking to the American public as well as our adversaries."

GUANTANAMO HAD DEVELOPED into an international flashpoint by 2006, prompting President George W. Bush to publicly muse that he would like to close the prison. But behind the scenes, plans were quietly underway to make the place a lot more permanent. That is, until Carol Rosenberg found out about it and managed to save American taxpayers about $100 million.

Carol is a dogged *Miami Herald* journalist and Guantanamo's unofficial historian. She was standing on a hill overlooking the tarmac on January 11, 2002, when the first planeload of twenty detainees arrived. She will likely be there the day the last one departs. After the first six months and more than one hundred days of reporting at Gitmo, she just stopped counting trips.

Journalists used Carol as a Gitmo encyclopedia, since she was faster than Google and more reliable than Wikipedia. She had thousands of facts (both significant and insanely trivial) stored away in her forever-churning brain, and if one somehow escaped, she could find it seconds later in her well-organized binders or databases. We called her the "Dean," while some of the PAOs called her a pain in the ass, or something much worse. There was no doubt Carol was relentless, but if not for her persistence, the public would not know all it does about Guantanamo. And she outlasted everyone: presidents (2), U.S. attorneys general (3), Guantanamo commanders (10), rotations of PAO units (14 and counting).

Carol had many scoops over the years, but in November 2006 she was the only one to get her hands on the secret Pentagon solicitation for bids to construct a new Guantanamo legal compound where the alleged 9/11 conspirators would be tried for war crimes. The only legal facility at the time was a hilltop makeshift courtroom, which had once been used as an airport terminal. It was there that Omar Khadr, Australian David Hicks and other high-profile detainees had made court appearances since the first trials began in 2004. But the facility was too small and posed security problems for a trial of KSM and his four co-accused. The Pentagon's plan was to construct a massive new legal compound, which would include a high-tech courtroom, permanent housing for 1,200, dining, conference and meeting facilities, and a 100-vehicle motor pool. The projected cost was as high as $125 million and because of the "national security implications and extreme urgency," the Pentagon was invoking a little-used authority that would allow it to fast-track the plan without congressional approval. Had Carol not discovered that document, it might have slipped through. Instead, the plan created a furor among both Democrats and Republicans in Congress. Less than a month after Carol's report, U.S. Defense Secretary Robert Gates dismissed the plan as "ridiculous."

In its place a new tent city was erected, and because every area in Gitmo seems to require a name, it was called "Camp Justice" (quickly dubbed "Camp Injustice" by civil rights advocates). Unlike in the original plans, this $12 million legal complex was completely portable. The M*A*S*H-style village of khaki bivouac six-bed canvas tents sat on the hot asphalt below the original courthouse on McCalla Hill (named after the first U.S. commander to lead a successful attack in the Spanish-American War). There were rubber shower and latrine tents, and a battlefield morgue normally used to store the remains of fallen soldiers kept the bottled water cold. A cavernous hangar that served in the 1920s as an experimental blimp station was converted into our media centre, with three air conditioned rooms and porta-potties (a decrepit foosball table was later added). The centrepiece of tent city was a squat, windowless courtroom surrounded by razor wire. The room had been outfitted with a computerized system for displaying digital documents. Ten strategically placed cameras would beam the proceedings to the nearby media centre. A double-pane Plexiglas window separated a viewing area from the court. The judge would have the ability to cut off the sound system for classified evidence.

We lived in the tents of Camp Justice during the trials. Charlie 19 became my makeshift home away from home for many weeks, along with other Gitmo regulars: Carol, Reuters's Jane Sutton and New York sketch artist Janet Hamlin. Two tents over in Charlie 16 lived the irrepressible Al Arabiya journalist Muna Shikaki, who would round out our warped girl gang of aging campers. To keep mould and any critters out of the tents, they were cooled and inflated by noisy circular tubes that made it feel as though we were having slumber parties in the belly of a groaning c-130 as it flew over Greenland.

Our movements on the base were monitored and largely controlled by the public affairs units, which frustrated most of the journalists. Sometimes I felt sorry for a new crew when they arrived for their six-month rotation, woefully unprepared to face a pack of experienced, older journalists, most of whom knew more about the place than they did. There were PAOs I got to know over the years and really liked, and journalists whom I didn't. If our escorts respected the job we had to do, I respected theirs. I remember remarking sympathetically to one while being shuttled from the gym to get a coffee one day: "Bet you didn't join the military to drive reporters to Starbucks?" But some of the PAOs were unreasonable and high on power. Many of the restrictions were ridiculous, especially since they changed from one unit to the next and curbed our coverage and movements more than that of journalists embedded in Iraq or Afghanistan. Sometimes it meant we couldn't do our job properly. Or sometimes, it meant that journalists, who are by nature loners or at least used to working alone, would go crazy. As petty as it may sound, one point of contention for some of us was whether we could go for a jog, blissfully alone, along the main road. Just when one PAO crew would agree that was possible, the next rotation would arrive and deem it off limits without a jogging escort (I always pictured a pudgy Bill Clinton with his team of Secret Service officers stopping at McDonald's). It finally took enraged New York Times reporter William Glaberson to get the rule lifted after running in frantic small loops on the asphalt around our tents, as perplexed service members looked on. The Pentagon finally concluded that journalists could be trusted to go for a run and not veer off course in sweaty pursuit of a Camp 7 interview with KSM.

Simply put, Camp Justice was not the Nuremberg Palace of Justice.

Less than a year after World War II ended, Courtroom 600 was built in Nuremberg, Germany, and trials began for the first twenty-two captured Nazi commanders, who were accused of unspeakable crimes. The proceedings were rapid and transparent and are still praised today.

But Camp Justice was the embodiment of justice-delayed-is-justice-denied. Most of the time it was a bunch of empty tents, home only to the white barn owl that liked the high rafters of the media centre aircraft hangar. The handful of military commissions that did occur had not been broadcast to the world, but just to a small media centre less than a few hundred metres away, watched by journalists from news outlets that could afford to fly correspondents to Cuba. There were often technical difficulties with the video feed.

Sometimes the media became part of the story. One tale in Gitmowonderland involved Janet Hamlin, Guantanamo's exclusive court sketch artist. Nearly sixty journalists were brought to Guantanamo to witness KSM's first commission hearing in June 2008. There had been no images of him since 2003, when the Pentagon released the memorable photo of his capture, showing a dishevelled, stubble-chinned KSM squinting at the camera, his hairy chest peeking out of his white undershirt neckline. I thought the photo looked like a drunken celebrity mug shot and started calling KSM al Qaeda's John Belushi. As I later found out, that was just what the Pentagon wanted me to think.

One of the speakers aboard the November 2010 "Spy Cruise" I attended was former CIA spokesperson Bill Harlow. Harlow—who began his speech by saying being the chief spokesperson for a secret organization was a bit of an oxymoron, like "jumbo shrimp"—told the group that when KSM was first captured, the CIA was enraged by media reports that described him as the "James Bond of al Qaeda." *James Bond, eh,* they thought. *We'll show them.* And so a decision was made to release KSM's embarrassing capture-shot. It had the intended PR effect and I gave them points for deglamorizing KSM. But when listening to Harlow, I did wonder why that photo was cleared for release while we were forbidden from photographing captives.

Since we couldn't take pictures of KSM at Gitmo, Janet would be the first one to show the world what the prized captive looked like today. He bore no resemblance to that man in the 2003 photo. We actually gasped in the viewing area when we first saw him. His beard extended mid-way down his chest. He wore prison-issued pop-bottle glasses with an elastic safety strap and had a haughty smirk. He certainly did not appear to have physically suffered from the 183 waterboarding sessions.

When Janet first started coming to Guantanamo in April 2006, she was forbidden from sketching the faces of detainees. The explanation for the rule was the same one for photographs—the Geneva Conventions prohibited the exploitation of prisoners of war (even though these weren't prisoners of war, the U.S. administration said they would respect the "spirit" of the conventions). But by the time KSM came to court, the Pentagon had decided that the restriction did not apply to detainees charged with war crimes since they were no longer "enemy combatants," but defendants. (That rule, however, still did not apply for photographs.)

Janet's pencils flew across her sketch pad the second she saw KSM. Within minutes she had the outlines of his face. She was focused but admitted later she had been slightly unnerved by his vanity and his habit of craning his neck to see her, almost as if he were posing. By the morning court break, Janet had her sketch but felt uneasy. She knew she had nailed his beard and the thick glasses and obscured eyes, but the nose? She could barely see him from behind the double Plexiglas without the opera glasses she some-times used in federal courts, which were forbidden in Gitmo. Janet, who is as gentle and caring as she is funny, later remarked, "Hmm. I gave him quite the beak."

As it turns out, Janet was not the only unhappy one. For some unexplained reason, the court security officer tasked with approv-ing all of Janet's sketches before they could be transported down the hill to the media room, photographed and released, had brought the sketch over to KSM himself during the break. KSM was not pleased. Janet watched as he waved his hands dismissively over her drawing. She was later told, "KSM does not want to okay this." He didn't like the nose. The security official relayed what the terrorism suspect had told him. "Tell the artist to go get the FBI picture off the Internet and use that as a reference. Then I will approve," Janet recalls him saying.

"The thing is," Janet conceded, "he was right."

She ended up giving KSM a nose job. The story of the al Qaeda suspect reprimanding Janet became part of Gitmo folklore.

IN THE SPRING of 2010, as Khadr's trial was grinding forward, our banning fiasco occurred. We were covering hearings to determine what evidence a jury could hear. Joshua Claus, the former military interrogator who had been convicted in the death of a detainee at Bagram and had been Khadr's chief interrogator, was a key witness.

It was well known that Claus had pleaded guilty for his role in the death of an Afghan taxi driver. The killing was the subject of the Oscar-winning documentary *Taxi to the Dark Side*. Claus admitted at his court martial that he had twisted a hood over the head of the taxi driver, Dilawar (like many Afghans he only went by one name), and forced water down the innocent man's throat. The twenty-one-year-old interrogator also confessed to making another detainee lick the boots of a U.S. soldier.

But after a week of hearings, and the night before we were scheduled to fly back to Washington, the press pack was informed (on deadline) that the Office of the Secretary of Defense would stop some of us from coming back to Gitmo. My name was on the hit list along with Carol Rosenberg, *Globe and Mail* reporter Paul Koring and CanWest's Steven Edwards. I was really more stunned than upset. Our crime was that we had named Claus in our reports. Did the Pentagon really want to wage this battle on behalf of a convicted abuser? Had Joshua Claus not already waived his right to anonymity in an interview with me two years earlier? More critically, we did not believe we had violated the ground rules. The rules protected information revealed in a Guantanamo courtroom. I knew about Claus before he was called as a witness. He had confirmed his identity as Khadr's interrogator when I interviewed him in 2008.

Our only chance to fight the ban, we were told that night in Guantanamo, was to appeal to the very person who had banned us in the first place. They had to know we would fight this vociferously.

The issue was never the need for protective orders, although this was how some spun it later. Journalists understood that there were witnesses still in the military who could be deployed elsewhere, or who had legitimate security reasons for their identities to be shielded. Respecting publication bans in Canadian court cases was never a problem. If our paper disagreed with the need for a ban, we would challenge it, arguing that the public's right to know outweighed the need for secrecy. A judge would rule and we would abide by the decision. But this was Guantanamo, and the Military Commissions Act under which these detainees were charged was a new law that denied the media—and thus the public—standing. We had even tried to contact the judge that week to talk about the protective orders, but had been ignored.

What was especially troubling with the ban was the fact that it wasn't the military judge who found us in contempt of court. The judge did not say we had violated his order. Instead, Bryan Whitman, a mid-level Pentagon public affairs official, had decided from Washington that we broke Guantanamo's Ground Rules. Since the Pentagon controlled our access to the base they had this power to revoke our travel privileges. But if the military commissions were intended to be the "full, fair and open" procedures that Pentagon officials claimed they were, the ban was akin to a spokesperson for New York Mayor Michael Bloomberg barring select journalists from his city so they couldn't cover a Manhattan case. It also felt personal, since our news outlets were not barred, just the four of us. That didn't sit well with the press corps. "Allowing the news groups to send different reporters does not erase the harm of banning four veteran journalists who have spent years covering Guantanamo and bring a depth of knowledge to their coverage that novices would lack," noted a *Washington Post* editorial. Scott Horton of *Harper's* wrote: "The Pentagon public-affairs officers would prefer a different sort of reporting—one that regurgitates their own news feed, perhaps with a slight admixture of comments from defense counsel who are themselves subject to tight restrictions about what they can say to the media. Unfortunately, that is exactly what the bulk of major media covering the proceedings at Guantanamo produce."

The McClatchy Company (which owns the *Miami Herald*) hired a New York lawyer who specialized in First Amendment rights, and the Pentagon Press Association protested on our behalf. The case was embarrassing for an administration voted in on the promise of transparency, and eventually the ban was overturned. The Pentagon concluded that Claus had waived his right to anonymity by talking with me.

But now the Pentagon had further headaches, as the case had drawn unwanted attention to Gitmo's reporting Ground Rules—which we had long criticized, to no avail. Douglas Wilson, the Pentagon's affable deputy assistant secretary of defense for public affairs, convened a roundtable to discuss the issue that he would co-chair with the department's senior counsel, Jeh Johnson. The "Gitmo four" as we had been dubbed, were invited to attend.

On August 2, 2010, Carol and I (Paul and Steven could not make it), with visitor badges clipped to our suits, were led into a Pentagon meeting room, marvelling at the fact that in less than three months we had gone from being disgraced and barred journalists to advising a room of close to forty senior and uniformed officials about the trials of reporting on Gitmo's trials. Carol later bought us shot glasses at the gift shop that said "Someone in the Pentagon Loves You."

The meeting lasted ninety minutes and the sometimes-heated discussion ranged from weighty questions about why the Geneva Conventions precluded photographs of detainees' faces, to whether it was punitive to force reporters to use porta-potties when there was indoor plumbing available to other court observers. Changes were promised. A few were delivered.

DANIEL FRIED GREETED visitors in his sixth-floor State Department office with a grin, a boisterous "How are you" and a handshake that you could see coming. He would slowly extend his elbow back and swing his arm forward with such gusto that you feared if you didn't clasp his palm, his hand would continue upward and smack you in the jaw. Fried thought he had a great job. Most of Washington pitied him.

Fried was a career diplomat and Obama's "Gitmo czar." It was a fancy title for a special envoy whose job was to travel the world begging countries to take Guantanamo detainees the United States no longer wanted. Certainly no easy task when the prisoners had been described as the "worst of the worst," but a job made only more complicated by the fact that in May 2009 Congress forbade any of those detainees from stepping foot on U.S. soil. Even so, most agreed if anyone was up to the task it was Fried. (His name is pronounced *freed*, a fact I found wonderfully appropriate, but when I mentioned it, Dan said, "Huh, I never thought of that.") Dan had a disarming nature, and while he may have had a lifetime of diplomatic niceties on the cocktail circuit, he exuded sincerity. He also respected and understood the influence of the media. Which is why he granted few interviews, and getting one with him required some State Department gymnastics. One condition of being able to trail him was that any published comment would have to be vetted first. "I like what I'm doing because it's advancing justice in the world. It's advancing national security, actually," was the type of thing he could say on the record.

A day after the U.S. Senate voted in 2009 to deny Obama the funds to close the prison, the president vigorously defended his plan in a speech at the National Archives, vowing to "clean up the mess at Guantanamo." He called the prison a "misguided experiment."

"We will be ill-served by the fearmongering that emerges whenever we discuss this issue," Obama said. "There are no neat or easy answers here." Speaking of fearmongering, former vice president Dick Cheney was at the same time less than a mile away, giving his own speech warning that Obama's national security policy was putting American lives at risk. Confused Americans now had their new president on one shoulder whispering *Calm down* and the former administration's most forceful spokesperson perched on the other yelling, *Be very afraid.* "Obama's is the speech of a young senator who was once a part-time law professor—platitudinous and preachy, vague and pseudo-thoughtful in an abstract kind of way," *Weekly Standard* editor William Kristol wrote. "Cheney's is the speech of a grown-up, of a chief executive, of a statesman. He's sober, realistic and concrete, stands up for his country and its public officials." Few at the time noted that aside from calling for Gitmo's closure (which Bush also said he'd like to do) and closing CIA sites, Obama's national security policy largely followed that of the Bush administration's final years. It was just packaged and articulated a lot more nicely.

With this political backdrop, Fried was quietly racking up frequent flyer points jetting around the world asking foreign friends for favours. Being discreet was not easy for the naturally gregarious Fried, but he managed to keep his cards and people close, which was probably why no one had any idea what he was up to in the spring and summer of 2009.

Of the remaining detainees, more than sixty-five had been cleared for release but could not be returned to their birth countries, such as Uzbekistan or China, for fear of persecution. Fried's job was to convince third countries to give these men refuge. By June, and with only six months until Obama's self-imposed deadline to close Gitmo, Fried had managed to convince only France and Britain to take one detainee each.

The most high-profile cases at the time concerned seventeen Chinese citizens belonging to the persecuted Uighur minority, who had been in custody since their 2002 capture in Afghanistan. Muslim separatists from China, the Uighur prisoners had argued they were captured by mistake as they fled their homeland—they regarded the United States as an ally, not a foe. In the public debate, they became a Guantanamo Rorschach test: some saw innocent victims; others saw Islamists in cahoots with a global al Qaeda conspiracy. The Pentagon claimed they were members of the East Turkestan Islamic Movement and had received weapons training from the Taliban while in Afghanistan.

One of the detainees, thirty-one-year-old Abdullah Abdulqadir, tried to convince a Guantanamo tribunal that they had been running for their lives and were not part of al Qaeda. "I will speak for myself and for all Uighurs. You are accusing us of participating in action with al Qaeda and the Taliban against the U.S.," he told the panel members. "It does not explain the Uighurs, we are not part of al Qaeda or the Taliban. We have nothing against the U.S. government. We have to solve our own problems with our own country's independence. We have only one enemy, and that's the Chinese. They have been torturing and killing us all: old, young, men, women, little children, and unborn children."

Finally after seven years, the Bush administration declared that they were "no longer an enemy combatant," which in Pentagon-speak meant they were not considered dangerous and could be released. But until Fried could find them homes, the men were stuck in Gitmo. The Uighur detainees should have been among the most sympathetic cases, making their settlement easy. But Fried had difficulty finding a country willing to risk the ire of Beijing by offering refuge. Not to mention that the Uighurs had been portrayed as too dangerous for U.S. soil, so why should any other country accept them?

"There was a wild series of hyperventilations on the floors of the Senate and the House by Congressmen who couldn't wait to tell everybody about the throat-slitting terrorists that Obama was about to bring into their midst," Boston lawyer Sabin Willett, who represented many of the men, said in reaction to the political debate. "The heat became enormous and the White House didn't manage it at all. They didn't get out in front of it and say, 'No, no, no. These are people who have been cleared.' They were just silent."

You can check out but you can never leave.

In June 2009, I was part of a small tour that was brought to Guantanamo's Camp Iguana, the oceanside prison where the Uighurs lived. One of the rules we faced during these tours that made us most uncomfortable was not being able to talk to detainees should they approach. More than once I had stood mute in Camp 4 when one of the men on the other side of the fence asked where I was from or simply said "hi." But saying "hello" back could land you in trouble, as Getty Images photographer John Moore would later discover.

John, an experienced photographer who had worked extensively in Iraq, Afghanistan and other war zones and usually got along with his military hosts, was the sole photographer on a September 2010 tour when a Camp 4 detainee greeted him with a wave. "*Salaam alaikum*," John replied and continued shooting. Either the young sailor escorting him didn't understand that he had just said "hi" in Arabic (or, literally, "peace be upon you"), or he was determined not to make an exception to the communication rule, but either way John was in trouble and a report was sent to the Pentagon. The same office that had banned us earlier that year issued a formal complaint to Getty Images concerning John's violation.

In his written reply, John explained:

> When I was greeted by other detainees, with a wave, I felt it would seem rude or aggressive to ignore the acknowledgment and simply to start shooting pictures. By acknowledging their presence, without exchanging information, I was only hoping to maintain a compliant subject who would allow me to take a photograph. Indeed, I have been told in the past that photographers had caused problems for guards at Guantanamo by taking photos of detainees who did not want their photos taken. I did not want to cause problems, and did not believe I was violating the ground rules simply by acknowledging a wave or saying hello in response to a greeting to facilitate taking a photograph.

In the end, the Pentagon said essentially, *Whoops, our bad,* and John was welcome to return to Gitmo.

When detainees approached the fence during that June 2009 trip in Camp Iguana, our escorts ordered us to stand back. We all moved slightly and said nothing. On other tours the Uighur detainees had gone inside to avoid scrutiny, but something was different this time and they seemed excited to see us. As we later found out, they had been waiting.

A week earlier they had tried to give a statement to a touring television crew but were quickly told that any such clip would be destroyed. So this time, in anticipation of the next journalists, they had scrawled their message on a large sketchpad. They began turning pages and we started shooting what was Guantanamo's first publicly captured protest. Our escorts shuffled uncomfortably behind us.

"We are the Uighurs," read one sheet of paper.

Said another: "We need to freedom."

"We are being held in prison but we have been annonced innocent a corrding to the virdict in caurt."

One compared their treatment by the U.S. government to that of the Nazis: "America is Double Hetler in unjustice."

They turned the pages as quickly as they could before we were abruptly ushered out. "Is Obama communist or a democrat? We have the same operation in China," someone yelled as the gate was locked behind us.

That night when our images were subjected to OPSEC review, there was confusion. Did this constitute communication or pose some sort of national security risk? Could our images be transmitted, or should they be deleted? For fourteen frustrating hours we sat on the photos as questions moved up the chain of command. The real problem—as was later explained quietly to me—was that no one in Guantanamo wanted to be responsible for Washington waking to a photo on the front page of the *New York Times* of detainees comparing Obama to Hitler (or Hetler). If the Pentagon couldn't prevent it, at the very least they wanted time to prepare for any fallout.

But the move ended up being counterproductive for the Pentagon (concerning my paper anyway). Had I filed immediately, the story and photos likely would have been buried inside. But as time ticked by they became more newsworthy, in the eyes of my editors. Was the Obama administration trying to restrict a free press and shape the news?

When we finally got the green light to transmit the photos the next day, the story and protest picture ran on the *Star*'s front page under the headline, "The Guantanamo Photo Washington Didn't Want You to See."

ON JUNE 11, 2009, ten days after we took those photos, a Gulfstream jet touched down on Guantanamo's landing strip just before 3 AM. Daniel Fried was on board with his deputy, Tony Ricci, a retired U.S. Army colonel with previous posts in Bosnia, Afghanistan and Iraq. Obama's senior counsel Greg Craig was on the flight too, as were Sabin Willett and his colleague Susan Baker Manning, who also represented the Uighur detainees. With them was Bermuda's home affairs minister, Lieutenant-Colonel David Burch.

Soon after the plane landed, a bus pulled up on the tarmac and guards moved in to surround it. Four disoriented Uighur detainees, blinking in the lights from a soldier's video camera, walked toward their lawyers and a beaming Fried. Their identification bracelets were snipped off. They were no longer 278, 285, 295 and 320, but Khelil Mamut, Abdullah Abdulqadir, Salahidin Abdulahat and Ablikim Turahun.

After nearly eight years in captivity, no matter the circumstances, the transition to life on the outside was going to be strange. But the contrast once aboard the Gulfstream could not have been more stark. As Guantanamo faded from sight, the four former detainees reclined in the plane's plush interior, looking at the Bermuda tourist brochures and deciding if they would eat one of the sandwiches from the fridge.

The secret deal had come together in just weeks. Since Fried's appointment, Willet and other lawyers for the remaining detainees had been meeting with administration officials, jockeying to get their clients released. Willet was fast losing hope, believing the prospects for his Uighur clients were slim, since the United States had slammed the door shut. "It was the middle of May and we were in heated negotiations with the White House," Willett later told me. "At some point in the midst of all that they said, 'We've got this other idea—Bermuda.'" Willet remembers turning to Greg Craig and saying the equivalent of "Yeah, right." Craig promised he could personally make it happen.

In just four weeks, what started as a casual offer of help from Bermuda's prime minister during a White House visit gave way to intense negotiations between Bermudian ministers and Fried and Craig. They hammered out the details in a flurry of meetings, deciding what the United States would spend for settlement expenses, finding housing and job prospects in Bermuda, and even locating the Gulfstream at the last minute when it was discovered an American pilot scheduled to make the Guantanamo flight did not have the proper paperwork to land at the base at night. During one meeting with David Burch and Premier Dr. Ewart Brown, Fried enquired whether the Bermudians would monitor the Uighurs weekly to "check on their status." Willett, who was also in the meeting, recalls Premier Brown asking, "Their status? Do you mean whether they've married or not?" Everyone laughed. "Ambassador Fried, this is Bermuda," Burch replied. "There's no one I need to meet with every week in Bermuda."

No one wanted the story to leak lest furor erupt in the United Kingdom about Bermuda, a British territory, taking four detainees. (Well-founded fear, as it would turn out, because Britain later did react angrily for not being consulted.) Luckily for the organizers, journalists were in the dark, focused instead on another tropical island. On June 9, the government of Palau announced they were considering taking some of the Uighur prisoners. The president of the Pacific archipelago said he was making the offer for as many as seventeen Uighur detainees as a "humanitarian gesture." Palau would end up accepting detainees, but the Bermuda four would be first. The arrival at Bermuda's Hamilton Airport in the soft morning light was postcard-perfect. The Gulfstream passengers even saw dolphins frolicking in the ocean. For the first two hours, Bermuda's four newest inhabitants had time to explore the island with their lawyers, in peace. When the island's premier held a press conference to break the news, Fried and his crew were already on a flight back to Washington. I sent the news alert to my editor, Alison Uncles. I knew she couldn't resist a good prison-to-paradise yarn and got an immediate reply: "When can you get there?"

Later that afternoon, on the three-hour flight from Toronto to the island of cotton-candy-coloured cabins, I was still smugly thinking that finding four Uighurs on an island half the size of Guantanamo would be a cinch. But in what turned out to be a frustrating and comical evening, I walked, took buses and cabs, and even started accosting confused tourists, only to keep narrowly missing the men at every stop. It seemed everywhere I went they had just left, and I was unable to reach Willett by phone or email. "They just bought pants here," one storeowner told me. I found where they ate, what they ate, whom they met, what they said, but still had no idea where they were or would sleep that night. Dejected, I finally canvassed all of Hamilton's hotels until I found where Sabin was staying. Then I sat in the lobby nursing a beer until about 1 AM, hoping to run into him. Just as I gave up and returned to my own hotel up the street, Willett sent an email apologizing for being offline. Sure, the guys would be happy to see me. Could I go in the morning?

The former Gitmo prisoners were just waking when I knocked on the door of their pink oceanside cabin. I immediately recognized one of them from the Camp Iguana protest. He had been holding the signs and I had brought prints of my photos to Bermuda with me (which only showed him from the neck down to comply with Guantanamo's restrictions on identifying detainees). "That's me!" he said incredulously, as I handed him a print.

They hadn't slept much but were energized by their new life, and we spent the day eating together, hanging out in their cabin and going fishing from the rocks behind it. It was amazing how similar the geographical surroundings were to Guantanamo and yet were now a world apart. "This may be a small island," Abdullah Abdulqadir said to me. "But it has a big heart."

MAYBE, SAUDI ARABIA'S king suggested to White House counterterrorism advisor John Brennan during a March 2009 meeting, the United States could put chips into the Guantanamo detainees returning to Yemen? The electronic monitoring would allow them to track the men's movements. It works for falcons and horses, King Abdullah offered. "Horses don't have good lawyers," Brennan replied.

Kuwait's Ministry of Interior suggested to the country's U.S. ambassador that Gitmo detainees should just be sent back to Afghanistan "where they could be killed in combat." Slovenia was pressed to "do more" if it wanted to "attract higher-level attention from Washington." An official in Finland's prime minister's office confided: "Chinese diplomats in Helsinki have repeatedly warned them about the damage to bilateral relations should Finland accept any Uighurs."

Those were the types of closed-door comments being made around the world as the United States bartered for homes for the remaining Guantanamo prisoners. Closed-door comments, that is, until revealed as part of the 2010 WikiLeaks dump of thousands of secret State Department documents. Reading through the classified cables gave the impression that Obama was relying on his appeal as the most popular kid in the playground and had his buddies cajoling, begging, bullying and trading friendships for favours. *You want to sit at the cool picnic table? Take a Palestinian. Enjoy your lunch money, do you? How about giving a home to an Algerian and an Uzbek to keep buying fries at noon?*

Each negotiation was unique, but one source of tension seemed to be the American refusal to accept any detainees. Congress's NIMBY measure to block the transfer of prisoners cleared for release irked many American allies. A September 2009 cable from Strasbourg, France, made that clear. "The U.S. could not expect European countries to accept detainees from Guantanamo if the U.S. were not willing to accept some on U.S. soil," said the Council of Europe human rights commissioner, Thomas Hammarberg. Canada refused to even entertain the notion of taking detainees, making it unique among U.S. allies.

Gitmo remains open and will be for the foreseeable future. By 2011, there were 171 detainees remaining, and Obama had lifted the suspension on military commissions. Civil rights advocates continue to denounce Guantanamo's military tribunals as inherently unjust, with flawed rules allowing hearsay evidence and crafted to ensure convictions. The nearly sixty Yemeni detainees, not slated for prosecution, but considered too dangerous to be returned to the impoverished and unstable Arab nation, are being held indefinitely.

President Obama's first act as president was to issue an order to close the prison. Five months later, in that National Archives speech, he talked again about regaining the "moral high ground" and mentioned the prison twenty-eight times. In his January 2011 State of the Union address he did not once utter the word Guantanamo.

Four months later, on April 4, 2011, U.S. Attorney General Eric Holder announced that, against his better judgment, KSM and his co-accused would be prosecuted in Guantanamo. On the same day, Obama officially launched his re-election campaign.

> "Ruling Yemen is like dancing on the heads of snakes."
>
> YEMENI PRESIDENT ALI ABDULLAH SALEH

6 Sanaa

OSAMA BIN LADEN'S former bodyguard lives in the shadow of the U.S. embassy in Yemen's capital. The embassy is more of a fortress, really; a mess of barbed wire and tanks greets visitors. After two carloads of suicide bombers drove up to the entrance in September 2008, killing eighteen, the embassy grounds were expanded, gobbling up city blocks and further alienating neighbours.

It is strangely fitting that Nasser al Bahri, a one-time al Qaeda insider who still thinks fondly of the days when he walked a few paces ahead of Osama bin Laden, ready to take a bullet or a bomb, lives just a short stroll from the U.S. embassy's gates. This is Yemen. People who know the country often explain bizarre anomalies by saying, "Well, it's Yemen," followed by a chuckle if they're fond of the place, or a derisive shake of the head if not—either way, delivering the line in the tone used for an eccentric uncle who no longer lives within societal norms.

Nasser is largely known by his *kunya*, Abu Jandal, which roughly translates as "The Powerful One." He has been a jihadist in all the hotspots—Bosnia, Chechnya, Somalia—and if he were younger, and not being watched so closely these days, he says he would happily return to Afghanistan.

In the summer of 2009, about four months before Yemen would become the next pariah state, I went to Sanaa with *Star* photographer Lucas Oleniuk to learn not just about al Qaeda's past but its future. We were also interested in finding out more about the bookish-looking U.S.-born cleric, Anwar al Awlaki, who was living in Yemen and whose online preaching had inspired members of the Toronto 18. Awlaki was not yet on the public radar, but he was watched closely within the intelligence community.

The main point of our trip, however—and how I sold it to my editors—was Yemen's connection to Guantanamo. Barack Obama was nine months into his presidency and the Guantanamo quagmire was starting to dog his administration. He was still figuring out what to do with the prisoners. Almost half of the camp's detainees were from Yemen and there was concern about returning these men into this impoverished nation. The Pentagon considered some of the detainees too dangerous to release, but it did not have enough evidence to prosecute them. Others may not have been violent going in, but eight years in custody had given them time to develop a serious grudge. Would they not become easy recruits without proper monitoring or assistance? Yemen's government promised that if it received financial help from the United States, it could handle the returning detainees. Few believed those assurances, especially since Yemen, the poorest of Arab countries, was in trouble.

The statistics were horrifying. Yemen was suffering from dwindling oil and water reserves. Poverty was crushing. Almost half of the country's 23 million people survived on less than $2 a day. At least a quarter were unemployed, illiterate or starving, and often all three at once. Government corruption was rampant under President Ali Abdullah Saleh, "The Boss," as the man who had ruled for three decades was known. The birthrate was increasing steadily and the population's median age was seventeen. In the mountains north of Sanaa, the "Houthi rebellion" (named after a deceased rebel leader) had claimed thousands of lives since 2004, as Shia insurgents clashed with government soldiers in the Saada Province, near the border with Saudi Arabia. In the south, a secessionist movement threatened to pull the country apart. The prospect of civil war had loomed constantly since the bloody days in 1994, when it had consumed the country. These socioeconomic and domestic threats were far greater concerns than al Qaeda, but as history had shown, fragile states were perfect incubators for burgeoning terrorist organizations.

Visiting Yemen as a national security reporter was like trekking to Graceland as an Elvis fan. Dozens of men named on the U.S. and UN terrorist lists lived freely in Sanaa, like bin Laden's spiritual advisor, who ran the city's government-funded university. Former Afghan jihadists and senior al Qaeda lieutenants and countless low-level foot soldiers lived in "retirement" in the mountainous tribal region, or in the crumbling stone buildings of the ancient city, largely unnoticed. Every household had at least one gun (according to the Small Arms Survey, Yemen was second to the United States as the world's most armed nation).

Saleh, who had once been nicknamed "Little Saddam" after his former Iraqi ally, was the longest-serving ruler in the Middle East after Libya's Muammar Gaddafi and Oman's Sultan Qaboos bin Said. When he took power in 1979, the Washington Post quoted an unnamed U.S. intelligence analyst who predicted that Saleh would be lucky if he lasted six months. But Saleh was wily and understood the need to dole out costly patronage to keep the tribal and religious leaders onside. He famously said that governing Yemen was as dangerous as "dancing on the heads of snakes." If so, he had been the ultimate snake charmer for more than three decades.

We picked up Abu Jandal on a street near his home in Saawan, a dusty neighbourhood punctuated by concrete barricades, which made it feel as if you were driving through a pinball machine. Abu Jandal was standing on the street, checking his watch, as we approached. He looked nothing like I had imagined, more business executive late for a golf game than the fabled jihadist. He wore a white polo shirt and khaki pants instead of the traditional thawb, the long white robe worn by most men. As he took his seat, his cologne filled the car's interior. Abu Jandal turned and flashed a beatific smile.

Beside him, in the driver's seat, was Khaled al Hammadi, one of Yemen's best-known journalists—if not the most famous, then definitely the most patient. Tall, lean and with an uncanny resemblance to a lanky Speedy Gonzales, Khaled, who had arranged our interview with Abu Jandal, seemed unflappable. We had learned that within minutes of meeting him at the airport a few days earlier.

We had arrived exhausted in Sanaa just after 3 AM and were told that there was a problem with our visas. Or, more accurately, there was a problem after customs agents discovered Lucas's camera and video equipment, even though we were travelling on visas issued personally by Yemen's ambassador in Ottawa. This was not good, but also not uncommon, as foreign journalists were closely monitored in Yemen. But one of the warnings we had been given was that it was unwise to linger at Yemen's airport, since scouts were watching for foreigners with price tags on their foreheads. The road from the airport was deserted at night and a great place to snatch disoriented travellers.

Airport agents told us that Ottawa had failed to inform the Ministry of Information of our arrival, which prompted four officious, sweaty men to make a flurry of calls. As the airport slowly emptied of all other passengers, we wondered if they were not just calling each other. When Khaled arrived to bail us out, he smiled and cooed deferentially, not the slightest bit condescending to the agitated security staff, or to us. He apologized profusely for the misunderstanding, as we grinned our best *silly us* Canadian smiles. It eventually cost us a palmed $10 U.S. and a promise to report to the ministry a couple of days later.

We had secured Khaled as our fixer before coming, and in Sanaa he became our everything: driver, translator, producer, tour guide and save-your-butt-in-a-foreign-country friend. Khaled was stringing for the wire service Agence France-Presse and worked as a full-time correspondent for the London-based Arabic paper *Al-Quds al-Arabi*. He had been questioned, shunned, roughed up and jailed for stories, and also celebrated in a country where the government bragged of press freedom but really appreciated it if that press unctuously covered President Saleh. Khaled had been the first reporter to interview Abu Jandal and he had spent six months, and likely bottomless cups of tea, to secure his story. His excellent nine-part series for *Al-Quds* served as an important backgrounder to al Qaeda's inner workings.

With Abu Jandal and Khaled in the front, I sat in the back with Lucas. Lucas had begun to sweat and shake just hours after arriving in Yemen. We later concluded it was a vicious flu, perhaps the swine flu that had started to infect the country. It would take a few agonizing days to get through his system. But, not knowing if we would get another chance to talk with Abu Jandal, he had come along and was propped up against the back window, his eyes closed behind his mirrored shades as he begged his stomach not to hurl what little was left in it. Khaled drove the three of us along pebbly, narrow back roads to somewhere quiet, without the prying eyes and ears of government snoops.

We settled on an outdoor courtyard at the Arabia Felix Hotel (the "Happy Arabia"), inside the gates of the Old City. We ordered glasses of frothy lemonade and bottles of water as Lucas set up a video camera and Abu Jandal settled in.

ABU JANDAL'S PATH to al Qaeda began as it had for many others. Born in Saudi Arabia in 1972 to parents of Yemeni heritage, he grew up in a comfortable middle-class family, raised on stories of jihad fought during the Soviet invasion of Afghanistan. The Arab world was not only awash with romanticized images of their Muslim brothers fighting communist oppressors, but the Kingdom was financing fighters to travel to Afghanistan. He spent Fridays absorbing sermons in Jeddah's mosques about how it was every Muslim's duty to fight, or listening to tales of valour on cassettes that were widely circulated among the youth. He watched the mujahideen return home as heroes after the Soviet withdrawal. Abu Jandal had told Khaled that a photo he was shown of a Jewish soldier breaking the arms of a Palestinian child had profoundly affected him. He never forgot that image.

When the conflict in Bosnia broke out, Abu Jandal left Saudi Arabia to fight and never returned. After Bosnia, he went to Somalia in the tumultuous years after the U.S. withdrawal and then to Yemen to recruit others into the mujahideen life he had grown to love. One day in 1996, he went to the Martyrs Mosque in Sanaa and approached a group of men. One of them was Salim Ahmed Hamdan, who would later become bin Laden's chauffeur and a famous Guantanamo Bay detainee. Hamdan was trying to get work as a taxi driver but spent most of his days chewing the leafy stimulant qat and living in a room at a local boarding house. Abu Jandal was younger than Hamdan by a couple of years but quickly adopted the role of wiser older brother. An orphaned only child, Hamdan had longed for a mentor and sought direction in his life. Besides, he needed a paycheque. Abu Jandal offered all of this and eventually convinced Hamdan and the rest of the group he had met that they should go to Tajikistan, where the Soviets continued to battle Islamic insurgents.

In 1996, with their flights financed by Saudi charities, Abu Jandal, Hamdan and a group of nearly three dozen others left Yemen for Jalalabad, Afghanistan, where they began a gruelling journey to the border. They travelled first by Jeep, then on foot, taking nearly six months to reach Tajikistan. But ultimately, they would fail. Abu Jandal believed he was sold out by a Tajik guide who had warned the Soviets about a group of thirty-six Arab fighters marching through Afghanistan. When news reached them that Soviet troops were gathering at the border, and fearing they were walking into an ambush, the group turned back. Yemenis are known for their fortitude. They are "mountain Arabs," growing up in terrain similar to Afghanistan's wilds and considered the toughest of the Arab fighters. But after six months, they were starting to get discouraged.

Abu Jandal decided to take his men back to Jalalabad, where word was spreading about a wealthy Saudi sheikh named Osama bin Laden. Bin Laden had recently returned from exile in Sudan and set up camp outside of Jalalabad. It was 1996, and al Qaeda was growing. Abu Jandal and Hamdan knew little at the time about the organization they were joining but were persuaded to fight for the cause after spending three days listening to bin Laden preach about America's creeping influence in the Gulf. Bin Laden was an admirable and imposing figure, with his six-foot-five frame towering above the men, his soothing voice waxing poetic about the struggle ahead, and his avowal to live a modest life despite his family's wealth. Abu Jandal and Hamdan stayed.

More than a decade after this meeting, talking with us as he sat in the Arabia Felix Hotel, Abu Jandal tried to recall what it was like when he first met bin Laden. He was slightly defensive, perhaps having been asked this question too often.

"Osama bin Laden is very normal person," he said with a shrug. "Osama is your average father or friend or husband. Bin Laden never treated us as followers ... he treated us like he was our older brother and we his younger siblings. Really, he is a normal guy but many people think otherwise because a lot of the media is antagonistic to him. He is a man that believes he has a righteous cause. So he defends his cause with all the means available."

He had been more effusive in his interview with Khaled years earlier. "Our love for Sheikh Osama springs from the fact that we went hungry together and were filled together," he said, according to an English translation of their interview. "We felt afraid with him and felt safe with him. We wept and rejoiced with him. We were joined by a common destiny. We lived a full life with him without discrimination. The man was very simple in all his dealings and in everything in his life. Nevertheless he bore the nation's concerns, and he did that very cleverly. In that aspect of his character, he was very astute. His simple way of dealing with others and his tolerance towards those who offended him made everyone around him love him dearly."

Abu Jandal pledged allegiance, the bayat, to bin Laden and eventually was selected as a chief bodyguard. Sometimes, he would travel days ahead of bin Laden to check out a locale and make sure a city was safe, much in the same fashion as the U.S. Secret Service would do for a president. Abu Jandal believed dying for bin Laden would have been an honour. And he was also tasked with making sure the leader was never captured. If someone came too close, he said, his job was also to put a bullet in bin Laden's head. During their four years together, the men grew close. Then Abu Jandal returned to Yemen.

ON OCTOBER 12, 2000, a tiny Yemeni fishing boat pulled up alongside the $1 billion destroyer USS *Cole* in Aden's harbour. The two men on the boat waved to the American sailors on the ship as it refuelled. The sailors waved back. When the fishing boat kept moving forward to strike the ship, it exploded, punching a hole in the destroyer that nearly sank it, and killing seventeen U.S. sailors.

At the time, little was known about al Qaeda, even though it was suspected that its members had been behind the bombings of U.S. embassies in Kenya and Tanzania two years earlier. Al Qaeda would later gloat that the *Cole* bombing was a military triumph, a David-versus-Goliath success and a deadly warning about U.S. meddling in the Middle East. But the threat posed by al Qaeda was never fully appreciated even after the *Cole* bombing—one of the tragic missteps that led to the 9/11 attacks. U.S. President Bill Clinton had vowed to seek justice and retribution after the attack, warning the terrorists: "You will not find a safe harbour." But Clinton later told the 9/11 Commission that he was never provided conclusive evidence that bin Laden was behind the attack.

Abu Jandal insisted he had had no warning about the bombing, despite the proximity he had to bin Laden and al Qaeda's inner circle, but instead had come to Yemen after arranging a marriage between bin Laden and his fourth wife. In other interviews he said he had grown tired and disillusioned with al Qaeda and was looking for a way out. Whatever the circumstances, he was rounded up with more than one hundred other suspected al Qaeda members in December 2000. Abu Jandal was kept in solitary confinement in Yemen's political prison and questioned about his knowledge of al Qaeda. But he said little. Then 9/11 happened, and a week later, FBI agent Ali Soufan, one of the bureau's foremost experts on al Qaeda, came to his cell.

Ali Soufan had a reputation as a shrewd interrogator. He was fluent in both Arabic and English and well versed in al Qaeda's hierarchy and its players. He had been part of the *Cole* investigation, but he met Abu Jandal for the first time when dispatched to Yemen in September 2001.

At first, Abu Jandal refused to cooperate, ranting to Soufan and his partner from the U.S. Naval Criminal Investigative Service about the evils of the West. But slowly, through patience, persistence and with the agents' extensive knowledge of al Qaeda's inner workings (which Abu Jandal admitted to me impressed him), he began to talk. It didn't hurt that Ali Soufan played to Abu Jandal's ego and tried to befriend him. He noticed that Abu Jandal never touched any of the biscuits they provided with tea, and it dawned on Soufan that he was diabetic. So next time they served sugar-free cookies, and Abu Jandal ate them heartily. It was a small gesture, but it showed respect, and slowly, he began to talk.

Abu Jandal's cooperation is credited as vital in the early days following 9/11, when it was essential to prove to doubting allies that al Qaeda had been involved. He was also reportedly the first to confirm the identities of seven of the hijackers. "Through our interrogation, which was done completely by the book, including advising him of his rights, we obtained a treasure trove of highly significant actionable intelligence," Soufan told a U.S. Senate Committee in 2009. "Abu Jandal gave us extensive information on Osama bin Laden's terror network, structure, leadership, membership, security details, facilities, family, communication methods, travels, training, ammunitions and weaponry, including a breakdown of what machine guns, rifles, rocket launchers and anti-tank missiles they used. He also provided explicit details of the 9/11 plot operatives, and identified many terrorists who we later successfully apprehended."

Soufan had also been involved in the early interrogations of Abu Zubaydah, one of Guantanamo's "high-value" detainees. Trying to repeat the success he had had with Abu Jandal, he began these interrogations by making sure the wounds Zubaydah had received during his capture were treated. Soufan claimed it was during this time that the FBI learned of the importance of KSM. But Soufan was pulled off the case when the CIA took over. U.S. Vice President Dick Cheney later said that Abu Zubaydah coughed up information about KSM during waterboarding sessions, to which he was subjected eighty-three times under the CIA's watch.

Abu Jandal was kept in jail until 2002, when, almost twenty months after his arrest, he was released on strict conditions. When we met, almost seven years later, he claimed he remained under surveillance.

He said his views on al Qaeda had shifted over the years, and the organization itself had changed dramatically. He had gone to school for business administration and with French journalist Georges Malbrunot had written a memoir. But he remained frighteningly pragmatic about al Qaeda's mission and expressed no sympathy for its victims. "Ordinary Americans don't know what the U.S. is doing abroad; they need to feel the suffering that other peoples are going through. Bin Laden didn't target the civilians in September. He simply hit targets, and civilians happened to be around."

YEMEN WAS ONCE a relatively safe country for journalists and intrepid tourists, but after the U.S. embassy bombing in 2008, things became more complicated. Kidnappings of foreigners had been a lucrative business for decades, but the kidnappers were reputed to shower their hostages with Arab hospitality. There were even tales of gonzo tourists hoping to get snatched for the experience, and other tales of hostages not particularly eager to be freed. But by 2009, kidnappings were less Lawrence of Arabia and more Iraqi-style, which meant you were snatched for ideological purposes, or as barter for a prisoner release, or to fetch outlandish ransoms. A couple of months before Lucas and I arrived, nine foreigners were kidnapped in northern Yemen and three of them—a South Korean teacher and two German nurses—were later found dead. In another case that year, a group of South Korean tourists was killed in a bombing. When investigators and relatives of the victims arrived after the attack, a suicide bomber struck again, hitting their convoy as it left the airport. Only the bomber died.

Sanaa was chaotic, but still a far cry from the war zones of Afghanistan or Iraq. It was just that the uncertainty of the security threat in Yemen made it, well, uncertain. Canada did not have an embassy there, only an honorary consul general, who was on holiday outside the country that summer. The advice from the U.S. embassy in Sanaa was not to stay in any one place for longer than fifteen minutes, although most of the American staff regarded this as ridiculously overcautious. American diplomats lived in a guarded compound and their movements were restricted. Yemen was considered a dangerous posting, which meant they could not be married or have children.

The best advice I received probably came from maverick spy Jack Hooper. Jack, who retired as the head of CSIS in 2007, was old-school—blunt, crude, he wore cowboy boots and had an ass-kicking personality to match. He was famous around Ottawa's stodgy headquarters for his "Jackisms," which were politically incorrect metaphors he dropped at all the wrong times. Unabashedly sexist and aware of my passion for running in exotic places, he warned me before I left for Yemen, "Don't go jogging in Sanaa. Even fat, ugly chicks can't get away with that."

Decisions made under Jack's watch had been scrutinized in various post-9/11 federal inquiries and investigations. Most damning were accusations that information passed by his agency to Syrian and Egyptian authorities led to the detention of Canadian citizens in Damascus and Cairo. I had first met Jack at the Ottawa inquiry into the case of Maher Arar. Canada eventually paid Arar $10.5 million after a federal inquiry found that RCMP agents had given the CIA erroneous information linking him to al Qaeda. When Jack appeared as a witness at the inquiry, he deftly dodged uncomfortable questions about CSIS's role in the affair, sitting for hours, with one elbow bent, his hand gripping the armrest. He looked like a grinning jack-in-the-box, ready to bolt if given a chance.

In the summer of 2007, I interviewed Jack at his retirement home in Peachland, British Columbia, a stunning, if ridiculously named, western valley town, with snow-peaked mountains, glacial blue lakes, and orchards of fragrant apples and pears. I told Jack he would die a slow death of boredom. He vowed he had found peace at the time, but I wasn't surprised when after a couple of years he was back east in Toronto working as a consultant. Jumping into his gas-guzzling behemoth of a sports utility vehicle that summer, I was prepared to be professional and courteous, but ready to dislike him. He was a misogynist, a self-professed redneck, about as right as I was left, a gruff-talking, the-world-is-black-and-white-and-screw-you-for-exploring-the-grey type of guy. But we went on a wine tour as we talked, during which he sipped Merlot (and later denied that fact, since he was a Scotch and bourbon man and was ribbed mercilessly when I wrote about his red-wine tasting), and then had a lakeside dinner with his sweet wife, Maureen. By the end of the week I had to admit, sheepishly, that I was thoroughly charmed. We agreed to disagree on much, but vowed to stay in touch—and we did.

Jack loved Yemen. "You're living my dream," he emailed me before I left.

> I always like to tell people to avoid staying where Westerners congregate. In Sanaa, your options are unattractive. I stayed at the Moevenpick, which was great. Westerners congregate there. You can actually get a drink. The food is good. I actually found Sanaa to be quite secure. You just can't spend enough time in the market, particularly at night when it really comes alive. Avoid travel by cab mid-afternoon, when all the drivers are in a qat-induced euphoric state. Not that there is a lot of respect for the rules of the road at the best of times. Avoid restaurants where the cook and wait staff are naked from the waist up (a long story). The best honey and coffee in the world. Buy some coffee to bring home. In my enthusiasm I bought a 5-pound pail of honey. Doesn't pack well.

Signing off, he wrote cheerily: "If the fundamentalists don't get you, the elevation will. Avoid cigars; breathing becomes an interesting experience, but you're in good shape. That's all I can think of for now. Have fun!"

Well, neither got me. In fact, despite the city's elevation of 7,500 feet, I'd never felt better, even as I jogged on the hotel treadmill. The fundamentalists? They were the ones we were looking for.

We decided to stay in a couple of different hotels but avoided the Moevenpick, which was too far from the city's downtown and just seemed to stick out like a diamond on the pudgy finger of a tourist in an Indian slum. Jack was right about the enchanting market behind the walls of the breathtakingly beautiful old city, a UNESCO World Heritage Site. And he was right about the ubiquity of qat.

Unfortunately, I never got the story of the naked wait staff as Jack, only fifty-seven, died of a heart attack in Toronto in late 2010.

FOREIGN HOTELS CRAWLED with government spies. Everyone knew that in Yemen. So when an old gentleman made a great show of snapping his newspaper open and sat in a chair directly beside us, even though the lobby of the Taj Sheba Hotel was nearly empty, Khaled and I exchanged knowing looks. It must have been a very engaging story, as we noticed he never turned the page.

We were waiting to meet Nabil al Hila, a younger brother of one of the Guantanamo detainees. I had hoped he could tell me more about his brother, considered a high-profile captive. Quietly, we got up and retreated to the far corner of the lobby with our backs to the wall and a clear view of the room. But you could only play chess in the small lobby for so long.

When Nabil arrived, so did a rather tall, muscular man who also sat uncomfortably close. Yemeni men tend to be short, but this stranger had to be well over six feet. His shoulders were also extremely broad, and aside from Abu Jandal, he was the only person I had seen so far wearing a polo shirt (faint pink) and khakis. As Khaled translated my questions and then patiently listened to the answers, I watched our friend read the English magazine Yemen Today. While I continued to stare, one of his hands slipped down slowly under his leg, which was crossed with his ankle resting on his other knee. From that little triangle of space near his crotch his hand emerged with a point-and-shoot camera. I had to stifle a giggle, as the move was pure Inspector Clouseau. Just as he was about to snap the money shot, I drew back sharply. Khaled and Nabil did not notice but he did, abruptly turning his head before returning to the magazine where he now hid the camera.

A couple of hours later, Khaled got a call from the Political Security Organization, Yemen's powerful public security and intelligence service, which runs its own detention facility and reports directly to the president. It was a casual chat that he dismissed later as "routine." They just wanted to know what Khaled was up to these days. In his typically unruffled fashion, he explained that he was working with two Canadian journalists and promised he would take us to the ministry the next morning. (Which he did, and despite my speech about the importance of a free, unfettered press, we were politely assigned a government minder, who accompanied us for the rest of the trip. For his company we paid $40 a day.)

Nabil's older brother, forty-one-year-old Abdel Salem al Hila, had been detained since the fall of 2001 and was one of the better-known Guantanamo cases in Yemen. Posters bearing his photo and calling for his release were plastered around Sanaa. Hila was a popular tribal leader and prominent businessman when he was snatched in the fall of 2002 from the Semiramis InterContinental, a five-star hotel in Cairo overlooking Tahrir Square and the Nile. His brother told me he had gone to Egypt for a meeting with representatives from the construction company where he worked, which was a ruse to get him out of Yemen.

Human Rights Watch called his kidnapping a "reverse rendition." Renditions, the covert intelligence operations in which terrorism suspects (such as Maher Arar) are sent to countries known for using torture as part of interrogations, had begun in the United States under former president Bill Clinton, but it wasn't until 2002, when the Washington Post's Dana Priest broke the story about the program, that it became widely known and criticized. Hila's case was unique, because he was snatched in Cairo, likely at the behest of the United States, and then transferred into U.S. custody on a Gulfstream jet to Afghanistan. Hila was imprisoned in the U.S. detention centre in Bagram before he was sent to Guantanamo two years later.

The Pentagon's unclassified allegations claimed Hila was a member of al Qaeda; had acquired fake passports for members of the Egyptian Islamic Jihad and al-Gama'a al-Islamiyya; was associated with imprisoned terrorists and had arranged the release of al Qaeda members. Allegations also stated he had "detailed knowledge" about a planned attack on a U.S. embassy and a western oil company.

During the 1990s, Hila had been a colonel with Yemen's Public Security Organization and had dealings with Yemen's "Afghan Arabs," as the mujahideen returning from Afghanistan were known. The Republic of Yemen had only been formed in May 1990, after the south and north were united for the first time in centuries and the country's northern leader, Saleh, was declared president. The foundation was still shaky when the Afghan-Arabs were returning and Saleh was eager to keep the jihadists onside, or, to help direct them outside the country so they would not cause problems at home.

How Hila fit into this picture is still unclear, but during an impassioned plea before a military panel in Guantanamo in 2004, he denied allegations concerning his involvement in al Qaeda and demanded evidence. "I will not be considered an enemy to anybody. I will not fight anybody. I hate fighting from the bottom of my heart. This is not because I'm here today; this is a fact," he told the panelists. "I want to let you know that I am a father. Even though I am not important in the American people's eyes because I am a prisoner, I am very important to myself. My kids and my wife think that I am important as do my mother and family. I hope that you consider that. I've already spent twenty-eight months. I am in prison without any reason for being there." He remains in custody.

During his years of captivity since that hearing, Hila's mother passed away and his two sons—twelve and nine—were killed in a tragic accident. His brothers told me that the boys had stumbled on a grenade while playing, finding it in a closet that was supposed to be locked. David Remes, an outspoken and passionate corporate-turned-human rights lawyer, was one of Hila's lawyers and visited him shortly after he heard about the death of his two sons. His client was completely despondent.

Hila was one of about a dozen Yemeni detainees in Guantanamo whom Remes represented pro bono. Remes had travelled often to Yemen to try to lobby for the repatriation of his clients and raise awareness of an unpopular cause. He may have had twenty-five years of corporate law and sixty U.S. Supreme Court briefs under his belt, but he will likely be best remembered as that lawyer who took off his belt to show his briefs. During a 2008 Sanaa press conference in the office of the human rights organization HOOD, the Boston lawyer dropped his pants to make a point about the humiliation his devout Muslim clients were enduring in Guantanamo. Flipping his red tie over his shoulder, he let his dress pants slip down as he described how guards would run their hands along the top of a prisoner's underwear during daily searches, demonstrating with the elastic of his own white briefs. The move would have shocked any room of journalists, but in conservative Yemen no one was sure quite what to do. He certainly brought attention to the issue, but his clients remained in Gitmo. When Remes left his corporate law firm in 2008 to focus exclusively on a human rights practice, a *Wall Street Journal* blog announcing his departure was titled: "David Remes, Who Dropped His Pants in Yemen, to Leave Covington."

The relatives of the Yemeni detainees had lost all hope until Obama's January 2009 announcement that the facility would be closed. The cautious optimism was still evident nine months later when we visited Sanaa. Nabil and his brothers, whom I would meet at their home, where we sat one afternoon chewing *qat*, said Obama's earlier outreach to Muslim citizens gave them confidence that Hila would soon be out. They stressed to me that they were not asking for an unconditional release. If the U.S. or Yemeni government had proof of a terrorist connection, then hold a trial to assess their brother's guilt. "We don't oppose any trial if it is fair. Let everyone measure up to their responsibility," Nabil said. But he felt confident a trial would show his brother's innocence. "The only time he was in Afghanistan was when the Americans kidnapped him and took him there," Nabil argued.

Also among the Pentagon's public allegations was a claim that Hila's "brother was extremely close to those who conducted the terrorist attack on the USS *Cole*."

At his hearing in 2004, Hila explained: "He went to fight in Bosnia without any of my family's approval when he was a very young man. Maybe he knew these guys in Bosnia… We don't know what happened until he got arrested and was jailed. He was in six years. He was in prison from 1997 up until the time I got jailed in the year 2002, my brother was still in jail."

When I asked Nabil about that as we sat drinking mint tea and hot chocolate in the hotel lobby he simply replied, "Yes, that was me."

GEOPOLITICS WAS NO doubt the main reason why only fourteen detainees had been repatriated to Yemen and more than half of Guantanamo's remaining population is Yemeni. Hundreds of detainees had been sent back to Saudi Arabia, Egypt, Afghanistan or other allied nations. Many of them faced allegations more serious than those levelled against some of the still-detained Yemenis. For instance, if a Taliban connection was grounds for imprisonment, then why release the Taliban's one-time ambassador to Pakistan, Abdul Salam Zaeef? Just in case Zaeef's credentials were ever in doubt, which they weren't, he later wrote of recruiting Mullah Omar in his memoir, *My Life With the Taliban*. Many Saudi detainees were accused of holding high-level al Qaeda positions, but there were few Saudis left in Gitmo. (It was rarely noted that fifteen of the nineteen 9/11 hijackers were Saudis.)

More than one hundred Saudi prisoners had been released, in large part due to the Kingdom's well-financed "rehabilitation" program, which had been praised by Bush and other Western leaders. Saudi Arabia was considered a pioneer in this field, but the program actually followed what Yemen had started. With little fanfare, Yemen was the first country to establish a counselling program for suspected terrorists following 9/11. But by the time we visited in 2009, the Yemeni program had been disbanded and was dismissed as a failed experiment.

The "Committee for Religious Dialogue," as the program was known, had been heavily based, as the name suggests, on religious cognitive therapy. Hamoud al Hitar, the former director, described it to me as engaging militants in "theological duels." Hundreds underwent these jailhouse sessions conducted by Hitar and a rotation of Islamic high court judges. They would counsel the men, either in groups or in private sessions, that Islam does not promote violence. Hitar, who in 2009 was the Minister of Religious Endowments, claimed the program was "98 per cent successful" but the lack of funding and political will killed it after just a few years.

Other assessments were not as rosy. There were stories of many of the 364 participants disappearing or leaving Yemen to fight in Iraq. Abu Jandal took part in the rehabilitation program and had been counselled by Hitar. During their three sessions, they talked about the nexus between religion and militancy and debated whether bin Laden's version of Islam was flawed. Hitar would later use Abu Jandal's apparent transformation from al Qaeda bodyguard to business administrator as an example of the program's success.

There was no doubt, in rehabilitation parlance, that Abu Jandal was "disengaged" from al Qaeda, but was he "deradicalized"? ("Disengagement" refers to a change in behaviour, whereas "deradicalization" is a change in beliefs.) Abu Jandal later told me he wasn't sure himself, but he was certain that Hitar's program had had little impact. He believed the program was doomed to fail since it took place in prison under the watch of the political security force. He said he eventually turned his life around because he had a supportive family, was well educated, and was tired of "life on the lam." As for the papers Hitar asked him to sign promising he would reject all violence and past contacts, he told me: "I'd have signed anything just to get out."

Trying to pin down where Abu Jandal stood and whether he could pose a danger was difficult. There was no doubt that like many former fighters he romanticized his days in Afghanistan and elsewhere. "People are categorized; some people say that I am a member and others say I am a supporter," he told me in 2009. "I am a supporter today of al Qaeda, not a member. The difference between a member and a supporter is that a member has the capability to execute, but I support. As supporters, we back whatever al Qaeda does against the U.S."

The failed Yemeni program and the celebrated Saudi one were distinct in their approach, but the main difference came down to money.

Saudi Arabia's costly carrot-and-stick rehabilitation plan lavished prisoners with cars, jobs, arranged marriages and posh weddings if the jailed jihadists agreed to reject violence and start anew. It was "soft" rehabilitation in a country not known for leniency. Religious counselling was part of the program, but not the focus. The premise was that these men should not be treated as Islamist zealots, but as criminals who deserved a second chance. If recruits joined al Qaeda because the organization offered a job and the chance to belong to something bigger, then the government would make a better offer. As Christopher Boucek, an associate at Washington's Carnegie Endowment for International Peace, told me, "They figured out they needed to support people and their families, because if they don't, someone else will." Boucek had heard stories of the wives of detained militants getting cash-stuffed envelopes from al Qaeda saying, "We're going to take care of you while your husband is away."

Successful graduates of the Saudi program were given further financial and emotional support after rehab. But step out of line and reaction would be swift, not just for the former prisoner, but also for his extended family. The Kingdom declared the program 100 per cent successful. There were, however, some high-profile exceptions, and for those Yemen would suffer.

MORNINGS SEEM TO yawn awake in Sanaa as the cacophony of calls to prayer prompts sleepy Yemenis to rise, stretch, unfurl prayer mats and face east. Shop owners shuffle to their stalls in the Old City market and slowly lift tarps and roll back doors to reveal a dizzying array of brightly coloured candy wrappers, pashminas, polished gold and silver plates and bin upon bin of saffron, cardamom and salted pistachios. The blenders purr with tart lime shakes, while stray cats meow at the feet of butchers. It takes a while for the caffeine in the goopy coffee served in reused evaporated milk tins to kick in.

It was sometime during this calm, one February morning in 2006, when twenty-three Yemeni prisoners crawled their way to freedom. The great escape from their basement cells through a 140-foot tunnel to the yard of a nearby mosque was *so* great, in fact, there was little doubt they had inside help.

Among the escapees were Jamal al-Badawi, the alleged brains behind the 2000 USS *Cole* bombing, and Jaber al-Banna, a Yemeni with U.S. citizenship and a spot on the FBI's most wanted list. The prison break was an international embarrassment for President Saleh, who was considered a Bush ally and had assured the United States that he could handle his country's terrorists. Saleh had been one of the first foreign leaders to pledge support after 9/11, personally visiting Washington that November to shake hands with Bush.

But Yemen's initial efforts to target al Qaeda leaders in the months after 9/11 largely failed. An attempt in late 2001 to catch top al Qaeda figure Abu Ali al-Harithi was bungled by Yemen's counterterrorism unit. Harithi managed to escape and a number of the unit's forces were captured or killed. By November 2002, the United States had quietly stepped in and an unmanned CIA drone finished the job, striking a convoy of vehicles about a hundred kilometres east of Sanaa with a Hellfire missile. Harithi was among the dead. Saleh would pay a high price at home when it was revealed that he had condoned the U.S. strike, but by 2003, with this loss of al Qaeda's leadership, and hundreds of Yemeni jihadists leaving to fight in Iraq, it appeared as if al Qaeda had been defeated in Yemen. The country faded from the news until the prison escape of 2006. Saleh acted quickly and most of the escapees were quickly recaptured or killed.

But two important ones got away.

Qasim al-Raymi and Nasser Wihayshi were not well known outside Yemen, but they should have been. Wihayshi was a thirty-three-year-old veteran of the Afghan war and a smart bin Laden underling. His fiery and outspoken counterpart, Raymi, was also an Afghan veteran. The twenty-eight-year-old had been convicted in 2004 for his role in bombings two years earlier, as well as a plot to attack foreign embassies. He was unrepentant during his trial and threatened to cut off the public prosecutor's leg (the attorney's home was subsequently hit by grenades). After breaking out of prison, Raymi and Wihayshi managed to disappear to Yemen's mountainous region, where they hid and carefully regrouped.

In January 2009, when Washington was in the grip of Obama-mania and I was in Guantanamo, Raymi and Wihayshi were in a two-storey safe house in Yemen's northern desert, preparing their own inaugural speech. As a camera rolled, the escapees sat cross-legged in front of al Qaeda's black flag. Beside them were two Saudis, and together, the four were making a video to announce their new organization: al Qaeda in the Arabian Peninsula. The group, which would become better known by its acronym AQAP, was a merger of local al Qaeda fighters from Saudi Arabia and Yemen.

The Saudi leaders in the video—Said al-Shihri and Muhammad al-Awfi—were former Guantanamo detainees 372 and 333.

Princeton scholar Gregory Johnsen was in his New Jersey apartment with Obama's inauguration speech on the television when he came across an Arabic press release from a jihadi site. Greg, a PhD student and Fulbright Fellow, was just thirty but already one of the United States' foremost experts on Yemen. He was as modest as he was impressive, spoke Arabic fluently, and had lived and studied in Sanaa during a time when most people couldn't find Yemen on a map. Greg also had a nonchalant style that laid-back Yemenis appreciated. His advice was sought from the highest levels of both the U.S. and Yemeni governments, but it wasn't uncommon for Greg to saunter into a ministry building in Sanaa, carrying his notes and a water bottle in a plastic bag, in much the same fashion as he would arrive for an afternoon qat chew.

Greg read the press release more than once. Former Guantanamo detainees had joined forces with the two escaped prisoners. Raymi and Wihayshi may have faded from the news since their 2006 escape, but Greg had been tracking their activities. To build his forces, Wihayshi had been taking advantage of Saudi Arabia's crackdown on extremists, which had sent fighters fleeing across the border into Yemen. He had been active, with suspected involvement in a variety of small attacks on local oil and gas facilities that rarely made international news. In June 2007, a suicide car bombing targeted Spanish tourists visiting a temple in central Yemen, and six months later, gunmen opened fire on a tourist convoy in the Hadramawt region in eastern Yemen, killing two Belgians. Then came the

September 2008 U.S embassy bombing, which, barring the wars in Iraq and Afghanistan, was the first direct hit on a U.S. target since 9/11.

Greg immediately understood the importance of what he was reading. An al Qaeda-affiliated group was now rooted in an unstable country and two of its leaders were former Guantanamo detainees. He looked toward the television at the image of a confident and beaming President Obama. "I knew he would never be as popular as he was at that moment," he later said about that day. "He was going to have to disappoint too many people."

On January 23, the video announcing AQAP's creation was posted online. But it wasn't until almost a week later—after Obama had signed an executive order to close Gitmo on January 24—that Greg called his friend, *New York Times* journalist Robert Worth, to show him the video. The front-page *Times* story of the two former Guantanamo detainees created a predictable media storm and greatly embarrassed Saudi Arabia (since the two Guantanamo detainees had participated in the much-vaunted rehab program) and the Obama administration (which had just committed to closing Gitmo).

A month after the video was posted, Awfi (formerly Guantanamo inmate 333) surrendered to Saudi authorities. Shihri remains an important figure in the group.

THE CONVOY WAS kicking up clouds of dust as we raced through the streets behind Yemen's counterterrorism unit. Women in flowing folds of black cloth yanked children onto the sidewalk, and drivers leaned heavily on their horns. It didn't matter that this was only a training exercise and most of the commandos were carrying automatic rifles loaded with blanks. This was how they always travelled when outside their fortress-like Ministry of Interior base: fast.

Nearing Saawan, the dusty, rundown Sanaa neighbourhood where Abu Jandal lived, the convoy slowed briefly outside the fortified gates of the U.S. embassy. We had been warned not to lose the group and Khaled struggled to keep up. Seconds later, we understood why. The gates to the diplomatic enclave rolled opened briefly to let the convoy use an otherwise forbidden stretch of embassy road. Guards stared warily, but waved us through.

The race through Sanaa ended at a training site in a barren valley outside the city limits. The counterterrorism unit had been planning this training exercise for weeks, and dozens of uniformed and heavily armed agents had converged for a mock takedown of a suicide bomber and high-value target. They had invited us on the condition that Lucas would only photograph those commandos who gave us consent. After years of Guantanamo restrictions, that seemed reasonable.

There were female commandos in the unit, who were celebrated as the first in the Arab world. Berlin Salah, just twenty-six, was the unit's articulate, English-speaking commander. She told us that the unit had been formed three years ago because of concerns that women were involved in terrorist attacks or hiding weapons for the men. In conservative Yemen, even during arrests or times of crisis, male commandos would not approach women. "If there's anything with women, we have to do it. Searching women, arresting them, all that kind of stuff," Berlin told me. As we stood preparing for the drill, the women, many with their identities shielded with a balaclava under their camouflage hats, watched from the sidelines.

The counterterrorism unit was known as Yemen's CTU. The pop cultural reference would have been lost in Yemen, but my mind went immediately to Jack Bauer. Watching the Fox TV series 24, starring Canadian actor Kiefer Sutherland as Bauer, was one of my guilty pleasures. Every week, with the 24-hour clock ticking in real time, the maverick agent saved the world. He was part of the Los Angeles–based counterterrorism unit, the CTU. Bauer's general belief was that "the ends justify the means." If there was a ticking time bomb (and there was each week), Bauer would eschew the moral high ground Obama liked to preach about, and with unsettling efficiency could suffocate, shoot, beat, extort and, in one case, employ an electric drill to a kneecap, to extract life-saving intelligence. Bauer did everything on that show except eat, sleep or pee, and apparently national security reporters weren't the show's only fans. The military loved it too, and this caused problems. There was concern among army brass that the show was having a toxic effect on American soldiers and interrogators. In November 2006, Jane Mayer reported in the *New Yorker* that the problem was so dire, the dean of the United States Military Academy at West Point, along with the three of the United States' most experienced military and FBI interrogators, flew to Los Angeles to voice their concerns to producers on the set of 24. "They should do a show where torture backfires," U.S. Brigadier General Patrick Finnegan optimistically suggested, according to Mayer.

Shortly after we arrived at the training drill, we met an American, who did not identify himself by name or organization, but who clearly seemed in control. After he shouted instructions, a dozen Yemeni agents began to run low and fast down an incline to the home of the "suspect." Our Yemeni hosts encouraged Lucas to go closer so he moved in. The Yemenis were proud to showcase their counterterrorism unit and more than one posed for Lucas.

The American, who we presumed was CIA, did not share their excitement. "Who are you?" he asked, storming up to me, as Lucas shot in the distance. When I explained what we were doing and the stipulation that we would not photograph any Americans who were part of the drill, he just sneered and said he would call "Washington." As I attempted to explain further, he ignored me. "It's just a little tense," explained his British counterpart apologetically. He seemed happy to talk as long as I didn't quote him and was unfazed by our presence.

Less than ten minutes later, the American returned and announced it was "over." With the petulance of a sore loser taking his ball and going home, he stopped the exercise mid-drill and sped away in a cloud of dust. The Yemeni commandoes were left either confused or infuriated by the abrupt end. "You should report that," one of the senior officers shouted to me in Arabic as we also left. "We invited you."

In the summer of 2009, the fact that Americans were training local forces was a poorly kept secret. I understood the reluctance to acknowledge the U.S. presence since a large American footprint would fuel insurgencies opposed to foreign meddling. And yet the abject denial of any U.S. presence—which most Yemenis knew was an outright lie—only inspired conspiracy theories of even greater Western influence.

At the Ministry of Interior base later, we were approached by a representative from the American team who described his role as "spokesperson" but did not have a card handy to give me. He apologized profusely for the misunderstanding. They had not been informed that journalists would be tagging along for the drill. "He was completely unprofessional," I sputtered, as the public relations officer nodded sympathetically.

"Thing is, we could have arranged something for you if only we had known. How long are you here?" he tried, even though I was certain that would not happen. "Listen, seriously let's arrange that. We could get you something *sick*." When he left, I wrote that down. That's exactly what he said.

He was a nice guy, just doing his job and trying to undo whatever damage his hotheaded counterpart had wrought. But we had no intention of writing about the American involvement in the drill— because that too had been a condition of accompanying the Yemeni team. However, being told that we could get something *sick* just made me feel sick. I later wondered how the dozens of Yemeni commandos regarded the dramatic cancelling of training that day. When U.S.-Yemeni relations were at their most precarious, could one agent hamper future cooperation?

Months later, when an attack in the United States would catapult Yemen onto the world's stage, the U.S. training of local counter-terrorism forces was no longer considered a secret. Senator Joseph Lieberman, chairman of the Senate Homeland Security Committee, was one of the first to confirm that U.S. forces had been training local units when he warned on Fox News that "Iraq was yesterday's war. Afghanistan is today's war. If we don't act pre-emptively, Yemen will be tomorrow's war."

But by July 2010, judging by a report from CNN's Jane Ferguson, it seemed not a lot had changed in terms of figuring out how to acknowledge the U.S. presence in Yemen without inciting the wrath of Yemenis (or journalists). "The anti-terror headquarters in Sanaa has a number of foreign guests these days, but until now they have never been caught on camera," she wrote in an online story accompanying her video.

> Beneath hats and behind sunglasses, U.S. and British military trainers put Yemeni security forces through their paces—teaching them how to fight al Qaeda. At the training grounds in the mountains surrounding the ancient city, they were finishing up classes for the day. Such classes are secretive. They are acknowledged by the governments involved but rarely openly discussed. The trainers were less than keen on publicity and CNN was ordered to stop filming despite having rarely granted official permission to visit the base. Their numbers have not been confirmed. Over the course of a few days I spotted around ten. Their responses to a Western journalist ranged from cordial chats to passive aggressive. Most skulked off when they saw me.

Guess they still weren't up to showing journalists something "sick."

THERE WERE NO good options for Guantanamo's Yemeni detainees. The country did not have a credible justice system or the political will to keep tabs on them, nor social programs to ease the transition from prison back into society. Even well-funded programs, like those the Saudis provided, did not guarantee success.

But what were the possibilities? Indefinite detention? Aside from the civil rights implications of holding people without trial, there was a dangerous ripple effect. Every detained man had brothers, cousins, neighbours or close tribal relations, who every year grew increasingly enraged about the United States' handling of Guantanamo. It fed anti-Western sentiments for a generation nurtured by the grievances of their elders. Yemenis loved to talk. Every afternoon was devoted to *qat* chew discussions. When Barack Obama took over from George W. Bush and immediately promised to close Guantanamo, there was a chance to chip away at some of the well-entrenched biases against the West.

"Both options are bad," Greg Johnsen said one night in Sanaa when Lucas and I met him for dinner. "You can continue to keep these guys and allow al Qaeda to score rhetorical points and gain more and more recruits as younger and younger people get radicalized and continue to tell about the abuses allegedly going on in Guantanamo. Or you can release them and face the potential of having some of them carry out attacks and, worst case scenario, having some of them carry out attacks that take the lives of innocent civilians and maybe Western civilians. The potential for disaster is quite great, without much of an inverse payoff."

As Abu Bakr al-Qirbi, Yemen's foreign minister, noted during a meeting with me in his office, "We have to be realistic, that sometimes injustice is one of the factors that leads to terrorism." Then there are those, he said, "who will always find a reason to fight" and need to be stopped. "This is the dilemma we face fighting terrorism."

In Obama's speech at the National Archives in Washington in May 2009, he said, "the existence of Guantanamo likely created more terrorists around the world than it ever detained. So the record is clear: rather than keeping us safer, the prison at Guantanamo has weakened American national security. It is a rallying cry for our enemies... by any measure, the costs of keeping it open far exceed the complications involved in closing it."

Obama had not dismissed the prospect of indefinite detentions of Guantanamo detainees (or "long-term" detention, as the White House prefers). "I have to be honest here—this is the toughest single issue that we will face," he said. "We're going to exhaust every avenue that we have to prosecute those at Guantanamo who pose a danger to our country. But even when this process is complete, there may be a number of people who cannot be prosecuted for past crimes, in some cases because evidence may be tainted, but who nonetheless pose a threat to the security of the United States." He vowed to seek the "strongest and most sustainable legal framework" rather than make decisions that would "service immediate politics." But six months after that speech and shortly after we returned home, everyone was talking about Yemen. And despite his promise otherwise, politics would play a role in Obama's actions concerning the Guantanamo detainees and Yemen.

In November 2009, U.S. Major Nidal Malik Hasan, a disturbed army major, went on a shooting rampage on his base at Fort Hood, Texas, killing twelve soldiers and one civilian. A month later, Nigerian Umar Farouk Abdulmutallab attempted to detonate plastic explosives hidden in his underwear while on board Detroit-bound Northwest Airlines Flight 253 on Christmas Day.

American online orator Anwar al Awlaki, whom we had tried to find during our summer visit to Sanaa, was hiding by late 2009 in Yemen's Shabwa region, where his tribe held sway. In online postings, Awlaki publicly praised Hasan and Abdulmutallab. Reports later claimed that Hasan, who is Muslim, had emailed Awlaki before the shootings, asking if it was permissible under Islam to kill his fellow soldiers. Awlaki told him it was, and they continued their conversation in more than a dozen emails. Abdulmutallab reportedly told the FBI that he had been instructed by Awlaki to carry out the airplane bombing (he has not yet been tried or spoken publicly).

Our hunt for Awlaki in the summer of 2009 had ultimately failed. At the time we went looking for him, he hardly seemed like the American-born Yemeni boogeyman he would become. His online videos were only a footnote at the Toronto 18 trial, and I vaguely remembered his name from the 9/11 Commission Report. After watching his videos on YouTube, I could understand how he would appeal to young, frustrated Muslim kids looking for a cause. He was unique in his understanding of both the Western and Arab worlds, which made his preaching seem credible and also easily understood by a Western audience. He even seemed to take a cue from U.S. president hopeful Sarah Palin in his I'm-just-like-you approach, sprinkling his speeches with glib references to "Joe Sixpack." But there was so much jihadi noise on the Internet, I wondered if his preaching was any more powerful than other voices.

Born in New Mexico in April 1971, Awlaki had returned with his family to Yemen as a child. At the age of twenty, he moved back to the United States to complete his university studies, beginning at Colorado State University. In the decade he remained in the United States he earned a master's degree in education in San Diego and started a PhD in human resource development at The George Washington University in D.C. While studying, he also served as an imam in California and Virginia.

Awlaki had been on the FBI's radar before 9/11, but agents questioned him directly when it was discovered that two of the hijackers had prayed at the Dar al Hijrah Islamic Center in Northern Virginia, where Awlaki had been an imam. The 9/11 Commission Report later concluded that the hijackers—Nawaf al Hamzi and Khalid al Mihdhar—respected Awlaki as a religious figure, but that there was not enough evidence about Awlaki's relationship to the men to "reach a conclusion." Awlaki moved to Britain in 2002 and two years later was back in Sanaa, lecturing at Al-Imam University.

The university had acquired a nefarious reputation thanks to its high-profile graduates, such as the so-called American Taliban, John Walker Lindh. The school was run by one of Yemen's most controversial public figures, Shaikh Abdul Majeed al Zindani, a reputed former spiritual advisor to bin Laden. Zindani was listed by the U.S. Treasury Department as a "specially designated global terrorist" in 2004, and the UN classified him as an associate of al Qaeda. Lucas and I managed to run into him inside a VIP lounge at the airport in Sanaa. Zindani did not give interviews, but Khaled spoke to his aides, explaining that we were Canadian (i.e., not American) and wanted to hear his views about the closure of Guantanamo. He reluctantly agreed.

The lounge was packed with people, and to get close I had to crouch at his feet with my tape recorder raised while his men formed a semicircle around me and Lucas took pictures from above. "First, what is required is that those who imprisoned these innocent people—the jailers who kidnapped many innocent people and treated them in the worst ways possible and reminded us of medieval times and the times of the Inquisition and the injustice and oppression that befell Muslims then—be held accountable. It is a stain of shame on the face of the West that always claims to uphold human rights," he said. "We consider that we have begun a new era and the U.S. under the leadership of Obama has begun to rectify these aggressive policies against Islam and Muslims that were declared by Bush and that has planted hatred between Muslims and Bush and those who stood by him . . . the oppression of one detainee is the oppression of the entire nation."

Zindani did not often pay the United States lip service, so his praise of Obama was significant. But as I tried to press further or ask him about his status on the U.S. terrorism list, or Awlaki, he rapped my shins with his cane. My time was up.

Chances are that, like everyone, he would have had little to say about Awlaki. The most common reaction we got in the summer of 2009 when asking about the online orator was: "Awlaki who?" No one we spoke to with knowledge of AQAP, inside Yemen anyway, believed he was a major player within the organization. By early 2011, however, he had surpassed Osama bin Laden as "Terrorist Number One"—according to the label given him by U.S. congress-woman Jane Harman—and made history as the first American citizen included on the CIA's list of approved killings. Obama autho-rized the use of lethal force against him.

There was little doubt that Awlaki was dangerous. But even crit-ics of the Obama administration who considered the president "soft" on terrorism questioned the legal and ethical implications of the CIA's kill order of an American citizen. "I hate to play the squish, but am I the only one who is just a little bit queasy over the fact that the president of the United States is authorizing the assassination of American citizens?" online National Review writer Kevin D. William-son asked. "Odious as Awlaki is, this seems to me to be setting an awful and reckless precedent."

The Terrorist Number One label elevated Awlaki to near mythical status. Greg Johnsen had told me he believed Awlaki was a mid-level player, noting that in the first twelve editions of an Arabic online magazine AQAP published, Awlaki had been mentioned only once—and only in disputing media reports that he had been killed. "I personally don't think that he's even one of the top ten most dangerous figures in al Qaeda in the Arabian Peninsula, let alone al Qaeda worldwide," Greg told me in early 2010. "It seems that people in the U.S. government and people outside put a lot more importance on his role than he actually seems to have in the organization."

Maybe a newly emboldened Awlaki felt the same way, for later that year, AQAP started publishing an English magazine as well. Called *Inspire*, it read like *Cosmo* for al Qaeda. Awlaki was one of its editorial stars. AQAP was a serious group, of course, but the magazine was part of the tragicomedy terrorist mosaic. There were tips on how to be a better jihadist and one of the features was titled: "How to Make a Bomb in the Kitchen of Your Mom."

Yemen's prominence in the news because of Awlaki and AQAP forced Obama's hand in the Guantanamo question and he bowed to political pressure. Eleven days after the failed bombing of the Detroit-bound flight, Obama suspended the release of any Guantanamo detainees to Yemen.

In Sanaa, supporters and relatives of the men were outraged.

"They could not break my spirit. If they break your spirit you cannot go anywhere. They only took my hand and foot."

ISMAIL KHALIF ABDULLE

7 Harstad

IN A FRIGID, dark field, more than two hundred kilometres north of the Arctic Circle, under a sky rippling with the greens and rusty reds of the Northern Lights, Ismail and Sahal were laughing hysterically. They stood arm in arm, doubling over as they giggled, and then rigidly arching their backs and stamping their feet like hens clucking and pecking for seeds.

"You're going to kill us," Ismail screamed in Somali.

"He says you're going to finish what AC Milan started," translated Sahal, his words sparking another round of violent hilarity.

I had not been able to figure out why Ismail started calling al Shabab, the Somali terrorist group that maimed him in a public amputation, after the Italian soccer team AC Milan. He wasn't sure how to explain it either. One day he just got sick of saying al Shabab, tired of giving the group legitimacy by using the name they had chosen. So he started calling them AC Milan and suddenly it became funny. He renamed Fuad Shangole, the leader who ordered Ismail's leg further mutilated, #9—the number worn by AC Milan's striker position. Ismail loved to laugh and thought this was one of the best jokes he had ever made. Perhaps he had hung around too many journalists and acquired our dark sense of humour or something was being lost in translation. Or maybe it was just that Ismail had an unbreakable spirit.

But was it too much to ask for just thirty seconds of complete stillness so my Somali friends would not be blurry black blobs in what I had envisioned as the quintessential photograph (albeit at this point contrived) in Norway's hinterland? Apparently it was, and the −15° Celsius temperature on that January 2011 night made us all delirious. Besides, even though I knew they wouldn't freeze to death, when I looked at their black patent leather shoes stamping in the snow, frostbite seemed a real possibility. As I feigned anger, they snickered all the way back to the car.

One year earlier, I had left seventeen-year-old Ismail Khalif Abdulle in Mogadishu as he frantically looked for the tiny Canadian pin lost beneath couch cushions. The start of the new decade was the start of a new life for the teenager. He was in Harstad, a coastal island town in Norway, population 23,500, where the winter sun did not rise above the horizon, and for a few days in the summer the sun never set. Despite its latitude, Harstad's proximity to the Western coast Gulf Stream meant that it was spared brutal winters and had a climate more like Chicago's or Toronto's. But try to explain to a teenager from Mogadishu that this wasn't really cold. It was as hard to explain every other surprise he encountered within his first twenty-four hours in Harstad: his barrel-chested guardian; his petite, soft-spoken Norwegian "mama"; a new six-foot-eight Somali friend named Osman who understood the horrors of Shabab; the apartment, the grocery store; the very fact that he was being given a fresh beginning.

This life was made possible thanks to a group of committed Somali-Canadians and Sahal Abdulle, the former Reuters journalist who could not fix his war-torn country, or save his pet Tortoise, or mend his traumatized soul, but who rescued one teenager no one could forget, and in doing so, brought hope at a time when it seemed there was none.

AMONG SO MANY tragic terrorism stories, Ismail's was just one. But it was one that touched many.

After six weeks living in the Horn of Africa in early 2010, I came home and wrote about Ismail as part of a three-part series on Somalia's desperate state. Ismail's story seemed to strike a chord; *Star* readers phoned, emailed and linked the article to other websites, giving it an even wider readership. The teenager's defiance in refusing to join Shabab and the barbarity of his "punishment" was especially poignant for Somali expats, whose emotions often oscillated between gratitude for their adopted countries and guilt over leaving Somalia behind. The common reaction to the story was: "What can we do?"

But no one was more profoundly affected than Sahal, who was still struggling with journalism, his responsibilities as a father and life in general since the August 2007 Mogadishu bombing that killed his fellow Somali-Canadian journalist and friend, Ali Sharmarke. After convalescing in Toronto, Sahal had moved to Nairobi in 2009, bringing his two eldest sons with him. Little Liban, who had strained to reach the microphone in delivering his speech about his dad and Ali to the ballroom of Canadian journalists in Toronto a couple of years earlier, now towered at over six feet tall and was an extremely quick-witted fourteen-year-old. Abul Aziz, eleven, had a mischievous grin and, like his dad, a warped sense of humour and easily bruised heart. The Abdulle boys were born and raised in Canada, but adapted easily to life and school in Kenya.

Sahal had left Reuters after the bombing and no longer worked as a journalist. But he still thought like one. He had taken a position with an information support team that helped the African Union mission in Somalia (AMISOM), and had become an important Somali voice in the Nairobi office. Occasionally he would travel to Mogadishu with a delegation, which was a difficult adjustment since security demanded he ride with an AU convoy, a far cry from his former low-key travels armed with only his camera and notebook. His Mogadishu home near the Shamo Hotel was still in the care of his relatives (as were his livestock and plants), but he was unable to visit since the area was insecure.

During an April 2010 trip to Mogadishu, Sahal sought out Ismail. When they met, the teenager's eyes haunted him in the same way the *Star* story had a few months earlier. It was as if every time Ismail described what had happened to him he was transported there again, held down in the stadium, watching the sun reflect off the knife as it neared his arm and a voice in his head screamed, *But why?* That look was hard to forget and different from the deadened eyes of so many others who had seen or experienced too much and seemed weary of trying to sort it all out. They were the ones who just accepted the horror. Those were the most depressing eyes, the young who were old—dull gazes of those who had long ago given up hope.

Sahal whispered to Ismail that he would help and asked the teenager to trust him. Ismail told him he already did.

Sahal returned to Nairobi with a mission, or as he later described it to me: "I became obsessed." Quietly he plotted the teenager's escape with help from friends in Mogadishu and a handful of Somali-Canadians who would later form a committee in Toronto they called Project Ismail. They wanted to bring Ismail to Canada as a refugee, but first they needed to get him out of Mogadishu. Meanwhile, Sahal also had to win over Ismail's family. Ismail's mother was living outside of Mogadishu but kept in close phone contact with her son and was concerned about this stranger from Nairobi trying to take her boy out of the only country he had known. Sahal's kindness confounded Ismail too. "I don't even know your last name," he said during one of Sahal's trips to Mogadishu. They laughed when they discovered they shared the same last name even though they were not related.

Slowly Sahal's escape plan came together. Ismail got his passport, thanks to Somali-Canadians within the Transitional Federal Government. With his family's meagre funds and donations from Sahal and friends, Ismail collected enough for a flight out of Mogadishu.

Details about the rest of his escape in the fall of 2010 cannot be disclosed without risking the jobs and lives of his rescuers, and a few strangers Ismail met along the way, who have no idea how much they helped.

SAHAL WAS PACING, and nervous, and looking completely unlike his normally laid-back self. It was September 22, 2010, and Ismail was out of Mogadishu, but had not yet reached Nairobi. His journey by air, taxi, bus and foot lasted for three agonizing days and sleepless nights as Sahal waited like an expectant father, just hoping everything would go according to plan.

For the most part, it did. Then the battery died on a cellphone one of Ismail's rescuers had given him, and Sahal lost contact. I had come back to Nairobi to write about Ismail's escape, and the plan was that we would pick him up at the bus depot in the centre of Nairobi's chaotic downtown. But somehow the message had not reached Ismail. "I can't believe this. No, no, no," Sahal muttered out the cab window as we drove aimlessly around Nairobi. He rubbed his forehead over and over and stared at his silent cellphone. The cab driver kept warily looking at us in the rearview mirror, waiting for directions.

It was just minutes, but it felt like hours before the cell rang again. Ismail had borrowed a phone from an old woman he had met and he quickly told Sahal he would be dropped off in Eastleigh, before the prepaid minutes or the battery on that phone ran out. "No, no, no," Sahal moaned again as he hung up. This was definitely not part of the plan.

Eastleigh, a chaotic, busy neighbourhood known as "Little Mogadishu," was about a thirty-minute drive from the city centre. The area, with its predominantly Somali population, looks so much like Mogadishu that Somali singing sensation K'naan (Canadian citizen and Toronto resident) filmed one of his first breakout videos there, since the capital of Somalia would have been too dangerous for a film crew. While the neighbourhood provided a safe home for many Somali refugees, who were both legally and illegally in the country, the area also inherited many of Somalia's problems. Namely, al Shabab. The group's members had a strong presence, preaching their calls to jihad in the mosques and recruiting new members, while also laundering money through local Somali businesses and, worryingly, scouting areas within Nairobi to strike.

Countries near Somalia were considered "soft targets" for Shabab, meaning they were easy hits. Al Qaeda had bombed the U.S. embassies in Kenya and Tanzania in 1998, killing more than two hundred and injuring thousands of Kenyans. Even though the attack had been thirteen years earlier, few in Nairobi had forgotten al Qaeda's first massive attack, and many feared the group's latest offshoot would try to do the same. Shabab had the ability to strike Kenya, but likely held off because an attack would lead to a crackdown by authorities, thereby choking off vital transit routes across the border and increasing pressure on the group's benefactors. But the possibility still existed and the July 11, 2010, Shabab bombings that killed seventy-six soccer fans watching a World Cup match in Kampala, Uganda—the first strike outside Somalia—showed they were looking farther afield.

There was only one place in all of Kenya where Sahal did not want Ismail to go, and that was just where he was headed. "Eastleigh," Sahal sputtered to the confused cab driver, giving directions first in Somali and then switching to Swahili. Seeing Sahal like this was unnerving, like the panic that builds when you're a child and your parents become suddenly scared. How could it take nine months, including these last three tense days, only to have Ismail grabbed in Nairobi?

It was 3:30 PM and the sun beat down on Eastleigh as the cab driver pulled off the street near a market area, where hundreds milled about buying qat. Around this time each day, a qat shipment sent Somalis scrambling to snatch up the best leaves in Eastleigh. "Stay in the car," Sahal shouted and I watched him run until his flapping beige blazer was swallowed by the mob. Not wanting to draw attention, but also not wanting to miss what I optimistically hoped was the reunion photo, I slipped behind the cab with my cameras and waited. And waited.

When Sahal came out of the crowd with his arm draped around Ismail's shoulder it was hard to determine whose smile was larger. Ismail and Sahal slumped in the back of the cab as we drove away, and for a few minutes they just looked at each other grinning and talking in Somali. I had brought the front page of the January *Star* article featuring Ismail's story, and when I gave it to him he just stared at the picture of himself in his lap, shaking his head. When the cab driver pulled into a gas station before we returned to Sahal's apartment, Ismail leaned back and said to Sahal, "You are my second father."

LIFE IN NAIROBI was a series of firsts for the teenager, who had never ventured far from Mogadishu. "Wow" became his favourite new English world. In the car at nighttime, Ismail would sit, his chin held up by the palm of his hand, and just stare out the window at the passing lights. "People drive at night?" he asked Sahal. "It's after six and there are cars?"

A trip to a mall to buy him new clothes (he shivered when the nights dipped to a "cool" 18° Celsius) was like watching a newborn track colours for the first time. He would swivel around with his mouth agape as he passed display windows for the kitchen, clothing, book and hardware stores. "Wow," he said, stopping suddenly outside a department store featuring mannequins dressed scantily in chiffon tank tops and hot pants. Sahal and his sons had gone up ahead to look for Abdul Aziz's school uniform, and since Ismail knew little English we just stood in silence, as he grinned shyly and laughed. He looked at me repeatedly as if to say, *Are you seeing this too?* Before we moved on, he brought his hand to his lips and declared in English, "Bravo," before kissing his fingertips and raising them dramatically in the air as if he were praising the *Mona Lisa.*

Sahal had not been able to tell his sons about Ismail during his months of planning because he was afraid it would put them in danger or that they may let the secret slip. He worried about how his boys would react to their new houseguest. But the day Ismail arrived unannounced, the two boys instantly accepted him, almost as if they had been anticipating this moment. Abdul Aziz decided to give Ismail his cellphone, just until he could get his own, he said, and offered his room, telling Ismail it was no problem to bunk with his father. "I will make it perfect for him," Abdul Aziz said quietly to Sahal. The excitement faded only briefly in those first few hours of meeting, when Ismail removed his clunky prosthetic leg so he could kneel in Abdul Aziz's room for afternoon prayers. Suddenly the impact of what had happened and the realization of why Ismail was living with them hit. Embarrassed by the tears running down his cheeks, Abdul Aziz hid his head in his father's chest, saying, "It's just so sad... and painful." He retreated alone into Sahal's room.

A few days later I took the three boys to Nairobi National Park. Aside from Mogadishu's stray cats, Ismail had never seen wild animals. This was my sixth visit to Kenya, home of the world famous safaris, but since I had always come for work, I had not seen much of the famed wildlife either. We only made it to the small zoo-like orphanage, but Ismail was delighted, limping on his ill-fitted prosthetic from cage to cage. "Wow. Wow," he said, looking at the monkeys, hyenas and lions. He would have been happy to stay there all day in the shaded and peaceful sanctuary, practising his new English words. At one point he crouched down at the chain link fence, near a young spotted feline, repeating, "Cheetah. Cheetah. Cheetah."

Ismail was safer in Nairobi, but he was not out of danger yet. Shabab could find him here, and it was likely Ismail would soon become depressed hiding in Sahal's apartment with only a few escorted visits in town. But Sahal had been prepared to look after him in Nairobi for however long it took, even if it was years. Certainly word from Canada, where Ismail wanted to go, was not promising. The Nairobi embassy had a terrible backlog and while Ismail's case was certainly tragic and desperate, there were many others.

But again, it seemed Ismail's personality and Sahal's hard work paid off. Just over a month later, the United Nations High Commissioner for Refugees declared Ismail a refugee in need of protection and he was given what's known as a "mandate refugee certificate," which would enable him to file his application to countries outside Kenya. Ismail's father had died from an illness when Ismail was young, and his mother and siblings remained in Somalia. But his father had a previous marriage and children before he met Ismail's mother, so Ismail had older half-siblings around the world he had never met. Two sisters were in Finland and a forty-year-old brother lived in Norway. They had read about him in the local media in 2009 and then in the *Star* a few months later. They were prepared to give him whatever he needed, including a home, if their countries would accept him. Through the UNHCR, Ismail applied to Norway and Finland, although he confided to me often that his country of choice was still Canada. In Toronto, Project Ismail worked to get support for his Canadian application.

Canada, for many Somalis, was the mythical land of the free, and since Sahal and the members of Project Ismail were Canadian, it was little wonder that this is where he wanted to settle. When we were visiting Nairobi's park, Ismail confessed sadly that he had found that Canadian pin I had given him in Mogadishu, but in his rush to escape he had left it behind. I gave him a sticker of a Canadian flag I had with me, which cheered him up, and he promptly pulled off the backing and stuck it to his forehead, like a stamped package ready to be delivered north.

Before Sahal's brother drove me to the Nairobi airport in October 2010, I asked Sahal how long he thought it would take to get Ismail out of Kenya. "I don't know," he said. "I was told not to get my hopes up. It could be years."

This time, my last image of Ismail was of the teenager sitting with a fluted glass dish of strawberry ice cream, voraciously digging in with a long-handled silver spoon.

IT WAS NOT years later, but just weeks, when Norway accepted Ismail on an emergency basis as a refugee-in-need. "Are you sitting down," Sahal asked when he called me in Toronto. *Norway?* We laughed when thinking of how Ismail was cold even in Nairobi. Delighted he would soon be safe, I was a little sad that Canada had not jumped first and worried about Ismail's culture shock. He was not going to Oslo, where there was a sizable Somali population and where his half-brother lived, but to a small community on the country's northern coast. As I talked with Sahal, I Googled "Harstad." "It's pretty," I told him, looking at summer photos of the mountains and deep blue lakes.

It was December 2010.

A few weeks later, Ismail said his teary goodbyes at Nairobi's airport. Sahal, a big fan of surprises, had not told Ismail that he had a plane ticket too, as he wanted to make sure that Ismail arrived safely in Norway. When he surprised him at the departure gate, Ismail was again overcome with emotion and relieved not to be alone, stepping on a plane for only the second time in his life. He later told me that he had glanced at the clock before boarding and it read 8:45 AM— the same time Shabab had dragged him into the Mogadishu stadium where his limbs were amputated. "I was scared both times," he said.

His flights took him from Nairobi to Brussels to Oslo and then on the final two-hour leg north of the Arctic Circle to Harstad. I joined them in Oslo for the last flight. When I found them (again, a surprise) Ismail was at one of the airport's public Internet terminals showing the Norwegian immigration representative the *Star* article about him.

The world outside the airport was white with snow and Ismail said he couldn't wait to touch it. "I will play soccer in the snow," he announced as we waited for the Harstad flight. Before his leg and hand had been taken, Ismail, like so many Somali boys, loved soccer. His nickname on the field was *cagmadhige*, which translates roughly to mean one who runs so fast his feet don't touch the ground.

With just minutes until our flight, Live Synnevåg Sydness, a woman working with the Norwegian People's Aid who was responsible for Ismail transiting safely through Oslo's airport, was on the phone with Ismail's cousin. Ismail had never met this cousin, Quman Abdulahi Abdulle, but they had talked by phone. She lived in Oslo and was at the airport, desperate to meet him before the flight departed. "I'll try," Live said as she ran off to a security gate and we asked the ticket agent if we could have some more time before boarding.

Moments later, Quman came running through the airport in her stocking feet with a grinning Live trailing her. As she threw her arms around Ismail and broke down in tears, she explained how she had left her shoes on the X-ray machine and just ran, worried she would miss him. They continued hanging on to each other until we were the last to board the flight.

THE SCANDINAVIAN AIRLINES flight attendants had clearly read a local newspaper profile of Ismail, as never has service been so attentive for a trip that lasted less than two hours. "Would he like an apple muffin?" asked one, plopping the complimentary doughy mound on Ismail's tray. A day earlier, Ismail had discovered coffee and was sipping what was possibly his twelfth cup, and was continually offered refills. For most of the flight, he stared at a map of Norway in the airline magazine and traced with his finger the flight's path north. He became only briefly worried as he looked out the window at the early evening sky, and Sahal had to explain that it might be dark now, but in the summer there would be days when the sun shone for twenty-four hours. "What will I do for Ramadan?" he asked, trying to figure out how to break the daily fast, normally signalled by the sunset. Sahal rubbed his forehead thinking of an answer, and Ismail waved his hand and laughed as if to say, *A problem we can figure out another day*. The flight touched down at 5:30 PM. "Tell the pilot he doesn't need to stop," Ismail told Sahal. "I'm so excited I could jump out."

I'm not sure who was the most surprised—Sahal, Ismail or me—when we disembarked at Harstad's airport and walked into the embrace of a six-foot-eight Somali named Mohamed Osman. The thirty-year-old, with size 14 shoes and shoulders slightly hunched as if he were continually trying to avoid a low doorframe, was part of Ismail's welcoming committee and stood at the baggage carousel alongside Ola Steinvoll (whom Ismail would soon call *bastafar*, meaning grandfather) and the petite Nina Hellevik (soon-to-be nick-named *mama*). Over the next few months Ismail would meet many friends and supporters, but these three seemed to embody all the elements that made Harstad's refugee program perfect for him.

Most friends called Mohamed Osman just "Osman," except for Ola, who used the Norwegian nickname he had given him, which translated to "little buddy." Osman had been in Harstad since

November 2008, when he was granted asylum. Born in 1980 in Mogadishu, Osman was just young when the government collapsed and during those horrific days of Black Hawk Down a couple of years later. But like so many other resilient Somalis, Osman's family had managed to survive the ensuing years of fighting and the warlords' ruthless rule. In 2008, when Shabab bolstered its ranks, Osman, an only child, new husband and father, was working at Mogadishu's Coca-Cola plant. He had studied nursing, but his position at the plant making the soft drink's syrup paid him more, providing enough to support his parents and young family.

Shabab, however, wanted him. "I was told I had to be prepared like a good soldier, because I was so strong. I had to be prepared to hold big mortars," he told me. "I was told it was military and I said, 'No, no, I won't take a gun.'" Spurning Shabab turned Osman into a marked man. The group's leaders began telling others that since Osman worked for Coca-Cola he was employed by a Jewish company and should be killed. "My mother and father just said, 'Mohamed, don't worry, we will give all our prayers to you,'" he said. One day, while Osman was working at the plant, a couple of well-dressed Shabab members came looking for him. They found only his wife at home, so they visited his parents.

Osman told me his story in a small room at Harstad's refugee centre, and it was the only time since meeting him at the airport a few days earlier that he had stopped smiling. At this point in our interview he looked embarrassed as his eyes became glassy and he whispered, "It's a very sad story."

Then he continued: "My father tells them, 'Maybe he is at his job and he's working.' So they tell him, 'Oh it's okay with you that he works with the Jewish?' He says, 'Yes, he's working just for us.' And so they say, 'Then you are Jewish and he is Jewish.' So they killed him. They killed my father. My mother was saying, 'Don't kill him.' So they killed her, with a pistol."

Osman stared at his hands as a tear made a slow descent to his chin. He told me he had heard about the shooting in his neighbourhood, but didn't know until he came home that it was his parents who were killed. "My neighbours and family, they took my father to wash him, because I couldn't wash him. When I was at the grave, [a Shabab member] called and said, 'We see you are at the grave now. Let them dig your grave too.' I told them, 'I've died one time already with my father. They've killed my father and mother, why should I live?'"

Consumed by guilt and grief, Osman had to be convinced by his wife, neighbours and friends to go into hiding after the funeral, rather than find the men who executed his parents. His pregnant wife and young children were protected by friends and then made their way to a refugee camp outside of Mogadishu. Osman sold everything his family owned and took a bus to Nairobi, where he eventually met a human smuggler and with a false passport flew to Oslo. At the airport, he asked for asylum. "God took me from hell to paradise," he said of his flight from Somalia to Norway. "When you move from your country where people are killed, where your brothers are arrested, where there's no order and you come to a safe place; where people help you and you can sleep without being scared? It is like a paradise."

In this snowy paradise he met Ola and Nina, and just weeks before Ismail arrived, Harstad accepted Osman's wife and four children, reuniting his young family.

"I'll look after him too," he said of Ismail.

NORWAY IS KNOWN internationally for its progressive refugee policies, but in Harstad, where more than 150 young men and women from Africa, the Middle East and throughout Asia have been given sanctuary, part of the program's success was thanks to the kindness of Ola.

Ola had become involved with the system only two years earlier, at the age of fifty-two, when the married father of two university-aged sons decided to leave his career in the health care system to take the director position for Harstad's refugee program. "He is not the big boss; he is a father, he is our friend," said Ahmen Ayoub, a thirty-three-year-old Yemeni refugee who had lived in Harstad for two years. "If you need something he will give it to you. Every time you say, 'Thank you, thank you, thank you,' but it is not enough. You know, we have nothing to give."

And yet, that is not how Ola regards it. The refugees have given him a whole new outlook on life. He said he was quickly humbled and forced to confront the racial stereotypes he once harboured. "There are a lot of people who are against immigration in Norway," he said one day as we took a tour around the small town with Ismail. "A lot of people on the right wing do not want to see black people in Norway; this is a struggle even here." In his spare time he travels the country talking about the program. "I find some guy in the audience and I say, 'Refugees are like me and you. . . they need to be treated as individuals, with respect.'"

Respect is what Harstad delivers. Ismail, like the other refugees, is given housing, a small bank account, an intense language program and eventually the chance at a university education. (Within three months of arriving, Ismail was already cutting back on his expenses, so he could send money home to his mother and siblings in Mogadishu.) After a few years, Ismail can apply for citizenship.

Before I left for Toronto and Sahal returned to his sons in Nairobi, we sat drinking coffee and marvelling at the fact that it was dark at 2 PM. Sahal wore a woolen grey and pink toque he had borrowed from Ola and said he still would not forgive me for nearly giving him frost bite as we watched the Northern Lights. I told him he had been away from Canada for too long. Then we talked about Somalia.

"Whether it was Tortoise or Ismail, I just wanted to help. God knows I've tried to help Somalia, and I'm still not giving up," he said. "But there was an occasion last week when I was really quite down. You work and work and then you just get depressed because you see things going down, and some people you were hopeful could bring change, become corrupt." Sahal paused for a long time before turning his gaze to where Ismail was sitting with Nina watching a video that instructed him on how to care for his apartment.

"Cases like Ismail? I learned you have to walk before you can run. It's a start. Working in Somalia I did learn to manage my expectations. When you are young and out of school, you're an idealist and you think you can change the world overnight. Things don't happen that quick, but little by little ..." He stopped again. "Little by little, you can change the whole country."

Rescuing Ismail would not rescue Somalia from its misery, nor lead to the demise of al Shabab. The three other young men kidnapped and maimed alongside Ismail are still desperate and trapped in Somalia. The day I left Harstad, Somali reporters wrote about another amputation of a young Somali "thief." More "punishments" would follow in the coming months.

Yet as I watched Norway fade below, I felt an optimism I had not experienced in ten years of reporting on terrorism. Perhaps it was just the fact that travel always makes me happy. There is little about it I don't love, even getting excited as the meal cart bumps along the aisle, carrying trays of fat- and sodium-laden dinners that somehow smell the same no matter the airline, or whether the offering is salmon, lasagna or curried lentils. I just find clarity in the clouds. Something about being helplessly sandwiched against an airplane window where your BlackBerry doesn't work, as you rise above puffed white hills, makes things fall into place. Philosopher Alain de Botton writes in his book *The Art of Travel* that the mental levity travel brings begins right on the runway. "There is a psychological pleasure in this take off too, for the swiftness of the plane's ascent is an exemplary symbol of transformation," he wrote. "The display of power can inspire us to imagine analogous, decisive shifts in our own lives; to imagine that we too might one day surge above much that now looms over us."

I was excited for Ismail to get settled and one day visit Canada and elsewhere, telling his story about al Shabab. He had been especially upset to hear the reports of Western youths leaving the comforts of their lives to join the group he had fought so hard to escape. He wanted to tell the deluded teenagers that they were not joining freedom fighters in a war against Islam, but butchers.

There is no doubt Ismail would be a powerful speaker, and if terrorism was so often about controlling the narrative, could an eighteen-year-old really make a difference? Could Ismail bring home the horrors of these organizations to Toronto teenagers in a way no one else could? Moreover, could he help Western governments understand why his friends and neighbours had joined the group, that the roots of terrorism involved the repression of the people, the unyielding cycle of poverty and corruption? Could he explain how it was easier to just join the fight, especially when it was difficult to determine sometimes who the "good guys" were anyway?

Up in the clouds it wasn't about *realpolitik*, and I felt happy with my oversimplified theory of how to wade through terrorism's morass. I imagined that not only was Ismail's future brighter, but that he had the power to make a brighter future. What I didn't know then, but would soon find out, was that this scenario—one victim, with one sad story, changing history—was unfolding below.

A Tunisian fruit vendor named Mohamed Bouazizi would not only forever alter the political landscape of the Middle East and northern Africa, but almost a decade after the 9/11 attacks would empower a generation who had been trapped in a ten-year cycle of fear. Al Qaeda's loquacious propagandists would be left struggling for words.

> "It was the moral force of non-violence—not
> terrorism and mindless killing—that bent the
> arc of history toward justice once more."
> U.S. PRESIDENT BARACK OBAMA, on the
> ousting of Egyptian President Hosni Mubarak

> "Justice has been done."
> OBAMA, on the death of Osama bin Laden

8 The Arab Awakening: Back to Ground Zero

ON DECEMBER 17, 2010, a humiliated Tunisian street vendor decided he could not take another day of the corruption, violence and hopelessness that had consumed his life. Mohamed Bouazizi supported his mother, uncle and five siblings by selling fruit from a cart on a dusty street near his home in the impoverished Tunisian town of Sidi Bouzid. On that winter day, a municipal inspector had informed him that his fruit stand was illegal. When Bouazizi tried to take back the apples the inspector seized, he was slapped in the face. This was how other vendors described the dramatic scene, although there was some debate about its veracity. Soon it wouldn't matter, though, because the symbol of Mohamed became bigger than Mohamed the man.

Mohamed Bouazizi left his fruit stand that morning, and when complaints about his treatment went nowhere, he walked to a hardware store to buy paint solvent. Then he continued until he reached the steps of the municipal office in his small farming town. He poured the flammable liquid over his head and set himself on fire. Eighteen days later, the twenty-six-year-old succumbed to his wounds, never appreciating how his self-immolation would ignite revolutions across the region.

The waves of protests in early 2011 that began on the streets of Tunisia before moving through Egypt, Bahrain, Jordan, Yemen, Libya, Syria and beyond, were collectively dubbed the Arab Spring or the Arab Awakening. But really, they could have also been called the *Western* Awakening, for what followed not only forced the Arab world's autocrats to their knees—or at the very least made those knees quake—but compelled the West to justify a decade of politics and counterterrorism practices that had kept those dictators standing.

Tunisian President Zine El Abidine Ben Ali was the first to fall, fleeing on a jet to Saudi Arabia, from the country he had ruled for twenty-three years. Ben Ali always had an iron grip on his country, but like other Arab leaders eager to show the United States that his nation was tough on terror, his grasp clenched more tightly after 9/11. Postcard-picturesque Tunisia on the Mediterranean Sea, a popular tourist destination for Europeans, didn't figure much in the news. But human rights groups had been documenting abuses as the jails filled with Islamists and political prisoners. Just claim *terrorism* and it was case closed, normally without even a trial, or at least not a trial that came close to real justice.

In other Arab countries, such as Egypt and Yemen, the torture of political prisoners or terrorism suspects was well known, but even as Western governments condemned the abuses, they maintained close and lucrative military and intelligence ties in the name of fighting terror.

What propelled the Arab revolutions, though, was not anger over this Western hypocrisy, but frustration with the oppressive and corrupt regimes. The protests were about the daily drudgery of life in Tunisia (or Egypt, or Yemen, or Bahrain, or Syria); they did not include burning American flags. Bouazizi earned about $5 a day, and sometimes that was less than the bribes he had to pay officials or police. The young, the unemployed, the educated, the poor: they were frustrated. In death, Bouazizi became the everyman martyr. This is what made him a powerful force. By all accounts, he was a kind, simple family man whose greatest ambitions were to send his sisters to school and save enough for a pickup truck so he wouldn't have to haul his produce in a cart. His only real enemy was his country's pernicious system; that David-Goliath struggle resonated among youths living in the Middle East and northern Africa. They connected as young people around the world do—through Facebook, Twitter, emails and texts. Al Jazeera told their stories.

Ben Ali's ouster was the first shock, but the protests that followed in Egypt were the ones that shook the world. The impervious President Hosni Mubarak had ruled for nearly thirty years throughout times of incredible turmoil (with the powerful backing of the United States and Israel), and few predicted he could be toppled like Ben Ali. On January 25, 2011, the day Egypt's revolt began, U.S. Secretary of State Hillary Clinton said, "Our assessment is that the Egyptian government is stable and is looking for ways to respond to the legitimate needs and interests of the Egyptian people."

Egypt had a revolutionary martyr too. Six months before Bouazizi died, police killed an Egyptian blogger named Khaled Said in Alexandria, Egypt's second-largest city. Police went looking for Said on June 6, 2010, and found him behind a computer screen on the second floor of a cyber café. The twenty-eight-year-old blogger had seen the two arresting officers before—through the lens of his camera as he videotaped them allegedly making a drug deal. Once outside, in the full view of a street of witnesses, the officers beat Said to death. He was, according to those who knew him, battered beyond recognition. But with Egypt's ubiquitous and brutal security service, who would speak out?

It took Tunisia's example and safety in numbers for Egyptians to find their voice. Hundreds of thousands chanted on the street, "We are all Khaled Said," and after eighteen days, Mubarak, defiant to the end, was gone too.

Rallies followed in cities such as Benghazi, Deraa, Manama and Sohar, leaving many around the world scrambling for maps to try to find them in Libya, Syria, Bahrain and Oman. Squares became symbolic circles of democracy—Tahrir, Pearl, Freedom and Change.

The revolutionary fever was spreading "like the flu," Yemeni President Ali Abdullah Saleh complained.

TAWAKKOL KARMAN, one of the figures at the forefront of Yemen's uprising, was rarely still. Her hands, her eyes and most of the time her feet were in constant motion. It is hard to imagine the thirty-two-year-old human rights activist and mother of three sleeping, turning off that adrenalin that seems to course through her body.

I met Tawakkol within a couple of days of arriving back in Sanaa in February 2011, after Tunisia's revolt but before Mubarak had been forced out. She stood on the street amid a crowd of protesters, unfazed by the fact that she was one of less than a dozen women among thousands of men. Aside from a couple of female foreign journalists, she was also the only one who did not cover her face.

Tawakkol's cellphone rang constantly, at least every ninety seconds. Sometimes she answered; sometimes, she just glanced at the number, her eyes diverting briefly, without losing her train of thought as we talked. "The only solution for Yemen is that he has to go," she told me as a crush of supporters rushed her like a rock star. The "he," was of course Saleh, and for Tawakkol there was no point in discussing the rest of her revolutionary plan until the president stepped down.

Of all the Arab nations, Yemen's revolt caused the greatest concern in the West and Saudi Arabia—not surprising, since it was poor, armed and home to AQAP, the sophisticated al Qaeda franchise. The politically astute and American-backed Saleh had offered quick concessions in an effort to quell the protests. He vowed not to run again in the 2013 election and promised that his son, Ahmed, whom most believed Saleh was grooming for the presidency, would not run either. Problem was, no one trusted Saleh—and with good reason. He had made the same undertaking before. In 2006, he said he was forced to renege on his promise, as the people had demanded he return.

Aside from his pledge not to seek re-election, Saleh also promised to lower income taxes and tuition, raise the salaries of soldiers and civil servants and tackle unemployment. They were empty promises, as the economy could not sustain these measures; but, realistic or not, the more significant fact was that Saleh had made any concessions at all. It was a sign that he was worried. His ruling style had always been force first; the man's arrogance was legendary. Large portraits adorning the city showed the regal ruler looking down his nose or somewhere off-camera. Once, during a campaign, he portrayed himself as Napoleon, perched astride a white horse, Yemen's flag around his shoulders. Saleh's oversized ego was not all he shared with the French emperor. During his carefully orchestrated public appearances, there was always a step behind the lectern for the diminutive leader to stand upon.

When Cairo's Tahrir Square became the ground zero for Egyptian protesters, Saleh acted quickly to avoid a similar scene, ordering government tents erected in the Sanaa square that shared the same name. Over the weeks, as the protests calling for Saleh's departure got larger, so did the tents in Sanaa's Tahrir Square. Some genuine Saleh supporters camped there, those who had done well under the president, or those scared of what a post-Saleh Yemen would look like. In interviews they said they feared "the chaos." Other pro-Saleh "supporters" were tribesmen brought in from outlying regions and paid in food and qat for their patronage. They guarded the square, and if the student protesters tried to get close, they would fight. Yemenis called them the baltagiya, meaning thugs, and they were vicious.

Yemen's movement started on January 14, the day President Ben Ali resigned in Tunisia. Tawakkol posted a message on Facebook calling for others to join her in celebration. A group of students gathered at Sanaa University and marched to the Tunisian embassy. A week later, on January 22, Tawakkol was driving home when her car was forced to the side of the road by unmarked vehicles and men in street clothes. It wasn't uncommon for human rights workers to be arrested. Ali al Dailami, the director of a local democracy group, told me he had been taken into custody eight times since 2006. During one harrowing forty-day term, he said, he was sleep-deprived, beaten daily and refused outside contact. But it was unusual for women to be detained, and Tawakkol's arrest set off its own protest. Thirty-six hours later, she was released, but not before Saleh reportedly spoke with her brother Tariq, telling him, "Control your sister. Anyone who disobeys me will be killed."

Tawakkol had emerged as one of the revolutionary stars, but she was not a new headache for Saleh. She hadn't changed; it was just that the world around her had. Tawakkol had been staging sit-ins every Tuesday since 2007, protesting on behalf of women, journalists and political prisoners. She had formed an organization called Women Journalists Without Chains, but she advocated for all human and civil rights, not just a free press for female reporters. In 2010, she was nominated for one of the U.S. State Department's "Women of Courage" awards. Hillary Clinton is one of her heroes, she told me. She has pictures of her other idols framed in her home—Martin Luther King Jr., Gandhi and Nelson Mandela. They sit on a mantel alongside a family portrait of her husband, fellow activist Mohammed, and her six-year-old son and two daughters, aged thirteen and seven.

Dailami, also a well-known fixture at the protests in his beat-up brown leather jacket, met Tawakkol in 2004 when their organizations came together under the umbrella of the Yemeni Network for Human Rights. Like almost all Yemeni women, Tawakkol was covered in black cloth, with only her eyes showing. Dailami remembers the day three years later when he was having breakfast as a woman approached. "She sat down, and she said, 'How are you, Ali?' I didn't recognize her." Tawakkol had decided she no longer wanted to cover her face. When I later asked her why, she just shrugged. "It was time."

Describing Tawakkol was like trying to explain Yemen, where politics and tribal affiliations made it impossible to put people in tidy ideological boxes. Tawakkol was a member of the Islamic party, Islah, the second-most influential party in an alliance of six opposition groups, which included a socialist party that represented the interests of the south, and together they formed the Joint Meeting Parties.

Islah's membership was composed of a diverse group of tribesmen and businessmen (not mutually exclusive), fundamentalists, moderate Muslims who believed in the separation of state and religion, and a few feminists like Tawakkol. Yet Islah raised red flags in the West, where there was concern about the party's most outspoken member, Zindani, the former bin Laden advisor who had rapped my shins a couple of years earlier at Sanaa's airport to signal the end of our little Guantanamo chat. In October 2010, Islah made international headlines after its ultra-conservative members blocked a bill that would make it illegal to marry girls under the age of seventeen. In Yemen, there were instances of girls as young as nine becoming brides.

Fear of Islah becoming the country's governing party was one of the reasons the United States and other Western administrations supported Saleh, head of the leading party, the General People's Congress. Abdul Ghani al-Iryani, one of Yemen's best-known analysts and a favourite of journalists not only for his blunt observations but also because he spoke English fluently, laughed at this notion. "Zindani usually speaks from both sides of his mouth, as do politicians, but more so in Yemen than in sophisticated societies where people actually have a longer memory," he told me. Iryani argued that while Zindani purported to be a card-carrying Islah member, he was more often part of Team Saleh thanks to the president's crafty patronage, doled out to keep the Islamists on side. Zindani even publicly backed the president's re-election campaign in 2006, even though Islah fielded its own candidate. "Yeah, I think it's a problem for the West to support Islamic extremists," said Iryani, adding dryly, "as they are doing now... The most reprehensible figures of Islamic extremism are either outright members of the ruling party or they are clearly aligned to it. Even those who are still nominally members of Islah, such as Zindani and the entire pack of extremist clerics, are loyal to the regime."

This described what Yemenis derided as "decorative democracy." There may have been the veneer of a robust political system, but few Yemenis believed it worked. Add to this the fact that Saleh's sons and nephews controlled the country's most powerful security and intelligence operations, such as the American-trained counterterrorism unit and the Republican Guard, and politics took on even less importance.

As government forces increasingly cracked down on protesters and the *baltagiya* stepped up their attacks, word spread that Zindani would hold a press conference at his home. I went with *Washington Post* journalist Sudarsan Raghavan, whom I had met five years earlier at the Hostile Environment Training course in Virginia. Although there were more than fifty journalists, clerics and guards gathered in Zindani's backyard, only four foreign reporters were in attendance (Sudarsan and I, CNN's Mohammed Jamjoom and Al Jazeera's Hashem Ahelbarra). My gender had not yet been an obstacle in Yemen, and if anything it was a benefit, since I could photograph and interview women when my male colleagues couldn't. But I was very aware that day that I was the only woman in the backyard. At one point, as I crouched near Zindani, a furious cleric called one of the guards to usher me back to my seat. No wide-angle shots at this press conference, I guess.

Zindani had one of the most beautiful gardens I had seen in Sanaa, and his home—judging from the outside, at least—was palatial. If he had indeed been bin Laden's spiritual advisor, then he obviously did not abide by the same vow to live a life among the people.

After our bags and equipment were searched, we were seated on velvet-cushioned chairs, spread out in rows on the freshly mowed grass. This scene of serenity in his garden oasis was somewhat jarring after days of dodging rocks and security forces. He gave a twenty-five-minute statement as the sun crept over the backyard wall and highlighted the red in his henna-dyed beard. His main sound bite, which he gave repeatedly, was *ballots, not blood*. "Does any person have the right to express his views about issues without being punished, individually or collectively? Yes, they absolutely have the right to express these views without any fear of intimidation. It's not only a right, it's a duty of Muslims," he told us about the protesters. "[But] we're left with two choices. We have to be very clear on this. Bloodshed and chaos, or stability?"

As we listened to Zindani, Saleh was holding one of his many meetings with tribal leaders across town. They were orchestrated, narcissistic affairs, with much flag-waving and chants and speeches in praise of the president. Behind the scenes, Saleh lavished these leaders with cars, money and other bribes to maintain their support. We would later discover that Saleh was delivering the same message, indeed the same very words as Zindani. "Change," Saleh thundered, would come through "ballot boxes, not through chaos."

THE PROTESTS WERE biggest on Fridays, following the midday prayers. As the weeks went by, each one was given a name. There was Friday of Rage, Friday of Dignity, Friday of Warning and Friday of No Return. Saleh kept promising to step down, when he could do so "peacefully." I waited for organizers to dub one rally "Friday of Just Get On With It." It was no longer a question of whether Saleh would go, just when and how. Protesters wanted it yesterday. Some believed Saleh would fight to hang on until the 2013 election, or at the very least until he had negotiated leaving on his own terms.

As the weeks went on, Tawakkol distanced herself from her party, Islah, fearing that real change was not possible within the confines of Yemen's political system. She became part of a new apolitical group that was neither secular nor religious, but rather a street movement that was growing by the day. But the protests were disorganized and powerless at first. Greg Johnsen, the Princeton scholar who had been in Yemen last time I had visited, predicted that the greatest threat to Saleh was not the protesters themselves, but the possibility that their demands would unite the other fighting factions in the country (the northern and southern groups, the tribal leaders jockeying for power). "The danger in Yemen is that we already have so many different uprisings," he said during a phone call from Cairo, where he had recently moved. "So if all these different strands of the opposition would coalesce into a single strand against the regime of Saleh, then we're dealing with something the Yemeni government is quite worried about."

The demonstrations in Sanaa were really only half-hearted affairs when I first arrived. They followed a predictable pattern. It began in the morning with a small protest and gathered momentum as students marched through the downtown streets. Then at some point, usually an hour or two later, the group would turn a corner and encounter the *baltagiya*. They would fight, rocks and chunks of concrete would fly, and mobs of protesters would surge forth like waves, crashing and then retreating again with the tide. When caught in the middle I kept my photographer-husband's words in my head: "When the going gets bad, go high." I'd convince a kindly building owner to let me scramble up darkened and crumbling stairs, reaching the roof, or hanging out of a window somewhere. It worked until the day riot police decided to point their guns up every time I tried to poke my head or lens out too far.

The street brawls would last sometimes as long as an hour, ending in great clouds of tear gas or shots fired into the air. They wrapped up around lunchtime, with little fanfare, as people went to grab a bite before the afternoon *qat* chew. "What is Saleh's best weapon against protesters," began a popular joke at the time. "Tear gas? Live ammunition? Nope. Put a *qat* dealer on the corner."

But *qat* wouldn't crush the movement, as some predicted, and soon demonstrators erected a permanent camp outside the gates of the university, about a ten-minute drive from pro-Saleh headquarters in Tahrir Square. They renamed the area "Freedom Square," and it took on a carnival-like atmosphere, with fresh-squeezed orange juice and barbequed corn sold from carts and row upon row of rainbow-coloured tents. Volunteer doctors set up a medical tent to treat the injured protesters.

On February 19, I was again with Tawakkol, interviewing her this time at her home. "Yes, it is very dangerous for us, and soon it could explode," she said as the television blared in another room, bringing reports of protests from the south-central city of Taizz, considered the cultural and intellectual cradle of the country. Protesters had been killed in Taizz, as had many more in the southern port city of Aden, the heart of the separatist movement. But no one had yet died in Sanaa, where the government was based and international attention was focused. Tawakkol forecast that if government forces turned on protesters in Sanaa, it would popularize the movement in the way her arrest had a few weeks earlier. Less than a half hour later, Tawakkol's prediction would come true.

She had agreed to talk to me that morning in advance of a busy afternoon of meetings; but, prompted by a couple of phone calls, she decided to change plans and join the hundreds gathered outside the university gates. She bounced into the front seat of her car, her husband Mohammed taking the wheel, as her trusted supporter and videographer climbed into the back with me. The crowd swallowed her as we arrived, celebrating her presence by shouting even louder, "Saleh, go." Eventually I made my way out of the mob to take photos of other protesters and met Ahmed Hussein, a nineteen-year-old American of Somali heritage from Seattle. Ahmed had come to Yemen a year earlier to learn Arabic; he approached me wanting to know what the foreigner with the 300-mm lens was doing walking around alone.

We barely got out a hello and handshake before the shooting started. This time, the security services were not firing into the air but right into the crowd, right at us. I looked quickly for Tawakkol but could no longer see her in the melee. Worried I couldn't outrun the shooters, I darted into a restaurant, just as the owner rolled the door shut. Ahmed slipped in behind me. (He would later give me a quarter from his coin collection that featured an image of a stallion. As he handed it to me, he laughed, "Boy, you can run.")

We huddled in the restaurant's kitchen as the door was battered by rocks and bullets.

Now trapped, I leaned on a bag of carrots, and Ahmed made the lump of potatoes his seat. I began tweeting on my BlackBerry, writing about the protest 140 characters at a time and hoping my parents and husband weren't reading the reports in real time. I would later find out that as I worked, Ahmed was working too, calming one of the restaurant patrons, a Saleh supporter. The patron was asking the owner why he was protecting a foreign journalist and not forcing us to leave. But Ahmed convinced him we just needed to stay a little longer, and the owner said he would not expel his guests. Meanwhile,

I phoned my faithful and worried driver Mohammed. The road outside would puncture his tires in seconds, he told me, but he offered to come meet us, and we could then scurry to his car, a few blocks away. We finally left when it sounded like the government forces had moved on. I thanked the owner and slipped out the door. The street was littered with bullet casings from automatic weapons. I scooped up a few as souvenirs, foolishly thinking they could help me determine who was shooting at us—and forgetting that almost everyone here had a gun.

Ahmed went back to the restaurant the next day to thank the owner. Just minutes after we had left, the owner told him, three police officers had arrived to grill the owner about us. After nearly a year in Yemen, Ahmed had learned much about the country and its culture. He was able to blend in well and had adopted most of the customs (except qat, which he discovered he didn't like; instead, he would stuff slices of orange in his cheek so he could fit in with the locals with his bulging mouth). But, he told me when we met later for coffee, the restaurant owner had taught him an important lesson. "We had more equipment on us than what the whole cafeteria was worth, and [the owner] offered us lunch, even though he risked his life for taking us in," he said. The selfless hospitality amazed him. For someone who was nine on 9/11 and raised believing that anti-Western views were prevalent throughout the Arab world, the man's compassion would be unforgettable.

Soon after we fled, Tawakkol called to make sure I had not been injured, before I could call to make sure she hadn't been. We were both fine, but as we were hiding and running, twenty-one-year-old Bassim Abdu Othman lay near death on the street. He had been shot in the shoulder by government forces. His injury, the first serious one in Sanaa, would send even more protesters to the streets.

Then, one month later, on Friday, March 18, came the crucial turning point. As thousands of unarmed protesters and student demonstrators rose after performing noonday prayers, snipers on rooftops opened fire. They assassinated at least fifty-two, and dozens more were seriously injured. Many of those killed were shot in the head. Three days later, the country's most powerful military leader defected and joined the protesters. Another influential general soon joined him, splitting the army. The United States, Canada and other Western governments issued statements condemning the killings, as disgusted Yemeni diplomats around the world resigned. "This is on principle," Khaled Bahah, Yemen's ambassador to Canada told me as he denounced Saleh. Bahah had once travelled the world with the president as the country's minister of oil and minerals, and admired Saleh's political acumen. But on the Friday of the massacre he left his office in Ottawa early, barely able to speak. On Monday, he announced that he was resigning from Saleh's regime and was with "the people of Yemen."

TO REALLY UNDERSTAND Yemen, sometimes you needed to go inside, to chew the fat by chewing qat.

One February afternoon, Mohammed Abu Lehum, an articulate and refreshingly direct member of Saleh's ruling party, invited me to his home for an interview arranged by well-known journalist Nasser Arrabyee. A friend of Khaled al Hammadi (who was now working as a television producer), the dapper Nasser often sported a red polar fleece scarf an American filmmaker had given him, and would pepper his speech with much laughter and liked to say "no problem." He worked as a translator, journalist, blogger and sometime fixer, and seemed to have a cellphone number for just about everyone in the country.

As I arrived in Lehum's sitting room, where the setting sun made the stained glass windows glow, I interrupted a meeting he was having with six tribal members. Lehum is a sheikh with Yemen's second-largest tribal confederate, Bakeel, and he was mediating a discussion concerning a recent killing. Lehum had been a member of the opposition until the civil war in 1994, when he left Yemen for the United States. For ten years he had lived in D.C., and he had studied international relations at The George Washington University. In 2004, Saleh was in Washington for a meeting at the White House and later met Lehum, offering him the prestigious post of head of foreign relations if he would come back to Sanaa. Lehum agreed, but had never been a blind Saleh disciple, and on the day we met he seemed fed up with the president, fed up with the opposition and fed up with politics in general. (He would later form a new political party.)

"Sadly, political parties in the Arab world and particularly in Yemen, they haven't delivered anything," he said. "They just argue. I hoped the opposition would focus on health and education and things that touch people in Yemen. We cannot keep focusing all the time on politics, politics, politics, and sadly that's what we do. Always you see an action and reaction from the opposition and the ruling party and vice versa," he said. As he spoke his cheek bulged with qat. I tried to do the same and shove the leaves to the right side of my mouth, but instead had to keep dabbing at the rivulet of green goo escaping my lips and dribbling down my chin.

A brief note on qat, the leaf chewed every day in Yemen in a ritual that defies class. Almost the entire male population chews, and a growing number of women are organizing their own sessions. It is as much a part of Yemen's culture as jambiyas, the traditional curved knives men wear tucked into embroidered sashes. While its impact is often overstated, there were legitimate concerns about the economic and environmental dangers of qat. With the country's dwindling water resources, qat cultivation sucked up valuable reserves, and for some Yemenis, feeding the daily addiction took on the same importance as feeding their families.

Qat is illegal in both the United States and Canada, although its effect seems much weaker than that of alcohol. I will say this about qat: it makes everything seem more interesting, and it makes you content to sit. That's a benefit for Western reporters, who often find the culture shock worse than the jet lag. No matter how often I travel, it still takes me days to switch off my Toronto anxiety, which can cause a late streetcar to ruin a morning. I have learned to accept Somali time and Pakistani time, and even coped with Djibouti time (another qat-loving country). So in Yemen it is nice to have a little help relaxing when deadlines loom. Going for an interview and a few quotes over tea is never a ten-minute affair.

But at the risk of insulting an entire nation, I'm not sure I completely get it, when the effect is so mild. The experience is like chewing (or what I imagine it would be like to chew) bitter grass. Storing the qat in your cheek is difficult without swallowing; the pros look like chipmunks getting ready for winter. With enough use, it browns your teeth. I'm just not sure it's worth it.

As Lehum's guests left, we continued our discussion and chewing in a side room, where talk eventually turned to al Qaeda and the threat of AQAP. "Al Qaeda does not have a base in Yemen. Al Qaeda shouldn't have a base here. We do not want them ... I would hope the international community would see that a stable country would stop al Qaeda from spreading. Al Qaeda moves in the dark, and dark is corruption."

Was he denouncing his government as corrupt? "Once you reach a dead end and you don't have anything to give your family, people will take matters into their own hands," he said. "When you talk about the youth uprising, it's not just about poverty. It's more about integrity or liberty, or sharing power or democracy. That's what people are hungry for here in Yemen. The middle class vanished probably about ten or fifteen years ago. There are those who still act within the middle-class mentality but without the wealth of the middle class. Yemen is different from any part of the Arab world. We were built on democracy. Sit in any qat session, and everyone is open. Yemen is not Syria, or some closed society."

In other words, yes, the government to which he belonged had failed and was responsible for pushing its people to the brink.

"IN A COUNTRY where weapons outnumber people, half the population is illiterate, close to a quarter can't find work, and the internecine fighting is forcing thousands from their homes, the extremists come to play."

That was how I began my 2009 *Toronto Star* story concerning the Yemeni detainees in Guantanamo. The headline above my 4,082-word front-page opus highlighted the part that made me cringe: "Where Extremists Come To Play." I had lost the argument with a couple of editors who wanted to include that phrase, which was not mine. That's not an excuse, just a regret. It was my byline, my responsibility, and I should have fought harder. The story did provide context; but if you didn't read past the sensational headline, Yemen was reduced to a monolithic terrorist jungle gym, like the footage that looped endlessly after 9/11 of the Afghan training camp where al Qaeda recruits swung on monkey bars and shot Kalashnikovs into the air.

I felt especially guilty about that headline on the warm March 2011 evening when I stumbled upon a crowd of kids playing foosball on a Sanaa street. I love foosball and had the good fortune of growing up with a table in my basement, which meant that hours of fierce family competition with my parents and three sisters had honed my skills. Foosball could bridge the language and cultural gap, and I was amazed by how often during my travels I would find a table—even at Guantanamo, where many sweaty hours were spent battling other journalists in the media hangar (there was another table in one of the prison camps where the faces of the plastic figures had been chipped off so as not to offend detainees who objected to idolatry). The ten- and twelve-year-olds on the garbage-strewn street in Sanaa giggled as we battled, our palms blackened by the grease and dirt on the handles. They were shown no mercy or graciousness, and only laughed harder when I threw my arms up in arrogant victory. These kids were the ones playing, not the extremists.

But while al Qaeda may not be "playing," they certainly had a presence in the country, even if, as most Yemenis believed, Saleh hyped the threat to keep the U.S. dollars flowing. The concern in early 2011 was how AQAP would try to use the protests and the lapse in security (government forces were targeting the demonstrators and unarmed students, not going after terrorists, it appeared) to plot another attack. AQAP's failed plot to bomb a Christmas Day flight bound for the United States showed it had the West in its sights. But it was the near-assassination of Saudi Arabia's top internal security official that really showed the group's moxy. The August 2009 plan may have failed, but an AQAP operative had come close after convincing Saudi authorities—among the most suspicious in the world—that he was a repentant militant and wanted to turn himself in to the deputy interior minister, Prince Mohammed bin Nayef. He was in bin Nayef's Jeddah office, just metres away from the prince, when the bomb concealed in his underwear detonated prematurely. Only the bomber died, but the fact that he had reached the inner sanctum of the Saudi royals was significant.

One of my greatest journalistic failures had been not to pursue Anwar al Awlaki harder back in the summer of 2009, when he was still largely an unknown and, while it was unlikely, he may have agreed to meet a Canadian reporter for an interview. Now getting to the American-born orator would be impossible. A local Al Jazeera reporter had managed, and his story landed him in jail on terrorism charges.

While Awlaki seemed impossible to reach, his sixty-five-year-old father was not. Nasser al Awlaki had not given any interviews since Obama sanctioned the kill order against his son, but he agreed to come for a quick coffee at my hotel one morning. Our brief meeting turned into a two-hour interview.

Nasser was well known and connected in Yemen and came from the large, powerful and respected al Awalik tribe, which his grand-father once governed. He was the country's former agricultural minister and was a Fulbright scholar and friend of the embattled president, among other high-level figures in the government and security service. At first I kept my tape recorder off and notebook shut, since he said he wasn't interested in talking on the record. But as we discussed how his son had been elevated to "Terrorist Number One," in the United States he changed his mind and encouraged me to record the interview. "I don't care anymore," he said, shaking his head and staring at the dissolving Nescafé coffee crystals. "Do you know now Anwar is very popular in the Muslim world?" he asked me. "The Americans made a big thing of him. One year ago no one knew him in the Arab world, or even in Yemen. But now every Arab knows him." I could certainly attest to the fact that when I first went looking for him, few in Yemen had heard the name Anwar al Awlaki.

Awlaki's father said that the son he raised was a "moderate," attending Yemen's elite schools alongside Saleh's sons. It was after his son moved back to the United States to attend university, following 9/11, that he believes he became politicized, angered by the wars in Iraq and Afghanistan and the questioning and imprisonment of Muslims from his mosque. Anwar's two-year incarceration upon returning to Yemen, purportedly at the behest of the United States, only cemented his views that the West was waging a war against Islam. Nasser had convinced his son during his time in custody to cooperate with Yemeni interrogators and speak to two visiting FBI agents. "Anwar at the beginning was very reluctant to talk to them," Nasser told me. "I was called by the consul in the American embassy, and they said, 'Please tell your son to help us and talk to these guys. They came all the way from the United States'... I went to the prison, I met my son, and I said, 'Please, please, please meet these guys.' So he spent two days with them and do you know what they asked? All the questions were about September 11."

During his son's incarceration, Nasser visited often with his wife, an English literature scholar. They brought him Shakespeare, *Moby-Dick* and *A Tale of Two Cities*, among other literary classics. Nasser continued to advocate for his son's release. He was part of a government delegation that travelled to Britain for meetings in 2006, where he raised his son's case with Saleh.

When Anwar al Awlaki was eventually released, in December 2007, he remained in Sanaa for a few months, but later moved four hundred kilometres southeast to the Swaba region where his family's tribe is based. The last time father and son spoke was in early November 2009, before the Fort Hood shooting.

While he was vociferous in his criticism of the U.S. administration that had issued a kill order for his son, Nasser still praised much about the United States, where he had lived and worked for years. When he served as Yemen's agricultural minister in the late 1980s, he was close to the U.S. ambassador and USAID officials who helped fund Sanaa-based agricultural programs. He would often host the Americans for dinner, and his wife would make her famous cheesecake and apple pie, recipes she had perfected when they lived in Nebraska. His son used to like the American life too, he said. "If America would stop making him into Osama bin Laden and see Anwar as an educated man, born in the West, who used to love everything about America—he used to go offshore fishing, he used to go hiking, he was in every bit an 'all-American boy...'" He trails off and cringes. "It's just that he used to be like that, and then things changed his perceptions of America. He used to be open-minded. He never had an incident of violence or quarrel during all this life in America or Yemen." This timeline of Awlaki's radicalization is different from what some in the Western intelligence community believe, those who argue that Awlaki played a pivotal role in al Qaeda before 9/11.

However Awlaki arrived where he is today, his online postings and videos make it clear that he now adheres to al Qaeda's doctrine. In a November 2010 video, he advises, "Don't consult with anybody in killing the Americans. Fighting the devil does not require a fatwa, nor consultation, nor prayers, seeking divine guidance. They are the party of Satan and fighting them is the obligation of the time."

While I sympathized with Awlaki's father and understood why he was frustrated with Saleh's duplicity, or the role played by the Obama administration and the media in elevating his son's notoriety, I also knew his son's videos had inspired members of the Toronto 18 and countless other Western youths. I took particular offence to one posting that backed Somalia's al Shabab. "We are following your recent news and it fills our hearts with immense joy," he wrote. A reply from a purported Shabab member thanked him for his words and went on to complain about the media's coverage of his group; in particular, he highlighted the story of Asho Duhulow, the thirteen-year-old refugee who was stoned to death in Kismayo, Somalia—the sad little girl whose story I had investigated with Lucas at the Dadaab refugee camp. "The reality and truth is that she was over twenty years, married and practicing adultery," the posting lied.

"Listen, Anwar is my son and I have to do anything legal to protect him from the targeted killing by the United States," Nasser answered when I asked if he believed his son's words were powerful weapons. "I've never thought about helping him financially. I have never sent him one dollar. I thought my position was to help him peacefully, because I am a member of the political system in Yemen. I don't know how he lives but I am protecting and financing his family with my modest means. But I never had any contact or thoughts of helping him. He has to take responsibility for himself, and that's all."

ONE PERFECT SPRING morning, when Toronto's skyline reflected the pinks of the sunrise and Lake Ontario shimmered a deep blue, I picked up a couple of Starbucks lattes and went to see 9/11 widow Cindy Barkway for the first visit since we had met in New York. I had come home after my month-long visa for Yemen expired. I was trying to get another, but foreign journalists were barred and most of the young stringers who had been living in Sanaa had been expelled. Saleh was still hanging on.

Cindy lived about twenty minutes west of downtown, in a wealthy enclave with wide boulevards and houses. She had been generous with journalists over the decade, and I had followed her life through their reports, sending Cindy the occasional card. Her son was born healthy four months after 9/11. She named him after his dad, David Michael.

David was now nine, and her other son Jamie twelve. In the driveway of her home were a minivan and a hockey net, and I had a feeling it was the type of house that would soon have beds of tulips and daffodils, followed by carved pumpkins on the porch in October and Christmas lights lacing throughout the trees during the winter months. Cindy came to the door in jeans and a pink cardigan, and I was amazed how little she had changed. There were some extra creases around her eyes, a few early wisps of grey at her temples, but she was pretty much the same woman I saw walk off that Times Square hotel elevator four days after 9/11.

As Cindy described how her life had moved on, it was hard not to look at the wedding photos sitting on her piano, frozen in another time. "I'm still surprised when I cry now," she said, as a tear stubbornly pushed its way out of one eye. The tears had started when I asked about the day she brought her newborn David home. She described walking into her bedroom for the first time and seeing something sparkling in the carpet. Her husband had given her a pair of diamond earrings two years earlier, when Jamie was born, but in July 2001 she had lost one. After an exhaustive search on her hands and knees and weeks of refusing to vacuum the carpet, she had given up the earring for gone. But there it was, in plain sight, blinking up from the carpet six months later. She went immediately to her jewellery box to find the other one. It was there too. "It was as if David was giving me an earring for each boy," she said.

Cindy has gone with her sons to New York for almost every 9/11 anniversary, and they have stood at Ground Zero holding hands as the name of each victim was read out. Only once did she travel instead to Ottawa for a Canadian commemoration, and instantly regretted it. She had grown to love New York, to feel close to the city that shared her pain, and she preferred to be lost in the anonymous masses, rather than being one of just a few widows in Canada.

Life, for Cindy, is now happily fulfilled with being a hockey mom, and she has the financial stability that allows her to work at this full time. She has tried dating, a little, and says she is not opposed to the idea, but it just hasn't seemed to work out. Besides, she hates being away from her boys for a wasted evening. Although she follows the news periodically, Cindy hasn't become overwhelmed by it, as have some other relatives of 9/11 victims. I told her that it was likely the Pentagon would allow some relatives to attend the Guantanamo trial for KSM and his co-accused. "I don't think that would help me," she said. "I don't need that."

As I got ready to leave and let her get back to her fundraising planning for a school event, Cindy asked me what I had discovered in my travels. Had I figured out why we got to where we were, or where we were heading? I was tempted to flop back on her comfy couch and stay for the day, telling her about Ismail, Tawakkol, Tortoise, or Khawaja and Aweys; what a sorry part of history Guantanamo was, is; about the failed foreign interventions and hyperventilations in

Somalia and Yemen; or the problems in Pakistan. But there was no quick or easy way to explain all that had gone wrong. Just as there is no simple way to say what could happen now.

There is a writing technique known as "bookending" that journalists often use for long narratives. The general principle is that you end the story where you began, hopefully with some new insight. I think I had wanted Cindy to give me an easy, pithy anecdote to cap off the decade that we started together in New York. Instead, I left just happy knowing she had carried on with life and was doing so well. It would be another three weeks before I headed back to where it began.

Early on the morning of May 2, Cindy left a message on my cellphone. "Oh, hi, Michelle," she said, in her usual cheery tone. "I was just thinking of you, and our conversation, given the events." I had been thinking about Cindy too that morning. The man who had killed her husband was gone. Osama bin Laden was dead.

AT FIRST IT just seemed too difficult to fathom; a ridiculous, heroic Hollywood ending that could only have been conceived over martinis in Los Angeles.

In the early hours of May 2 in Pakistan, in the garrison town of Abbottabad about a two-hour drive from the country's capital, an elite team of U.S. Navy SEALs dropped into a high-walled compound. In the next forty minutes, the American commandos would kill a woman and three men. Among the dead was al Qaeda leader Osama bin Laden. They found him on the villa's third floor and shot him twice—once in the chest and once in the head. They left with his body and a treasure trove of intelligence, just as quickly as they came. After DNA testing, bin Laden was sent to a watery grave in the Arabian Sea. "Justice," Obama said in a late night television address from the East Wing of the White House, "has been served."

Bin Laden was not hiding in some cave in the border badlands between Afghanistan and Pakistan, but in a compound, living with three of his wives and some of his children. He took contemplative, circular strolls in his yard. He watched videos of his past speeches, like some aging former football star or washed-up actor. He had dyed his greying beard black. A trusted courier brought cases of Coca-Cola each week, and the local milkman was told to leave the bottles at the door.

Bin Laden lived in a neighbourhood favoured by retired Pakistani generals and his compound was near a military academy that was the country's equivalent of West Point. Eight days before bin Laden was killed, General Ashfaq Parvez Kayani, the head of the Pakistani Army, went to the military academy and, according to local journalist Pir Zubair Shah, told the cadets, "We have broken the backbone of the militants." The location of bin Laden's hideout would prompt the most pointed accusations yet of Pakistan's duplicity.

Bin Laden had not been a homeless fugitive, as presumed, but had lived there since 2005. He was not surrounded by a security detail; there were no bodyguards like Abu Jandal, who had told me in Yemen that he had been trained to kill bin Laden rather than have his beloved leader captured alive. In the end, it was one of bin Laden's wives who had tried to protect him and was shot as she ran toward the Navy SEALs team.

After years of criticism, the U.S. military and intelligence communities were hailed as heroes following bin Laden's death, as was their commander-in-chief for his gutsy decision to send the elite U.S. Navy SEALs team into bin Laden's lair. Until the moment that the al Qaeda leader was felled by bullets to his chest and head, Obama was not certain that they had their man. In a photograph of the situation room, White House photographer Peter Souza captured a poignant moment during the president's forty nail-biting minutes as commandos were in the bin Laden compound and Obama and his closest advisors got live reports. It was Hillary Clinton, staring wide-eyed at a screen, her hand covering her mouth, who made the photo iconic. She would later say she had "no idea" what was happening when Souza took that shot. "I am somewhat sheepishly concerned that [my hand] was my preventing one of my early-spring allergic coughs," she told reporters. But no matter: the image was ingrained in our memory as the moment the White House confirmed that bin Laden was dead.

Guantanamo, waterboarding and the CIA's black sites were among the talking points endlessly debated in the weeks that followed, since initial news reports stated that a vital nugget of intelligence about the nickname, or *kunya*, for bin Laden's courier resulted from the interrogation of KSM. Republican Peter King and former vice president Dick Cheney were among the first to boast. "We obtained that information through waterboarding," King said emphatically in interview with Fox News the day after the killing. "So for those who say that waterboarding doesn't work, who say it should be stopped and never used again, we got vital information, which directly led us to bin Laden." Cheney called for the return of "enhanced interrogation methods." I thought back to conversations on the Spy Cruise and wondered if this information about bin Laden's courier was what the former CIA bosses were alluding to as they used bar nuts to describe KSM's waterboarding.

But eventually, the narrative about the intelligence hunt for bin Laden evolved. Republican Senator John McCain, a war veteran who was tortured during his captivity in the Vietnam war, wrote in a May 11 *Washington Post* article:

> I asked CIA Director Leon Panetta for the facts, and he told me the following: The trail to bin Laden did not begin with a disclosure from Khalid Sheik Mohammed, who was waterboarded 183 times. The first mention of Abu Ahmed al-Kuwaiti—the nickname of the al-Qaeda courier who ultimately led us to bin Laden—as well as a description of him as an important member of al-Qaeda, came from a detainee held in another country, who we believe was not tortured. None of the three detainees who were waterboarded provided Abu Ahmed's real name, his whereabouts or an accurate description of his role in al-Qaeda.
>
> In fact, the use of "enhanced interrogation techniques" on Khalid Sheik Mohammed produced false and misleading information. He specifically told his interrogators that Abu Ahmed had moved to Peshawar, got married and ceased his role as an al-Qaeda facilitator—none of which was true. According to the staff of the Senate intelligence committee, the best intelligence

gained from a CIA detainee—information describing Abu Ahmed al-Kuwaiti's real role in al-Qaeda and his true relationship to bin Laden—was obtained through standard, noncoercive means.

The exact details of how the intelligence puzzle was put together may never be known. We may never fully understand why eliminating bin Laden, while a victory, was one that took nearly ten years.

One of the most startling facts about bin Laden's killing was the secrecy of the mission and lack of leaks . . . that is, unless you were among the few dozen Twitter followers of Sohaib Athar. The Abbottabad computer programmer and coffee shop owner wrote under the handle @ReallyVirtual, and in the weeks before the raid his posts largely catered to the technology crowd. "You hate Dora because she's the 'explorer'?" he wrote on April 9. "'Dora the Firefox' would have been a better name." *A little IT humour.*

His tweets began May 1 as the Navy SEALs circled above bin Laden's compound. They continued throughout the night and into the next day:

"Helicopters hovering above Abbottabad at 1 AM (is a rare event)."

"Go away helicopter—before I take out my giant swatter."

"A huge window shaking bang here in Abbottabad . . . I hope it's not the start of something nasty."

"All silent after blast, but a friend heard it 6 km away too . . . the helicopter is gone too."

"Seems like my giant swatter worked!"

"Since Taliban (probably) don't have helicopters, and since they're saying it was not 'ours,' so must be a complicated situation. #abbottabad."

"I guess Abbottabad is going to get as crowded as the Lahore that I left behind for some peace and quiet. sigh."

"(OBL killed) Uh oh, there goes the neighbourhood."

"Wondering what would be the right music to play in the coffee shop today."

And then the magnitude of what had happened dawned on Athar. On May 2, before he was overwhelmed by interview requests and became an instant Twitter sensation with more than 100,000 followers, he tweeted: "Uh oh, now I'm the guy who liveblogged the Osama raid without knowing it."

BIN LADEN'S DEATH will have wide-ranging implications for U.S.-Pakistan relations and the war in Afghanistan, but his death also forced a re-examination of long-held beliefs about what the post-9/11 al Qaeda had become. Many had presumed that bin Laden had been relegated to the role of figurehead, but computers seized from the raid revealed he still enjoyed a hands-on role. Seized material outlined plans for attacks to coincide with the tenth anniversary of 9/11. Bin Laden had been able to get his message out on thumb drives carried by trusted couriers and had managed to avoid electronic detection since his home had no phone or Internet connection. It was surmised that the still-elusive Zawahiri, al Qaeda's number two, had a similar system. This structure—the leadership connected to the rest of the organization only through messengers—explained why, as the common counterterrorism joke put it, being al Qaeda's number three was the worst position. A succession of number threes had been killed since KSM was captured in Rawalpindi in 2003. It made sense that they were most vulnerable: they were responsible for spreading the leader's message and for taking charge of the logistics of the attacks, which meant they had to use phones or some sort of electronic communication.

Bin Laden's death is no doubt a blow for al Qaeda, since no one within his organization—especially not the notoriously cantankerous and egotistical Zawahiri—could replace the charismatic figure. Some have predicted that the group may split into factions as greed and jealousy bubble up, transforming al Qaeda's members into squabbling siblings fighting over the will.

But al Qaeda's ideology is not dead yet. Since most of the group's adherents are opposed to Western military intervention or other interference in the Islamic world—including the conflicts in Palestine and Kashmir—these remain global grievances. Al Qaeda's goal of installing theocratic governments in all Islamic states worldwide had spread well beyond bin Laden's original organization and was adopted by domestic movements in Yemen, Somalia and elsewhere.

Journalism, it is said, is just the first draft of history. So maybe a contemporary book written by a journalist is just that—a draft, plus a spell-check. The tectonic political and social shifts continue throughout the Arab region and within the ranks of al Qaeda and its affiliates, which is why no one can really predict what comes next. It is why that dreaded cliché, denounced by every journalism professor, so aptly applies: *only time will tell.*

As I write, a *New York Times* article, headlined "Why Last Chapters Disappoint," taunts me. In his essay, David Greenberg, a professor of history and journalism at New Jersey's Rutgers University, tackles the problem of why the endings of books analyzing social or political problems always seem to fall short. "Practically every example of that genre, no matter how shrewd or rich its survey of the question at hand, finishes with an obligatory prescription that is utopian, banal, unhelpful or out of tune with the rest of the book," writes Greenberg. Maybe it is because readers expect them and editors demand them, the scholar continues. *Yes. I like this. Let's blame the readers, the editors!* But unfortunately, Greenberg concludes, "(I)n the end, most authors have themselves to blame. Having immersed themselves in a subject, almost all succumb to the hubristic idea that they can find new and unique ideas for solving intractable problems. They rarely do." Rest assured, I am not filled with hubris; I do not believe I have uncovered the terrorism vaccine.

We don't know how al Qaeda will respond, or whether bin Laden's death will embolden or weaken regional groups. The greatest unknown is what will happen in the Arab world when the post-revolution reality sets in; when the protesters and CNN go home, and the intoxication of the power-of-the-people movement gives way to the hangover of governing economically depressed countries. Besieged autocrats are now killing their own, trying to suppress movements by force, never quite comprehending that the violence only fuels the fury. Foreign journalists are being shut out of Yemen and Syria, while some of the most experienced war correspondents have been detained and killed in Libya. In Egypt and Tunisia, the fear is that new faces of corruption will fill the void. How will local terrorist groups insert themselves into this uncertainty?

However, as the cynical optimist I have become (if there is such an oxymoron), I'd like to think that the Arab Awakening gave al Qaeda a punch to the gut, which was followed by the uppercut of bin Laden's death. The writings of Awalaki and Zawahiri display a desperate effort to insert their organizations into the revolutionary picture, praising the protesters on the street as fellow mujahideen. The problem is that the people of Tunisia, Egypt and Yemen, as elsewhere, stole al Qaeda's narrative, and they don't see themselves as holy warriors. Al Qaeda's goal has always been to target not just the "far enemy" (the United States and Israel in particular), but also what they call the "near enemy," the rulers of oppressed Muslim nations. Egypt was of particular importance to al Qaeda. But because peaceful, secular, democratic demonstrations—not terrorism—pushed Mubarrak from his throne and forever changed Egypt, al Qaeda's message lost its resonance.

If real democratic change results in these countries, and the West moves past its strategy of using military might alone to fight terrorism, al Qaeda will further lose its appeal, and its access to the pool of young, angry and impressionable recruits. That would be a start.

THE SCENE AT Ground Zero was so hauntingly reminiscent of the days after 9/11 that I had to remind myself that nearly a decade had passed. Relatives had that faraway look in their eyes as they clutched photos of the dead. The Stars and Stripes adorned fences and buildings and hand-drawn cards hung everywhere. "Obama you da' man," read one. "Heroes" was another, outside the firehall nearest Ground Zero. Alicia Keys singing "Empire State of Mind" blared from a souvenir shop on Liberty Street as a nearby street vendor sold $2 flags. "Baby, I'm from New York. Concrete jungle where dreams are made of. There's nothing you can't do. Now you're in New York." It reminded me of the night when I was in the back of a cab following 9/11 and got teary as Billy Joel's "New York State of Mind" came on the radio. Even the weather was the same—sunny and warm, but not too hot.

On May 5, 2011, people had started to gather at Ground Zero near dawn, seven hours before Obama was scheduled to visit lower

Manhattan. The feeling was decidedly more sombre than it had been four days earlier, when spontaneous rallies broke out and jubilant Americans chanted "U-S-A, U-S-A" after the president told the world bin Laden was dead.

Before arriving at Ground Zero, Obama ate lunch with the firefighters at the "Pride of Midtown," the firehouse near Times Square (the meal was shrimp, scallops, creamy pasta, spring mix salad with Dijon balsamic vinaigrette and eggplant Parmesan; Obama ate a lot of the eggplant). Not many of the firefighters who had survived 9/11 were still working at the Pride of Midtown. Some of the probies who met Obama had been just kids at the time. But Lieutenant Patrick O'Brady was still there.

O'Brady was the one firefighter I had kept in touch with and visited whenever I was in town. Life had been pretty hard on him since 9/11, although you would never know it by his jovial demeanour. One morning in 2010, as we had breakfast following his overnight shift, he had told me about his beloved wife's death from cancer a few years after 9/11, followed by the death of his golden retriever, Finn. Now he was living and working for his two daughters and their university tuition.

But O'Brady remained a firefighter for more than just the paycheque. Every time I saw him, he said he would retire "in five years," but really he was waiting for a sign. "I'm not sure what it is, but there was a reason I was saved," he said about surviving 9/11. Perhaps he was going to pull a child alive from a burning Manhattan high-rise, help an elderly woman across the street, or just give a piece of vital advice to a rookie firefighter in his company. Whatever his greater mission, O'Brady hadn't found it yet, and he was determined not to retire until he did.

As Obama's motorcade left Midtown, at around 1 PM, a line of uniformed police officers, firefighters and Port Authority officers quietly marched into the area known as Memorial Plaza. This eight-acre garden and museum at Ground Zero was scheduled to open in four months, in time for the tenth anniversary. The design included two massive pools with cascading waterfalls, built in the footprints of the Twin Towers. The names of the victims would be inscribed on the pool walls, which measured one acre each. Around them, four hundred trees would be planted.

Much work remained; the plaza looked like a construction zone when Obama visited. The only striking feature was a Callery pear tree in the centre of the garden. Known to New Yorkers as the Survivor Tree, it had been planted in the World Trade Centre complex three decades earlier, but was badly damaged in the attack. Uprooted and taken to the Parks Department's Arthur Ross Nursery in Van Cortlandt Park, the eight-foot tree was nursed back to health and brought to the Memorial Garden in December 2010, and now stood over thirty feet tall. It was here in the tree's shade that Obama would lay a wreath.

I was in a press pack of about two hundred journalists who had received White House pre-clearance, and we stood crammed together to photograph the ceremony. The large floral wreath of red, white and blue flowers was designed by Flowers of the World, a chain of flower shops that had had a location on the ground floor of 4 World Trade Center.

Obama arrived at Ground Zero with Mayor Michael Bloomberg, as other politicians and dignitaries waited to the side, including former mayor Rudy Giuliani (George W. Bush had declined an invitation to attend). A group of about sixty relatives of 9/11 victims were brought in to meet Obama, and he shook their hands, hugged them and talked to each one individually. A photo of Christopher Cannizzaro beaming up at Obama was featured on the cover of the *New York Times* the following day. Christopher was only ten months old when his dad, Brian, a firefighter, died. I had spent time earlier that morning with Christopher's grandfather Sam. He too was a firefighter and stood at the gates of Ground Zero clutching a framed photo of Brian, wearing mirrored sunglasses to hide his watery eyes. He graciously gave interviews to one television crew after another. "People keep asking me how I'm doing," he confided to me after one such interview. "I'm not doing very well." He didn't mean he was having a hard time at that very moment. He just generally hadn't done well since losing his son.

As Obama bowed his head and observed a moment of silence that afternoon, the only sounds were the clicking of cameras and the faint buzz of a commercial aircraft crossing the sky high above, leaving a wispy, white tail.

Obama left New York that afternoon. At 2:51 PM, he saluted the small crowd that came to see him off, jogged up the stairs of the presidential plane Air Force One and waved once more.

At Ground Zero, the last of the 9/11 victims left. The spectators went home. Volunteers dismantled the metal detectors that had been erected for Obama's visit. The Secret Service agents, with their telltale dark suits and earphones, were long gone.

As the early afternoon rush hour in lower Manhattan began, an army of construction workers in yellow hard hats and fluorescent orange jerseys returned. One by one, they walked through the gates leading to Ground Zero and went back to work.

Acknowledgements

AS A JOURNALIST, I have two families to thank. First, the dysfunctional one.

The *Toronto Star* is where I have grown up since arriving as a clueless twenty-two-year-old summer student in 1995. To everyone in that madhouse we call a newsroom, thank you. A special mention to the godfather, John Honderich, and the succession of editors who over the last decade have agreed that going to Yemen, Bermuda, Somalia or Djibouti, or cruising with spies, made sense. Thank you Alison Uncles, David Walmsley, Colin MacKenzie, Jennifer Hunter, Michael Cooke, Mary Deanne Shears, Giles Gherson, Fred Kuntz, Bill Schiller, Martin Regg Cohn and John Ferri. Lynn McAuley, thanks for doubling as an editor who really understood these stories and as a book mentor whose blue marker attacked this manuscript. Thanks to Tom Walkom for convincing me this was a good beat, and to Haroon Siddiqui, Olivia Ward and Kathy English for the guidance. Bert Bruser, thanks for your legal/newspaper mind. Isabel Teotonio, one of the hardest working journalists I know, thanks for really digging into the story of the Toronto 18. To my photographer partners in crime and good friends, Lucas Oleniuk and Pete Power: I miss travelling with you.

To my reporter girlfriends Tanya Talaga, Rita Daly and Patty Winsa for enduring the book talk and keeping me company for hundreds of hours of spinning class therapy to stop my head from spinning. And to Betsy Powell, for always saying the right thing.

My journalism family extends beyond the Toronto newsroom and I would be dead, perhaps literally, without the help of my foreign relatives.

Sahal Abdulle, you've become like an older brother. Alisha Ryu, you are one tough, smart woman, and I'm sorry to ruin the steely image, but you're also one of the most giving. Matt Bryden (analyst, but I'm going to count you as part of the reporting family), thank you for your advice.

Khalid al Hammadi, I miss you, and if Yemen will just give me another visa I'll be back. Thank you for everything. Gregory Johnsen, you're frustratingly brilliant and now part of the writing club, so I look forward to reading your bestseller. Thanks for your patience in helping me understand. Thank you Nasser Arrabyee, for telling me "no problem."

Pakistan, I still don't understand you, but thanks to Declan Walsh I know more than I once did. Thanks for your friendship, Declan, and your help with this book, and for scaring me with your driving in Betsy. Tom Hussain, thanks for the careful edits and pistachio gelato, and for introducing me to the savvy Maulana Whiskey.

I have never hated or loved an assignment more than covering Guantanamo Bay, and the friendships I made there were intense and will never be forgotten. Charlie 19 tentmates Janet Hamlin, Dean Carol Rosenberg and Jane Sutton, I could have never survived without you incredible women. Our GTMO beverage and food coordinator, Muna Shikaki, is as kind and giving as she is smart. Paul Koring, I promise not to tell the editors at the *Globe and Mail* that we became such good friends we sometimes read each other's copy before filing.

Journalism can be a selfish profession, and I am so blessed to have such a supportive Shephard/Rankin family that has allowed me to indulge. Mum and Dad, I'm sorry for the sleepless nights when

I told you I was in Nairobi but you knew I was in Mogadishu. I still blame you both for giving me the love of travel (and Rochelle blames you both too). Dawn and Ron Shephard are my secret, unpaid editors and if there is a dangling modifier or comma blunder in this book it is only because I missed their neat pencilled-in correction. To my sisters Meg, Suzanne and Mary and their incredible brood of seven: I can't wait to supplement the shoeboxes of postcards with some actual time together.

Jimmie, I always knew I "married up." Thanks for letting this book become our roommate. You made coming home sweet and leaving so hard. If we endured these ten years, I know we have decades together to come.

Thanks to my agent, John Pearce, for thinking this was a story worth telling even when I wasn't sure. To everyone at Douglas & McIntyre, you have spoiled me. Scott McIntyre, thanks for getting excited about this book the first time we met. Peter Norman, your edits were terrific and I'm so glad you got to spell-check the spell-check. Trena White, you are simply great; a terrific editor, and now a good friend.

Index